ROME: A LITERARY COMPANION

By the same author

Italian Baroque and Rococo Architecture

ROME
A Literary Companion

John Varriano

JOHN MURRAY

For Wendy

© John Varriano 1991

First published in 1991
by John Murray (Publishers) Ltd
50 Albemarle Street, London W1X 4BD

A catalogue record for this book is available
from the British Library

ISBN 0-7195-4842-X

Typeset by Rowland Phototypesetting Ltd
Bury St Edmunds, Suffolk
Printed and bound in Great Britain
by Biddles Ltd, Guildford and King's Lynn

CONTENTS

CONTENTS

ILLUSTRATIONS

AP: Author's Photograph; BH: Bibliotheca Hertziana, Rome; PC: Private Collection

PREFACE

In a letter of 1337, Petrarch wrote to a friend, 'Nowhere is Rome less well known than in Rome'.[1] Astonished by the supine indifference of Romans to their own cultural heritage, he was humbled rather than elated to discover that a tourist from the Rhône was more conversant with the antiquities in the Forum than were the natives themselves.[2] A great many books have been written about the city in the six and a half centuries since the poet arrived from Avignon, but as he might have expected, many of the most perceptive and evocative of these were written by non-Italians. More than 1,400 British and American travel accounts are datable before 1860 alone, and there have been a prodigious number of titles in other languages as well.[3] Like the landscape paintings of the Roman Campagna by the Frenchman Claude Lorrain, the foreigner's accent and phrasing has sometimes been the most poetic and picturesque. It is the intention of the present volume to harvest the best crops from many literary gardens, to quote from poetry and prose, fiction and non-fiction, that originally appeared in eleven languages over the past 2,000 years and, wherever possible, to capture the innocence of fresh vision.

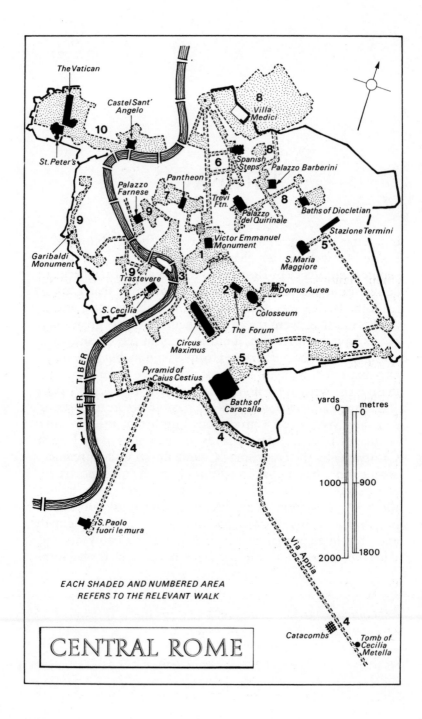

The Vatican

Castel Sant'
Angelo

St. Peter's

10

8

Villa
Medici

Spanish
Steps

Palazzo Barberini

6

Palazzo
Farnese

Pantheon

7

Trevi
Ftn.

8

Palazzo
del Quirinale

8

Baths of Diocletian

9

9

Victor Emmanuel
Monument

Stazione Termini

5

Garibaldi
Monument

9

Trastevere

3

S. Maria
Maggiore

S. Cecilia

2

Domus Aurea

Colosseum

The Forum

5

Circus
Maximus

Pyramid of
Caius Cestius

5

5

RIVER TIBER

4

4

Baths of
Caracalla

yards   metres
0   0

1000   900

S. Paolo
fuori le mura

Via Appia

2000   1800

EACH SHADED AND NUMBERED AREA
REFERS TO THE RELEVANT WALK

4

Catacombs

Tomb of
Cecilia
Metella

CENTRAL ROME

INTRODUCTION

THE LURE OF ROME

When Hannibal, one of Italy's first distinguished foreign visitors, crossed the Alps in the third century BC, his motives and style of travel had little to do with those of the modern tourist. Many centuries would pass before travel to Rome could be considered a cultural or civilized activity, removed from the exigencies of conquest, plunder, or religious pilgrimage. Even after the age of the Grand Tour in the seventeenth and eighteenth centuries, accounts of travel to the Eternal City were often guided by a variety of practical sentiments, often of a very personal nature. It is in the diversity of those sentiments, and the eloquence with which they are expressed, that the joys of travel writing are usually to be found.

The love of art and history are the most obvious reasons why travellers have flocked to Rome and classical lands, 'to mingle with those more refined nations, whom learning and knowledge did first urbanize and polish', as James Howell, a minor diplomat in the court of Charles I put it in the seventeenth century.[1] Rome's bibliography is dominated by the learned accounts of modern historians and art historians, but the Western preoccupation with objectivity and scholarly detachment has often deprived their writing of the feeling and sentiment one relishes in the better first-person or fictional renderings. Among travellers with less specialized interests, the quest for artistic and historical enlightenment was frequently spurred by secondary motives for visiting the Eternal City. Escape in one form or another – from failing or unsatisfying careers and relationships – was a common incentive. So was the search for creative inspiration, for romance, for health, and for ideal beauty.

Goethe left Weimar under an assumed name in the dead of night, abandoning a dull job and a stultifying relationship with a married woman many years his senior. Once in Rome, he wrote in his journal, 'Now I have arrived. I have calmed down and feel as if I had found a peace that will last for my whole life.'[2] The peace that Goethe found was based on the intellectual self-realization he experienced in Rome, but could never find in his native land. Henrik Ibsen shared this perspective when he wrote, 'Here in Rome there is blessed peace for writing', having fled from the failure of his Oslo theatre and his unappreciative critics.[3]

Rome's inducements to creativity were already recognized in the sixteenth century when Erasmus of Rotterdam listed among the city's 'great store of great advantages' the intellectual ferment that resulted from 'the delightful freedom, the many richly furnished libraries, the sweet society of all those great scholars, all the literary conversations, all the monuments of antiquity, and not least, so many leading lights of the world gathered together in one place'.[4] The contrast with London, where he was then living, is neatly evoked later in the same letter. For Turgenev, on the other hand, it was escape from habitual social obligations that spurred his creativity. 'I now feel the desire to get down to work', he wrote to a confidant, 'but that would be impossible in Petersburg; there I would be surrounded by friends, whom it would be a real joy to see, but who would prevent me from being alone; and without being alone there can be no work. Rome is just the sort of city where it's easiest to be by oneself.'[5] For Byron, Shelley, and Browning, Italy simply offered freedom from the moral and political strictures of their native land. Whatever their origins or work habits, ultramontane talents as diverse as Nicholas Poussin and Nathaniel Hawthorne, Nietzsche and Franz Liszt, migrated to Rome where they produced some of their best work.

Other creative individuals returned from Rome with the seed of an idea planted in their mind which only later would bear fruit. In what may be the most ingenuous passage in Gibbon's *Autobiography* (1796), the great historian matter-of-factly relates that 'it was at Rome, on the 15th of October, 1764, as I sat musing amidst the ruins of the Capitol, while the barefooted friars were singing vespers in the Temple of Jupiter, that the idea of writing the decline and fall of the city first started in my mind'.[6] Many are those of lesser talent and lesser ambition in whom Rome ignited a similar spark.

The lure of Rome has proved irresistible to so many expatriate authors that it is easier to gather names of those who never visited the city than of those who did. Blake, Poe, Tennyson, and Proust are among a select group who, for various reasons, stayed away. (Tennyson's reason, according to Browning, was that he turned back at Florence after realizing his favourite brand of tobacco was unavailable in Rome.) Certainly William Shakespeare never visited the city. While foreign travel in his day was not the commonplace it later was to become, his imagination was nonetheless so rich that he was able to depict the city in one narrative poem and five plays. *Shakespeare's Rome* (1983), a recent monograph on the subject, concludes that 'once inside Shakespeare's Eternal City, travellers soon discover that the streets, roads, and paths facing them are as many and as varied as those that lead to its gates'.[7]

'Roma', as every student of Latin learns, is 'amor' spelled backwards. Already in the sixteenth century the poet Joachim Du Bellay wrote of Rome as 'a mistress who resists the poet's courtship and lures him away from his mother country'.[8] Goethe went even farther when he considered *Erotica Romana* as the title for the book he eventually called *Römische Elegien* (1795), and later Freud dreamed of Rome and wrote of its seductive allure in *The Interpretation of Dreams* (1900) and in a series of letters to his friend Wilhelm Fliess.

On an ideal, platonic level, Rome can be as satisfying as it is seductive, but the quest for romantic or carnal love has rarely been as satisfactory. The young James Boswell had a prodigious appetite for local ladies, but his indulgence proved to be costly. In Rome for less than a month in 1765, he first contracted venereal disease and then crab-lice. Oscar Wilde had comparable cravings for young men, but the youths were a constant drain on his wallet and they unnerved him with their jealousies and petty crime. In 1891 Anton Chekhov wrote from Rome to a friend in Russia, 'The guidebooks say a love affair is a must for any tour of Italy. Well, what the hell, I'm ready for anything. An affair would be fine with me.'[9] Fortunately he was spared the heartache.

Even in fiction, few have found true love in Rome. Madame de Staël's Corinne died of a broken heart, Henry James's Daisy Miller succumbed to the poisonous night vapours (the 'malaria'), and Tennessee Williams's Mrs Stone ends her Roman spring in shameful debasement. Like a flame attracting moths, the city has often destroyed those frail characters who are so irresistibly drawn to it. Men are not immune to its disenchantments either. Hawthorne's Donatello (*The Marble Faun*) is consumed by guilt for a murder his lover encouraged him to commit, Henry James's Roderick Hudson falls off a cliff, a victim of his own cupidity, and Thomas Mann's Paolo Hofmann (*The Will to Happiness*), having forsaken Rome for a woman back in Germany, dies on his wedding night.

The narrator in Michel Butor's modern novel *A Change of Heart* (1969) saw the problem most clearly when, during the course of a train journey from Paris to Rome, he decides to end his extra-marital affair with the woman who awaits him at his destination. He does so only after he realizes 'you do not love her without Rome or away from Rome, you love her only because of Rome, because you first owed and you still owe your acquaintance with Rome chiefly to her and she is the doorway to Rome, just as Mary, in Catholic litanies, is called the doorway to heaven'.[10] Few fictional protagonists have ever been so wise. But Butor, of course, is French. Americans in particular have always had more difficulty seeing the city for what it is. Their puritanical heritage taught them that Rome's physical sensuality leads inevitably to sin. Since sin had to be punished, the American novel set in Italy had a ready, if somewhat predictable thematic structure. This is the plot that links authors as diverse as Nathaniel Hawthorne and Tennessee Williams. Henry James in particular saw Rome as a place where no good could ever come to innocent American romantics. His fictional characters 'remain in Rome only to be morally corrupted, artistically destroyed, financially ruined, physically maimed, or flat-out killed'.[11]

By the end of the eighteenth century a notion had advanced in some quarters that the warm Italian climate was responsible for overheating the passions and scorching souls. This view was put most succinctly in a couplet in Byron's *Don Juan* (1819–24):

What men call gallantry, and gods adultery
Is much more common where the climate's sultry.[12]

Originally proposed by Montesquieu and again by Madame de Staël, the theory of the climates, as it is called, found one of its most devoted adherents in Thomas Mann. In *The Will to Happiness*, Mann suggested that 'the warm wind carries across the sultry inertia of the orient', while in *Death in Venice* (1912), the sweltering torpidity of the atmosphere plays a major role first in Aschenbach's emotional release, and subsequently in his death.[13]

English authors from the beginning often took a more cynical attitude towards the Italian experience. In *The Unfortunate Traveller* (1594), Thomas Nashe finds Italy a place where foreigners learn 'the art of atheism, the art of epicurizing, the art of whoring, the art of poisoning, the art of sodomitry'.[14] Similar views are expressed in the travel literature of the next two centuries. The trend culminates in Samuel Sharp's *Letters from Italy* (1766), a volume so vituperative that it quickly provoked a two-volume rejoinder by the Italian Giuseppe Baretti. The English, morover, were renowned for their satirical portraits of both host and visitor, in first-person accounts and fiction alike. Few novelistic renderings can match the graphic depiction of Viscount Flimsey's dissipation in John Shebbeare's *Lydia* (1755). Immersed in a world of scoundrels and easy women, he returns home penniless and a hardened criminal, unenlightened and unredeemed by his experience in the Eternal City. Tales like this can only have stiffened the resolve of churchmen like the Reverend John Chetwode Eustace who, in the preliminary discourse of his

Classical Tour through Italy (1813) preached, 'But one final observation, I wish to impress strongly on the mind of the youthful traveller . . . moral improvement is or ought to be, the end of all our pursuits and all our exertions'.[15] More realistic perhaps was the view of Eustace's contemporary Joseph Cradock, who wrote in his *Memoirs* (1826–8) that 'foreign travel is knowledge to a wise man, and foppery to a fool'.[16] The same sentiment was premonitorily expressed in Henry James's tragic novel *Roderick Hudson* (1875) when, early in the book, Rowland Mallet says 'if Roman life doesn't do something substantial to make you happier, it increases tenfold your liability to moral misery'.[17]

Laurence Sterne describes twelve kinds of travellers in *A Sentimental Journey* (1768). The first of these leaves his native land for reasons of health, the second and third for 'imbecility of mind, or inevitable necessity'.[18] While it may seem strange today, a fair number of travellers in the past came to Rome for their health. John Keats was the best-known example of the failure of this regimen, but a Roman sojourn may have prolonged Shelley's life long enough for him to have drowned off the Ligurian coast in 1822. A consumptive like Keats, Shelley left England 'seeking health and sun and flying from the shadows of his first marriage'. Italy provided him with light and warmth. 'I depend on these things for life', he wrote, 'for in the smoke of cities and the tumult of human kind, and the chilling fogs and rains of our own country I can hardly be said to live'.[19]

In 1859 the English winter drove an asthmatic Edward Lear from Sussex to Rome. To a friend left behind he sent a poem *en route*:

> I send you this, that you may know
> I've left the Sussex shore,
> And coming here two days ago
> Do cough for evermore.
>
> Or gasping hard for breath do sit
> Upon a brutal chair
> For to lie down in Asthma fit
> Is what I cannot bear.

> Or sometimes sneeze and always blow
> My well-developed nose
> And altogether never know
> No comfort or repose.[20]

It is easy to imagine how, in an age of primitive medicine, one might be driven to desperation. In his *Diary of an Invalid* (1820), the Englishman Henry Matthews disclosed that 'in obedience to medical advice, I have determined to set out on a wild-goose chase after health, and try like honest Tristram Shandy . . . to run away from death'.[21]

Going to Rome to die may be the ultimate test of one's romantic idealism. The Protestant Cemetery contains the final plot of many a minor author who shared Chateaubriand's 'dearest dream' of 'eternal exile among the ruins of Rome'.[22] For others the lure may have been simple comfort. While an ailing Sinclair Lewis lived his final days in a lavish glass-walled apartment overlooking the Tiber, the philosopher George Santayana decided to end his life tended by nuns in a Roman nursing home. In his poem 'To an Old Philosopher in Rome' (1952), Wallace Stevens wrote:

> It is a kind of total grandeur at the end,
> With every visible thing enlarged and yet
> No more than a bed, a chair, and moving nuns,
> The immensest theatre, the pillared porch,
> The book and candle in your ambered room.[23]

THE FATAL GIFT OF BEAUTY

For the greatest number of travellers, the attraction of Rome lay not in its salons or hospitals but in the classical past. In the *Pleasure of Ruins* (1953), Rose Macaulay explains why this was so:

> The ascendency over men's minds of the ruins of the stupendous past, the past of history, legend and myth, at once factual and fantastic, stretching back and back into ages that can be surmised, is half-mystical in basis. The

intoxification, at once so heady and so devout, is not the
romantic melancholy engendered by broken towers and
mouldered stones; it is the soaring of the imagination into
the high empyrean where huge episodes are tangled with
myths and dreams; it is the stunning impact of world
history on its amazed heirs.[24]

During the Middle Ages, and sometimes afterwards, the
antiquities of Rome were used as stone quarries, with little or
no regard for the history or workmanship of the monuments
themselves. With the revival of classical learning in the Renaissance, the ancient remains came to be treated with new
respect. Humanists from Petrarch to Palladio celebrated the
ruins and were inspired by them in their own work. But
Renaissance artists and writers were also at times ambivalent
about what they saw. The strain of competition with long-
departed rivals is one of the major motifs in Joachim Du
Bellay's *Les Antiquitez de Rome* (1558), a work that has been
recently called

> a poem not so much about the ruins as about a man
> responding to ruins, trying quite explicitly to perform a
> necromantic resurrection . . . It is at once an accepted
> homage, a challenge, a ritual of summoning, a gesture of
> disinterment, a reconstruction, and a demystifying reflec-
> tion on all these attempts. They are all tinged with the
> suspicion of failure, even the demystification.[25]

The seventeenth and early eighteenth centuries frequently
viewed ancient monuments in more allegorical terms. John
Dyer's long poem 'The Ruins of Rome' (1740) exemplified the
trend to see emblems of *vanitas* in every fallen stone:

> Fall'n, Fall'n, a silent Heap; her Heroes all
> Sunk in their Urns; behold the Pride of Pomp,
> The Throne of Nations fall'n; obscur'd in dust . . .[26]

Like Milton before him, Dyer was a puritan whose moral
principles were in conflict with the sensuous beauty he found
in Italy everywhere he looked. The thoughtful Protestant
tourist of the later eighteenth century – not the fictional

Viscount Flimsey and his crowd – could either lose himself in archaeological study, or harp upon the disgraces that papal rule had imposed on the city since the Reformation.

But the writing of so-called 'ruin poems' and 'graveyard literature' continued through the Enlightenment, spurred no doubt by the decline of religious belief and growing interest in vaguer questions of existence and the destiny of the human soul.[27] The culmination of the genre came with Byron's *Childe Harold's Pilgrimage* (1818) in verses like:

> Oh Rome! my country! city of the soul!
> The orphans of the heart must turn to thee,
> Lone mother of dead empires![28]

Byron's poem was popular not only in its own day, but it exerted a powerful influence on subsequent generations. As one critic has recently pointed out, 'When Matthew Arnold turns his attention to the triumph of Alaric, or Dorothea Brooks visits the ruins of Rome in *Middlemarch*, or Thomas Cole begins his designs for a series of mammoth paintings on *The Course of Empire*, Byron's spirit weighs upon them with the force of centuries'.[29]

Byron's sentiments ignited dimmer lights as well. Inspired by the lines they had memorized in school, the memoirs of countless 'idle women' and 'gentlemen of Leisure' of the Victorian era are usually as conventional as they are seemingly self-indulgent. One of the better minds to take up the challenge was Violet Paget, better known as Vernon Lee. In *The Spirit of Rome* (1906), she makes the offhand remark that 'poets really make places', a belief that in a sense summarizes the outlook of the genre as a whole.[30]

THE JOURNEY

Whether bouncing by carriage on rutted roads or aloft at 30,000 feet with the aggravations of a modern airport left behind, few travellers past or present would say that getting there is half the fun. But for a bright and short-lived moment of luxurious ship travel earlier this century, the journey to Rome has never been an altogether pleasant experience.

Joseph Addison had yet to set foot on the continent when, disembarking at Calais, he fell straight into the harbour. Once in France, the early tourist had to pass through those 'high and hideous Alps . . . those uncouth, huge, monstrous, Excrescences of Nature' as James Howell put it in the seventeenth century.[31] Within Italy the roads in some places were little better. Lady Pomfret complained of a 'rough and dismal journey' going from Siena to Rome in 1741, as she and her party were 'obliged to get out and walk several times for fear of breaking our necks'.[32]

The trip could take weeks or months depending on one's pace. In the eighteenth century Walpole reported making about six miles an hour in a chaise over good roads, while Smollett managed but two 'at the risque of breaking your neck every minute' in the mountains.[33] But the nineteenth century saw some remarkable improvements. Napoleon opened the Mont Cencis Pass through the Alps early in the century and in 1870 this was replaced by a tunnel. Steamship service from Marseilles to Naples and across the Atlantic from America was introduced in the 1830s, while late in the same decade trains started to run in every European country. Rushing passengers to their destinations with a minimum of inconvenience, the railway system quickly led to an increased number of tourists. As travel became easier, the quality of the experience naturally diminished. It was thus with some nostalgia that Pauline Craven lamented in her novel *Anne Séverin* (1868) that

> Those who arrive at Rome by the railway, and rush like a whirlwind into a station, cannot imagine the effect which the words 'Ecco Roma' formerly produced when, on arriving at the point in the road from which the Eternal City could be descried for the first time, the postillion stopped his horses, and, pointing it out to the traveller in the distance, pronounced them with that Roman accent which is grave and sonorous as the name of Rome itself.[34]

Group travel inevitably followed, and in 1864 Thomas Cook offered the first conducted excursion of Italy. Not everyone was pleased with this development either, and an article soon appeared in *Blackwood's Magazine* which reported that some enterprizing and unscrupulous man [Thomas Cook] has devised the project of conducting some forty or fifty persons . . . from London to Naples and back for a fixed sum. He contracts to carry them, feed them, and amuse them. . . . When I first read the scheme . . . I imagined that the characteristic independence of Englishmen would revolt against a plan that reduces the traveller to the level of his trunk and obliterates every trace and trait of the individual. I was all wrong. As I write, the cities of Italy are deluged with droves of these creatures.[35]

The Grand Tour was thereby doomed. 'Travel is work', Paul Fussell has written, and with mass transportation and pre-arranged schedules, real 'travel is impossible and tourism is all we have left'.[36]

Lost luggage and delays of a few hours may seem like major vexations to the modern tourist, but the hazards of travel were naturally harsher in the past. Misadventures on the road to Rome ranged from Petrarch's being kicked by a horse and badly injured in 1350, to Walpole's dog being eaten by a wolf in 1739. Casanova was sexually assaulted by a policeman in 1761, a century after Francis Osborne's *Advice to a Son* warned, 'Who travels Italy handsome, young, and beardless may need as much caution and circumspection to protect him from the lust of men as the charms of women'.[37]

Apprehensions over crime were just as worrying. 'The country in general, especially Naples, swarms with pick-pockets', warned one eighteenth-century guidebook.[38] However the perils of petty crime paled before the more serious dangers posed by *banditti*. Few tourists, it is true, were actually murdered, but there is no shortage of hair-raising tales of anxious moments at the hands of roadside outlaws. The best-documented account is that of William Moens who, in *English Travellers and Italian Brigands* (1866), tells of being sequestered, starved, and terrorized in the mountains for four months until a ransom of 30,000 ducats was paid.

Some early travellers wagered the risks of a journey southward against high interest accounts payable upon their return. At the beginning of the seventeenth century, the rate from

London to Italy was 300 per cent. Shakespeare speaks of the practice in *The Tempest* and Fynes Moryson in 1617 decried its abuses by bankrupts seeking solvency and actors in search of notoriety. That travel in the twentieth century is safer than it was in the past is affirmed by E. S. Bates in *Touring in 1600* (1911):

> At the present day . . . the safest insurance company will not only lay fifty to one that the traveller *will* return, in place of the rate then of three to five to one that he would *not*, but will further insure him against accidents at a lower rate than if he became a London butcher.[39]

ACCOMMODATION

Apart from inveterate fault-finders like Samuel Sharp and Tobias Smollett, most foreign visitors were in the main pleased with Italian inns, at least those in the larger towns and cities. Montaigne's description from 1580 of the Orso and the Vaso d'Oro in Rome with their gilded leather and 'silks such as kings would use' would appeal, four centuries later, to the most discriminating tastes of today.[40] In Italy, one could sleep alone or with a companion of one's choosing. This was not the case in Germany, for example, where the innkeeper would choose one's bedfellows, who might turn out to be a gentleman or a carter, and 'all that could safely be prophesied about him was that he would be drunk when he came to bed'.[41]

Accommodation in Rome remained praiseworthy throughout the eighteenth and nineteenth centuries. Damp sheets, assorted bugs, unheated apartments, and high prices were the most common complaints, but the consensus, according to the Reverend Eustace, in his *Classical Tour through Italy*, was that 'the greater inns, particularly in Rome, Naples, Florence, and Venice, are good, and in general the linen is clean and the beds are excellent'.[42]

Those intent on longer stays sought furnished apartments, of which by the mid-nineteenth century 'the number to be let [in Rome] is great beyond conception'.[43] Some of the best-situated and noblest palaces in the city were rented to foreigners, as Keats's address in Piazza di Spagna and William Wetmore Story's in the Palazzo Barberini make clear. In the light of such past amenities, the modern middle-class expatriate would be wise to lower his own expectations. Seeking a furnished flat in the *centro storico* today is not the easy and rewarding task it once was. Bernard Malamud's short story 'Behold the Key' (1958) narrates the bizarre experience of a month-long and ultimately unsuccessful quest for housing by an American graduate student. Thirty years later, in *Playing Away* (1988), Michael Mewshaw indicates that the situation has not improved: 'Believe me, honest to God, this is gospel truth, *la vera verità*, as Italians put it. Renting an apartment in Rome is like no other agony that afflicts modern man'.[44]

READING ABOUT ROME

Serious sightseers require serious guidebooks with occasional supplements of inspirational literature. In the Middle Ages works like the *Mirabilia Urbis Romae* guided pilgrims through churches and catacombs, while poems like Hildebert of Lavardin's 'De Roma' sang the elegiac theme – originally sounded by Procopius in late antiquity – of the present Rome being but a pale shadow of its former self. For centuries, Hildebert's lines would resound timelessly:

> Rome, thy great ruins, still beyond compare,
> Thy former greatness mournfully declare,
> Through time thy stately palaces around
> Hath strew'd, and cast thy temples to the ground.[45]

With the invention of printing and the growth of secular tourism after the Reformation, the writing of travel books increased dramatically. These, as R. S. Pine-Coffin has pointed out, can conveniently be divided into two classes, those written for tourists and those written by them.[46] By the end of the eighteenth century, scores of Italian travel accounts had appeared in English and other European languages while in the first half of the nineteenth century the true guidebook came into being. In 1843 the authoritative and widely read

Murray's Handbook for Travellers in Central Italy was issued. Published simultaneously in London, Paris, Leipzig, and Florence, this handy tome was continually revised and in its final incarnation as *A Handbook of Rome and its Environs*, had appeared in nineteen editions by the year 1899.

By the end of the nineteenth century, the Murray guide had become a myth in its own right. Albert Bierstadt's 1855 painting of the *Portico of Octavia* (Plate 4) shows a tourist traipsing through the central fish market with its tell-tale red cover prominently tucked under his arm. Offhand references to it occur in many a written account. In the work of Henry James, the book is repeatedly used as a symbol of intellectual pursuit overshadowing the passions. Thus it seems like a major turning point in *Roderick Hudson* when, in the course of earnest conversation with Rowland Mallet, Mary Garland 'let the *Murray* slide down to the ground, and he was so charmed with this circumstance that he made no movement to pick it up'. A moment later, however, the girl recovers her composure 'and picking up her *Murray* she fairly buried her nose in it'.[47]

Before Thomas Cook and American Express put most of them out of business, freelance guides known as *ciceroni* were much in evidence. Of the many uncomplimentary tributes paid them, that in James Russell Lowell's *Fireside Travels* (1865) is perhaps the most amusing. A certain Leopoldo

> had found me in the morning celebrating due rites before the Sibyl's Temple with strange incense of the nicotian herb, and had marked me for his prey. At the very high tide of sentiment, when the traveller lies with oyster-like openness in the soft ooze of reverie, do these parasitic crabs, the *ciceroni*, insert themselves as his inseparable bosom companions. . . . Vain are thy poor crustaceous efforts at self-isolation. The foe henceforth is a part of thy consciousness, thy landscape, and thyself, happy only if that irritation breed in thee the pearl of patience and of voluntary abstraction.[48]

Fed up with importunate guides and inflexible guidebooks, the English journalist George Sala recommended in 1866 that

The best way to inspect the streets of Rome, if you wish
to study as well as see them, is to break your pocket-
compass and burn your maps and guide-books, as Pros-
pero did his conjuring apparatus, and forgetting that such
things as *ciceroni* ever existed, take Chance for a Mentor,
and lose yourself.[49]

Nevertheless, at the very beginning of *Roba di Roma* (1862),
William Wetmore Story flatly states that 'every Englishman
carries a Murray for information and a Byron for sentiment,
and finds out by them what he is to know and feel at every
step'.[50]

The habit of reading or recollecting a classic of literature
while standing before its subject is a long-standing one. Grand
Tourists with a classical education could, like Smollett in
1765, look over the Tiber and recite from Horace, Livy, and
Ovid. Stendhal asks rhetorically if there is a description of the
Apollo Belvedere in *Corinne* (1807); Berlioz read Byron in a St
Peter's confessional to escape the heat; and Herman Melville
could think only of Shelley's *Prometheus* (1818–19) while
prowling about the Baths of Caracalla.

Among the many preconceptions that travellers brought
with them were those they had read in the great books. The
well-read tourist of today still faces the problem. In *Italian
Days* (1989), Barbara Grizzuti Harrison steps into St Peter's
and her head fills with 'arguments derived from literature: St
Peter's is absurdly vulgar, it is absurdly pretty; it is vast, it is
disappointingly small; it is beautiful, it is pretentious. . . .'[51]

CULTURAL BAGGAGE

Literary preconceptions and those derived from guidebooks
like Murray's or Hillard's were only part of the traveller's
baggage. One's religious and political background played an
even greater role. From the time that Martin Luther arrived in
Rome a pilgrim and left a reformer, Christian visitors have
been of two minds when facing the many appurtenances of the
Catholic faith. Puritan iconoclasm blinded many visitors to
almost any painting, sculpture, or work of architecture
created in the late Renaissance or Baroque periods. Since the

pope remained Rome's temporal and spiritual leader until the Risorgimento, or Unification of Italy in 1870, such icono-clasm was usually accompanied by widespread discontent with the municipal governance as well. The sight of repugnant beggars in dirty streets only added to the distaste engendered by what John Evelyn called the 'unimaginable superstition' of Catholic ritual.

At its worst, anti-papal sentiment in the seventeenth and eighteenth centuries provoked a number of tracts whose attacks on popery were only loosely disguised by their travel-book format. Among the more popular of these was an anonymous volume, several times reprinted, entitled *A Pilgrimage to the Grand Jubilee at Rome, In the Year 1700*. On the title page, the reader is informed that the book contains, among other things, 'A diverting account of . . . the de-bauch'd Lives and Intrigues of the lustful Priests and Nuns'.

If the nineteenth century lacked the satirical nature of the eighteenth, it could be just as intolerant. In *Pictures from Italy* (1846), Charles Dickens freely offers his impression of step-ping into a Roman church:

> The scene in all the churches is the strangest possible. The same montonous, heartless, drowsy chanting, always going on; the same dark building . . . the same lamps dimly burning; the selfsame people kneeling here and there . . . There are the same dirty beggars stopping in their muttered prayers to beg; the same miserable cripples exhibiting their deformity at the doors; the same blind men, rattling little pots like kitchen pepper-castors – their depositories for alms; the same preposterous crowns of silver stuck upon the painted heads of single saints and Virgins in crowded pictures . . . the same favourite shrine or figure smothered with little silver hearts and crosses . . . the same odd mixture of respect and inde-corum, faith and phlegm – kneeling on the stones and spitting on them, loudly; getting up from prayers to beg a little, or to pursue some other worldly matter, and then kneeling down again, to resume the contrite supplication at the point where it was interrupted.[52]

Catholics naturally did not see it the same way. The *United States Catholic Magazine* printed an unsigned review of Dickens's book in 1847 in which the author roundly assailed

> the peculiar political bias or religious prejudices of certain writers who . . . are, for the most part, utterly incapable of giving us a correct picture of Italian language, and still less of Italian manners and feelings. They do not mingle much with the people, but are content to view them at a distance. Their associations are chiefly with their own set; with English or American travellers as ignorant, as frivolous, and as prejudiced as themselves.[53]

The reviewer's final point that his quarry remained aloof from the Roman people is inarguable. He might have further commented that for centuries foreign visitors had created stereotypes as quickly as stereotypes were in turn made of them. Professor Canepa's study 'From Degenerate Soundrel to Noble Savage: the Italian Stereotype in Eighteenth-Century British Travel Literature' illustrates but one aspect of the practice.[54] By and large, the reflected image of the Roman people has not been flattering. For the most part, they are thought unworthy of their cultural heritage, and their dark and passionate nature is found attractive only if the person described happens to be a woman. Shelley's remark that even 'countesses smell so of garlic that an ordinary Englishman cannot approach them' was not unusual for its day.[55]

It is one of the achievements of the modern age that travellers are freer of cultural prejudices to see with their own eyes, and value their experiences independently. The French have traditionally been better at this than Anglo-Saxons, but among English-speaking travellers for pleasure, one of the pioneers was the American novelist Edith Wharton. Given the stifling conventions of her own life, it is perhaps not surprising that her writing consistently questions the power of society to shape individual choices. Speaking strictly of art, her 1905 autobiography *Italian Backgrounds* vigorously protested the way 'the guide-book tourist has been taught to look askance [at objects], or rather . . . has been counselled to pass [them] by without a look'.[56] The objective sympathy that she advocates instead is laudable, although the detached attitude subsequently adopted in most contemporary guidebooks has rendered them heartless, soulless, and very dull reading.

With enough readers like Evelyn Waugh, who preferred all but the worst travel books to all but the very best novels, the old-fashioned travel memoir has recently made a remarkable comeback. Rambling and self-indulgent, but often witty and incisive, some of these may even provide a painless and practical alternative to Huxley's proposition that 'for every traveller who has any taste of his own, the only useful guidebook will be the one which he himself has written'.[57]

A MISCELLANY OF ROMAN IMPRESSIONS

For the present I know not where to start, overwhelmed as I am by the wonder of so many things and by the greatness of my astonishment. There is one thing that I do want to tell you, however, which happened contrary to what you expected. As I recall, you used to dissuade me from coming for a particular reason, which was that if the ruins of the city did not correspond to its fame and to the impressions I had received from books, my love for it would diminish. I, too, although burning with desire, willingly used to postpone my visit, fearing that what I had imagined in my mind, my eyes would belittle at the moment of reality which is always injurious to a reputation. Such reality I am happy to say diminished nothing and instead increased everything. In truth Rome was greater, and greater are its ruins than I imagined. I no longer wonder that the whole world was conquered by this city but that I was conquered so late.

Petrarch, *Rerum familiarium* (c. 1350)[58]

[The] state of affairs in Rome beggars description. You can find there a buying and selling, a bartering and a bargaining, a lying and trickery, robbery and stealing, pomp, procuration, knavery, and all sorts of stratagems bringing God into contempt, till it would be impossible for the Antichrist to govern more wickedly. There is

nothing in Venice, Antwerp, or Cairo to compare with
the fair which traffics in Rome. In those cities, right and
reason enjoy some respect; but here things go on in a way
that pleases the devil himself.

> Martin Luther, *An Appeal to the Ruling Class of*
> *German Nationality as to the Amelioration of the*
> *State of Christendom* (1520)[59]

I hardly slept the night before I arriv'd there with y^e
thoughts of seeing it – my heart beat high, my imagination expanded itself, & my Eyes flash'd again, as I drew
near the *Porta del Popolo*; but the moment I enter'd it, I fell
at once from my Airy Vision & Utopian Ideas into a very
dirty ill looking *place*, (as they call it) with three crooked
streets in front, terminated indeed at this End with two
tolerable Churches – w^t a disappointment! my Spirits
sunk & it was wth reluctance that I was drag'd in the
afternoon to see the Pantheon – but my God, w^t was my
Pleasure & Surprize! – I never felt so much in my life as
when I entered that glorious Structure: I gap'd, but could
not speak for 5 Minutes – It is so very noble, that it has not
been ye Power of Modern Frippery, or Popery (for it is a
Church you know) to extinguish Its grandeur & Elegance
– Here I began to think myself in *Old* Rome . . .

> David Garrick, *Letter* (1763)[60]

But my letter would never be at an end if I were to try [to]
tell a millionth part of the delights of Rome – it has such
an effect on me that my past life before I saw it appears a
blank and now I begin to live – in the churches you hear
the music of heaven and the singing of angels.

> Mary Wollstonecraft Shelley, *Letter* (1819)[61]

What a spring! God, what a spring! But you know what a
young fresh spring amid the crumbling ruins blossoming
with ivy and wild flowers is. How beautiful the blue
patches of sky are now – between the trees barely covered
with a fresh almost yellow greenery, and even cypresses,
dark as a raven's wing . . . What air! It seems that when

you inhale through your nose at least 700 angels will fly in
your nostrils. A wonderful spring!

Nikolai Gogol, *Letter* (1838)[62]

At last – for the first time – I live! It beats everything: it
leaves the Rome of your fancy – your education –
nowhere. It makes Venice – Florence – Oxford – London
– seem like little cities of pasteboard. . . . For the first
time I know what the picturesque is.

Henry James, *Letter* (1869)[63]

The young man asked Mrs Miller how she was pleased
with Rome. 'Well, I must say I am disappointed', she
answered. 'We had heard so much about it; I suppose we
had heard too much. But we couldn't help that. We had
been led to expect something different.'

Henry James, *Daisy Miller* (1878)[64]

I remember Rome chiefly as the place where Zelda and I
had an appalling squabble. In fact, that afternoon and
noon with you was the only luminous spot in our stay.

F. Scott Fitzgerald, *Letter* (1922)[65]

I don't know why one feels it to be so much superior to
other cities – partly the colour I suppose. It is a perfect
day; all the flowers are just out, there are great bushes of
azalea set in the paths; Judas trees, cypresses, lawns,
statues, among which go wandering the Italian nurses in
their primrose and pink silks with their veils and laces and
instead of being able to read Proust, as I had meant . . . I
find myself undulating like a fish in and out of leaves and
flowers and swimming round a vast earthenware jar
which changes from orange red to leaf green – It is
incredibly beautiful – oh, and there's St Peter's in the
distance; and people sitting on the parapet, all very distinguished, the loveliest women in Europe, with little
proud heads . . .

Virginia Woolf, *Letter* (1927)[66]

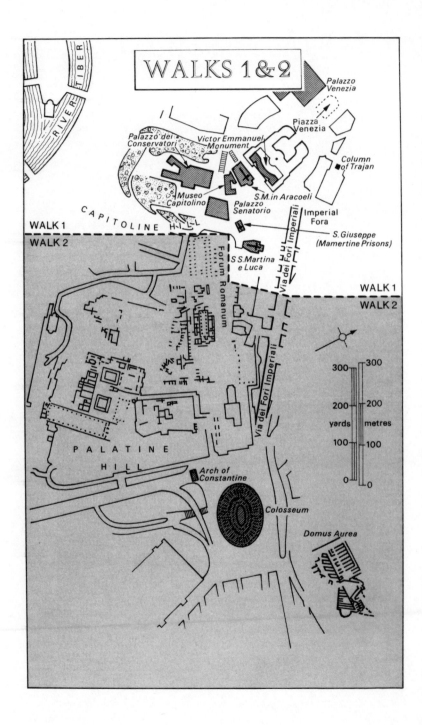

WALKS 1 & 2

RIVER TIBER

Palazzo Venezia

Piazza Venezia

Palazzo dei Conservatori

Victor Emmanuel Monument

Column of Trajan

Museo Capitolino

S.M.in Aracoeli

Palazzo Senatorio

CAPITOLINE HILL

Imperial Fora

WALK 1

WALK 2

S.Giuseppe (Mamertine Prisons)

Via dei Fori Imperiali

SS.Martina e Luca

Forum Romanum

WALK 1

WALK 2

Via dei Fori Imperiali

300   300

200   200

yards   metres

100   100

0   0

PALATINE   HILL

Arch of Constantine

Colosseum

Domus Aurea

1

FIRST WALK

*From the Piazza Venezia to the Capitoline Hill and
the Imperial Forums*

THE PIAZZA VENEZIA

The Piazza Venezia is the very centre of modern Rome and is
the city's principal hub of traffic and human activity. It is
rarely one's final destination, but twenty-three bus routes stop
there and to go almost anywhere in the city one must pass
through it. Pedestrians and motorists alike find navigating this
sea of chaos and clamour to be a nerve-racking experience.
Like an oriental bazaar, it is stimulating for some and exhausting for others. It should be kept in mind, however, that
Rome's traffic and noise and pollution are hardly the inventions of modern times. Some of the most vociferous accounts
of these urban ills are found in the writings of antiquity. Two
thousand years ago Horace warned in an Epistle, 'If pleasant
ease and sleep till sunrise be your delight, if dust and noise of
wheels . . . offend you, I shall advise you [to leave Rome]',
while Juvenal, in a famous Satire written some years later,
frets over the fact that 'The traffic of carts in narrow winding
streets, and the din when a herd of cattle is blocked, would rob
of his sleep even a Drusus, or a sea-calf!'[1]

While chaotic traffic and unbearable noise have always
played a part in Roman life, the Piazza Venezia is a com-
paratively modern addition. It was created only after Rome

was made the capital of the newly unified Italy in 1870. All that
remains of the original, more modest Renaissance square is the
Palazzo Venezia, a sombre palace built in the fifteenth century,
which now houses a disorderly art library and a museum
whose permanent collection is seldom on view. The original
owner, the Venetian cardinal Pietro Barbo, later Paul II, led a
somewhat unusual life. According to Kate Simon:

> He changed night into day, holding conferences and
> luncheon feasts at 3 a.m., and slept through the day, well
> protected from Roman noise by thick palace walls. A
> high and eccentric liver, his death was attributed to
> indigestion, translated by anticlerical Romans into a set of
> small devils piercing, pinching, chopping at his entrails.

Centuries later, Simon continues, 'one of the most memorable portraits of Mussolini has him standing on a balcony of
the Palazzo Venezia, the big jaw and forceful eyes like batter-
ing rams, exhorting thousands in the expansive piazza below'.[2]

Cardinal Barbo's gloomy fortress nowadays defers to the
monstrously imposing Victor Emmanuel Monument which
looms over the entire piazza. Dedicated to the first king of the
unified Italy, this bold structure was built in 1884–1911 and is
playfully referred to as the 'Wedding Cake' or the 'Giant
Typewriter'. The eminent architectural historian Henry-
Russell Hitchcock has called it 'the most pretentious of all
nineteenth-century monuments' and even the customarily
gracious Eleanor Clark found its 'cold and stupefying white-
ness' hard to praise.[3] Probably the most accurate and dis-
passionate assessment of the building is that of Carroll Meeks
who in *Italian Architecture 1750–1914* (1966) wrote:

> The form is unique . . . No traditional theme could have
> had equal power; no temple, dome, or triumphal arch
> could have been contrived on this scale, only a ziggurat or
> a pyramid. But neither of them would have the stamp of
> the nineteenth century so markedly. Artists and students
> have often dreamed of such fantasies, but they have
> remained on paper.[4]

The Capitoline Hill

The adjacent Capitoline Hill or Campidoglio is a welcome relief from the frenzy of the Piazza Venezia and the bombast of the Victor Emmanuel Monument. Nothing, alas, remains of the ancient Capitol or the venerable Temple of Jupiter Capitolinus, whose loss has been called 'the single most grievous gap in our knowledge of Roman architecture'.[5] Today one ascends a broad, aerobically demanding ramp to the complex designed by Michelangelo in the 1530s (Plate 1). This is probably the calmest, most serene, and architecturally satisfying urban ensemble in the world. Goethe revisited the site on his last day in Rome in 1788 and found it 'like an enchanted palace in a desert'.[6]

Surprisingly, most early visitors were not as enchanted as Goethe. In 1644 John Evelyn signalled what was to become a prevailing attitude when, with lukewarm praise, he described it as 'certainly one of the most renowned places in the world; even as now built by the designe of the famous M: Angelo'.[7] The Marquis de Sade went a step farther when in *Voyage d'Italie* (1775–6) he practically apologized

> for not having spoken of the Capitol, as the first object on which the traveller's attention should alight; but the few ancient beauties that remain there are completely swamped by the new ones, by façades, by vistas: in a word, this celebrated spot has been so cut down to size by all the modern beauties of Rome that it now has to be ranked as ordinary.[8]

The prejudice against 'modern' art and architecture – what we now call Renaissance and Baroque – ran deep, particularly among visitors from Protestant cultures. This in turn was combined with a deeper respect for the classical past than we may feel today. Joseph Forsyth, a retired schoolmaster, perhaps put it most plainly when in 1813 he wrote, 'the modern architecture [of the Capitol] struck me as unworthy of ground so sacred and so august'.[9] Feelings of disappointment on visiting the site are commonplace in the literature of the nineteenth century. William Wordsworth composed a sonnet

on this very theme, and Henry James did not mince words
when in 'A Roman Holiday' (1873) he wrote:

> I walked down by the back streets to the steps mounting
> to the Capitol – that long inclined plain, rather, broken at
> every two paces, which is the unfailing disappointment, I
> believe of tourists primed for retrospective raptures.
> Certainly the Capitol seen from this side isn't command-
> ing. The hill is so low, the ascent so narrow, Michael
> Angelo's architecture in the quadrangle at the top so
> meagre, the whole place somehow so much more of a
> mole-hill than a mountain, that for the first ten minutes of
> your standing there Roman history seems suddenly to
> have sunk through a trap-door. [10]

In a letter to his mother written in 1869, James, nevertheless, did admit to being moved by the equestrian statue of
Marcus Aurelius in the centre of the square:

> I like this grand old effigy better every time I see it. It
> commands the sympathies somehow more than any
> work of art I know. If to directly impress the soul, the
> heart, the affections, to stir up by some ineffable magic
> the sense of all one's human relations and of the warm
> surrounding frames of human life – if this is the sign of a
> great work of art – this statue is one of the very greatest. [11]

The Marcus Aurelius, in fact, is an ancient work, untainted
by the patronage of the Counter-Reformation papacy. The
only pope who can be associated with it is Paul III who moved
it from the Lateran Palace in 1538. Other pre-Christian remains on the Campidoglio were just as capable of stirring the
spirits of early visitors. George Eliot, in her Roman diary of
1860, reserved all her praise for the two *colossi* that stand at the
crest of the hill, adding that 'their large-eyed, mild might,
gives one a thrill of awe'. [12] Only in the twentieth century does
one begin to experience really appreciative sentiments for the
Capitoline ensemble as a whole. H. V. Morton in *A Traveller
in Rome* (1957) captures the exact essence of the place, past and
present:

The Capitoline Hill is, I think, one of the most perfect spots in Rome. Lifted above the noise of the city and undisturbed by the conflict between old and new, one passes, as it were, through a gateway into the sixteenth century, where all the beauty of that age is frozen in three sides of a square of exquisite, peach-coloured buildings. In the centre Marcus Aurelius, his curly hair and beard newly scented and barbered, rides his bronze horse, still touched with gilt, as if he were riding on some sunny morning ages ago. In all cities there are certain places, a church or a garden, where one may go as to sanctuary in moments of happiness or sorrow; and in spite of its grand and stormy memories, this piazza on the Capitol is such a place to me. The centuries lap at its feet and roll away in stormy vistas all round it, and the rock of the Capitol, where the philosopher rides his golden horse, is lifted like some ark above the flood of time.[13]

The post-antique buildings on the Capitoline Hill were originally constructed for the use of Rome's ceremonial and largely ineffectual civic government. Both the Palazzo Senatorio, which one faces from the ramp, and the Palazzo dei Conservatori, on the right, had their origins in the late Middle Ages. The incoherent design and shabby setting of these buildings proved a major embarrassment for the papacy when the Holy Roman Emperor Charles V paid a visit to the site in 1536. Pope Paul III wasted little time in subsequently commissioning Michelangelo to reconstruct the two *palazzi* and provide them with stylish Renaissance façades. Offended by the lack of symmetry, the great architect designed a third palace on the left of the square, whose only function was aesthetic, in exact imitation of the Palazzo dei Conservatori. Construction of this third palace was not immediate, however, and it was only built in the middle of the seventeenth century, long after Michelangelo's death.

Since the eighteenth century, the two side *palazzi* have served as public museums. Together, these collections – the Capitoline Museum in the new palace on the left and the Conservator's Museum and Pinacoteca (Picture Gallery) on

the right – contain thousands of works of art. Not surprisingly, most of these are works of classical antiquity. The
English essayist William Hazlitt came away with a composite
impression of the many 'old heads of senators, warriors,
philosophers' to be found there:

> They all have the freshness of truth and nature. They
> shew something substantial in mortality, they are the
> only things that do not crush and overturn our sense of
> personal identity; and are a fine relief to the mouldering
> relics of antiquity, and to the momentary littleness of
> modern things.[14]

If the theme of *vanitas* occasionally preoccupied visitors in
the past, travellers in our own secular age sometimes seem just
as silly in their quest for modern relevance. H. V. Morton, for
instance, suggests that

> The great number of Roman portrait busts in these
> galleries remind one again how closely the Victorians
> resembled the Romans in their appearance. There are
> Roman faces in the Capitoline Museum which might be
> those of mid-Victorian Birmingham manufacturers or
> temperance reformers; there are also among them Vic-
> torian statesmen, soldiers, and churchmen. Why the
> Roman type, which has now vanished from Rome,
> should have accidentally cropped up in England a century
> ago, I do not know, nor can I offer a guess. Having had
> the classics beaten into one with a birch rod can hardly be
> an explanation.[15]

The single work in the Capitoline Museum that most
frequently prompted comment from visitors was *The Dying
Gladiator*. This work, excavated in the 1620s, was already
described by John Evelyn in 1644 as 'much followed by all the
rare Artists, as the many copies . . . testifie'.[16] It remained
popular for centuries. Mrs Trollope found it so impressive
that 'it obliterated the recollection' of the other pieces in the
collection.[17] Nearly all accounts mention it, but surely the
most memorable is that found in the fourth canto of Byron's
Childe Harold's Pilgrimage:

I see before me the gladiator lie:
He leans upon his hand – his manly brow
Consents to his death, but conquers agony,
And his drooped head sinks low, –
And through his side the last drops, ebbing slow
From the red gash, fall heavy, one by one,
Like the first of a thunder shower; and now
The arena swims around him – he is gone,
Ere ceased the human shout which hailed the wretch who
      won.[18]

Such was the power of Byron's lines that in 1833, fifteen years after the canto was published, Ralph Waldo Emerson stood in front of *The Dying Gladiator* and could only think of the English poet. '*The Dying Gladiator* is a most expressive statue', he wrote, 'but it will always be indebted to the muse of Byron for fixing upon it forever his pathetic thought'.[19] In a letter written from Rome to her family in 1847, Florence Nightingale also quoted Byron in her account of viewing the statue, but her special sensitivity to human suffering moved her to write:

You see a dying man, the body dying in every sense and power, and yet you see a spirit, not there, but far away. It seems almost a miracle, and I lingered in that room, wondering at that art, which . . . has succeeded in enchaining all our sympathies to the soul, which yet hardly seems to animate that body which we see, but to be far off. The double life in that countenance, or rather the death in the face and the eternal life in the expression, is *really* like inspiration.[20]

If *The Dying Gladiator* was viewed by many as a romantic hero, even a Byronic hero, other statues in the Capitoline gallery appealed to different sensibilities. Is it surprising to learn that Shelley's favourite work (according to his wife) was the *Apollo with Lyre*?[21] Nathaniel Hawthorne, who had yet to publish *The Marble Faun* when he visited the museum in 1858, was enraptured by the so-called Praxitelean *Faun*:

I looked at the Faun of Praxiteles, and was sensible of a peculiar charm in it; a sylvan beauty and homeliness, friendly and wild at once. The lengthened, but not preposterous ears, and the little tail, which we infer, have an exquisite effect, and make the spectator smile in his very heart. This race of fauns was the most delightful of all that antiquity imagined. It seems to me that a story, with all sorts of fun and pathos in it, might be contrived on the idea of their species having become intermingled with the human race; a family with the faun blood in them having prolonged itself from the classic era till our own days. The tail might have disappeared, by dint of constant intermarriages with ordinary mortals; but the pretty hairy ears should occasionally reappear in members of the family; and the moral instincts and intellectual characteristics of the faun might be most picturesquely brought out, without detriment to the human interest of the story. Fancy this combination in the person of a young lady.[22]

Admirers of the languid *Antinous*, the Bithynian youth beloved by the emperor Hadrian, may have been swayed by other sentiments. Dare we speculate why the Anglican chaplain T. H. White found the dreamy youth so ravishing? Was it spiritual fervour alone that caused him to declare 'if you can imagine the union of masculine beauty with maiden modesty, this image of Adrian's favourite is their absolute personification!'[23] Hawthorne's good friend, the Boston lawyer George Stillman Hillard, de-sensualized the work but found it no less stirring. In *Six Months in Italy* (1853) he wrote:

> The statue of *Antinous* is not merely beautiful, but it is beauty itself. Like all his busts and statues, the expression is that of 'Elysian beauty, melancholy, grace', he has the air of a man looking into his own grave. The limbs, the figures, the turn of the head, which droops as if with a weight of unshed tears, are so admirable that they can only be praised in superlatives.[24]

In the Museo dei Conservatori across the piazza, one finds an outstanding picture gallery, or Pinacoteca, founded by

Pope Benedict XIV in 1749. To enter the gallery, one passes through a courtyard containing fragments (head, hand, and foot) of the colossal statue of Constantine the Great which in the fifteenth century was moved to its present location from the Basilica of Constantine. These fragments have provoked fewer comments than one might imagine for a monument of such striking dimensions. Francis Mortoft's diary of 1659 notes only that 'one of the toes of it [is] much bigger than my middle', but neither he nor subsequent visitors found much poetic or prosaic inspiration in the gargantuan fragments.[25] At least one artist found the work compelling, however. In the late eighteenth century, the Swiss painter Henry Fuseli drew a figure seated despairingly before the foot and entitled it 'The Artist Moved by the Grandeur of Antique Fragments'.

More consistently provocative works are found in the picture galleries upstairs. Of the handful of paintings that have drawn regular comment, Domenichino's *Cumaean Sibyl*, painted in 1620, was perhaps the most controversial. Recollections of this grand figure are found even in fiction. In Madame De Staël's *Corinne* (1807), the heroine is described early in the narrative as 'attired like Domenichino's Sibyl . . . her whole costume was picturesque without . . . appearing tainted by affectation. Her attitude was noble and modest; it might, indeed, be perceived that she was content to be admired'.[26] Mrs Anna Jameson, the art and literary critic, spoke for many in her *Diary of an Ennuyée* of 1826 when she declared the painting to be a 'magnificent creation' and 'one of the finest pictures here'.[27] As long as Ideal Beauty was the criterion of artistic excellence, as promoted, for example, in the *Discourses* (1769–90) of Joshua Reynolds, Domenichino and other members of the Bolognese school were held in the highest favour. But when in the mid-nineteenth century, John Ruskin and other critics decried the academic principles underlying Classic-Idealist art in favour of Sincerity and Spontaneity, Domenichino's reputation began to wane.[28] About Mrs Jameson, Ruskin went so far as to say that she 'knows as much about art as the cat'.[29]

The critical fortunes of the *Cumaean Sibyl* were kept afloat by amateurs throughout the nineteenth century, but more

'knowledgeable' critics felt compelled to deflate its prior reputation. William Makepeace Thackeray, for example, author
of the recently published *Vanity Fair*, whose heroine Becky
Sharp is a model of resourceful ingenuity, wrote in a letter of
1854, 'As for the Domenichino (it is at the Capitol, you
know . . .) Pish! It is a great clumsy woman affected ogling
and in a great turban'.[30] By 1886, at the height of the Victorian
age, John Addington Symonds put the picture in perfect
perspective when he declared that 'Domenichino's gigantic
saints and sibyls, with their fleshy limbs, red cheeks, and
upturned eyes, though famous enough in the last century, do
not demand a word of comment now. So strangely has taste
altered, that to our eyes they seem scarcely decorative'.[31]

A second painting in the Pinacoteca that has rarely escaped
notice is Guercino's *Burial of St Petronilla* (1621). This is the
work of an artist who, though a contemporary of
Domenichino, represented in his time a more progressive,
Baroque point of view. To be sure, Guercino's painting
possesses more energy and spontaneity, but stylistic issues
were eclipsed in the minds of many viewers of the past by a
picture's subject matter. The *Burial*, of course, is a fervently
religious work steeped in the attitudes of the Catholic Restoration and, as such, plain anathema to viewers from Protestant
countries. Why then has the painting been so renowned? Its
chief claim to fame evidently lay in its sheer size (it is almost 24
feet tall and was originally intended as an altarpiece in St
Peter's, where it is now replaced by a copy). Mrs Jameson
found the saint to be 'of very hypothetical fame', but it was
perhaps George Eliot who best typified the response of Anglo-
Saxon visitors when in 1860 she found the work 'a stupendous
piece of painting, about which one's only feeling is, that it
might as well have been left undone'.[32]

Many foreign visitors were more impressed by paintings
produced by artists who lived and worked outside Rome.
Works by Rubens or by the Venetians Titian, Tintoretto, and
Veronese were looked upon with particular favour. Veronese's *Rape of Europa* stood out among these, both as a superb
example of Venetian pictorial technique, and as a work un-
marred by Catholic sentiments. Nathaniel Hawthorne de-

scribed this painting as a 'joyous, exuberant, warm, voluptuous work', words that he is unlikely to have applied to a religious painting of equivalent stylistic character.[33]

S. MARIA IN ARACOELI

The Capitoline Hill is also the site of one of Rome's most venerable medieval churches. S. Maria in Aracoeli stands just behind the Capitoline Museum and is accessible either by its own monumental stairway (124 steps) or by a shorter, less strenuous flight leading from the Campidoglio to its right transept. Built on the site where the Tiburtine Sibyl is said to have informed Augustus of the Coming of Christ with the words *Haec est ara filii Dei* (hence the name Aracoeli, or Altar of Heaven), its origins date to the seventh century although its present Romanesque character is the result of a thirteenth-century reconstruction. The stairway, in turn, was added in the fourteenth century in thanksgiving for Rome's deliverance from the Black Death of 1348.

Charles Dickens in *Pictures from Italy* (1846), singles this church out for special mention, not so much for 'its long vista of gloomy pillars' that he found 'dark and sad', but for the miraculous waxen figure of the Bambino Gesù housed in one of the chapels. When after a certain amount of ritual the infant was finally revealed to him, Dickens found it

> in face very like General Tom Thumb, the American dwarf; gorgeously dressed in satin and gold lace, and actually blazing with rich jewels. There was scarcely a spot upon his little breast, or neck, or stomach, but was sparkling with the costly offerings of the Faithful. Presently [the priest] lifted it out of the box, and, carrying it round among the kneelers, set its face against the forehead of every one, and tendered its clumsy foot to them to kiss – a ceremony which they all performed, down to a dirty little ragamuffin of a boy who had walked in from the street. When this was done, he laid it in the box again; and the company, rising, drew near, and

commended the jewels in whispers. In good time, he
replaced the coverings, shut up the box, put it back in its
place, and locked up the whole concern . . . behind a pair
of folding doors; took off his priestly vestments; and
received the customary 'small change', while his companion, by means of a long stick, put out the lights, one
after another. The candles being all extinguished, and
the money all collected, they retired, and so did the
spectators.[34]

Other visitors to the church have recorded remembrances
of the daunting stairway, the 'broken flutings and scarred
granite' of the interior, and of having returned to France with
the convent key in his pocket (Montesquieu), but the image of
the infant Jesus, so crudely carved and tastelessly tarted up, has
made the greatest impression of all. Even Bernard Berenson,
the consummate connoisseur of our own century, found the
little figure irresistible. In his diary of 1950 he wrote:

At the Aracoeli, fascinated by a chapel crowded with
fervent worshippers of an infant Osiris, a baby face, the
rest of it covered in sparkling jewels. I love dolls. The
bedizening of this one appealed to the child in me. I am
aware of what is going on in me, and know that my
feeling is artistic, playful. But the worshippers – are they
not, unbeknown to themselves, inspired by similar feelings, perhaps to an even greater extent? Since every
manner of thing has been explored and pedantized, no
doubt German writers have published tome upon tome
on the psychology of religious worship. None have come
my way. I would like to write about it from my own
experience of long ago, still bright in my memory.[35]

AN OVERVIEW OF THE FORUM ROMANUM

The Roman Forum stretches behind and below the Capitoline
Hill (Plate 2). The most rewarding vantage points from which
to view the ancient remains are from either of two paths
descending along the flanks of the Palazzo Senatorio. Olave

Potter in *The Colour of Rome* (1909) captured the mournful tone of what is like to step from one world into another:

> As you pass the Senate-house the panorama of the ancient city unrolls itself before you. First the Palatine, with its heavy cloud of ilexes resting on the arched sub-structures of Imperial palaces; and then the Forum, with its broken temples and its slender solitary columns, with its wonderful majesty and its wonderful beauty, lying on the bosom of the Rome which it once cradled. The silver arch of Titus crowns the Velian; and beyond the Byzantine campanile of Saint Frances of Rome the great bulk of the Colosseum looms up against the misty Alban Hills. And while your lips are still pressed to the Circean bowl, a silent throng presses round you – the ghosts of those who never saw the Forum as it is, of those to whom the Capitoline was the goal of their hopes and their ambitions; the ghosts of those whose knell was tolled by the deep voice of the Patarina; Sovereigns and Popes. It has been a hill of death; it has been a hill of honour: Petrarch received his poet's crown here as the Generals of Ancient Rome received their crowns of victory; Rienzi died here, like the brother of Vespasian; and Arnold of Brescia and pale Stephen Porcari both wander on the hill of their unrealized ambitions, with the ghost of Tasso claiming the laurel-wreath he never wore.[36]

Elizabeth Bowen also recommends viewing the Forum from this high vantage point. In *A Time in Rome* (1960), she goes on to add:

> True, one looks down into a pit or trough of which the foreground is too near up under the eye. But in the main it *is* when one sees from here that porticoes, ranks of columns, exposed groundplans fall into the order of their relationship. For purely 'viewing' the Forum, this is the viewpoint; still better (because one looks along, instead of across) than the lofty Farnese terraces on the Palatine. . . . Could one only descend from here, without more fuss![37]

The Mamertine Prison

As one wends one's way to the Forum's entrance on the Via
dei Fori Imperiali, one passes the Baroque church of SS.
Martina e Luca on the right and the late Mannerist church of S.
Giuseppe dei Falegnami on the left. Neither has attracted
much literary notice, but S. Giuseppe, the guild church of
falegnami or carpenters, is renowned for the fact that it is built
on the foundation of the legendary Mamertine prison in which
St Peter is believed to have been incarcerated. Sean O'Faolain
has written what is perhaps the most evocative description of
this chilling structure in *A Summer in Italy* (1949):

> It is the dungeon called the Carcer Mamertinus, one of the
> oldest structures in the city. This city Prison contains two
> cells, one over the other; cold after the great heat, black
> after the incandescent sun, a frightening maw. The cell
> below was once reached only by a hole in the floor. Now
> there are stone stairs. This lower cell must have been as
> dark as a coalhole, as cold as an ice-box, as wet as a
> swamp. It is now lit by a single naked electric bulb.

O'Faolain was sickened by his guide's horrific tales of the
torture of St Peter and other prisoners who were 'decapitated,
strangled, and starved', but, nonetheless, he admits:

> I came out of that obdurate subterranean dungeon,
> blinded by the sun shimmering over the ruins of the
> forum, deeply stirred by the contrast and image of the
> triumph of failure. For days I could not forget it. This, I
> decided, would be my one sacred spot, free of all com-
> plications and speculations. I would remember it with
> feeling and intimacy; a mere hole in the ground; of no
> least aesthetic interest; impressive beyond words by its
> associations; a focus from which many thoughts could
> radiate to the verge of the empire, the old as well as the
> new.[38]

THE VIA DEI FORI IMPERIALI AND THE IMPERIAL FORUMS

Continuing onwards, one next approaches Mussolini's grand boulevard, the Via dell'Impero, now renamed the Via dei Fori Imperiali. Lying above (and precluding the excavation of) several of the Imperial forums, this roadway is nearly a thousand yards long and runs from the Victor Emmanuel Monument to the Colosseum. Professor Spiro Kostof provides some impressive statistics about its construction in *The Third Rome* (1973):

> By the time it was inaugurated, on 28 October 1932, 280,000 cubic meters of earth and 50,000 of rock had to be moved; 5,500 units of housing demolished; and 12,000 cubic meters of retaining walls erected. . . . Three churches . . . were pulled down, as well as the base of the colossus of Nero and the ancient fountain called Meta Sudans which impeded the view of the Arch of Constantine.[39]

Eleanor Clark, author of *Rome and a Villa* (1952), is admirably circumspect about the role of Mussolini in the planning of this modern thoroughfare:

> Via dell'Impero, Empire Street, [is] in line with the fascist dream; the maps of the ancient Empire in marble and bronze are still there, and a little of the hypothesis of archaism emanates from them even now. The problem goes beyond that; it is not only the original purpose of the street that is responsible for the depression one feels there. It is an age of platitude; the ruins were bound to be exposed and capitalized on in one way or another, and besides an avenue was needed, for modern traffic; the question is of the survival of the imagination under any system in this century.[40]

Walking down the boulevard in the direction of the Colosseum, one passes the Imperial forums of Trajan and Augustus on the left. Of these, the Trajanic complex (AD 98–117) consisting of his forum, a multi-storeyed market, the Basilica Ulpia, Trajan's Column, and originally a temple and

triumphal arch, is the most important. An eyewitness account
of the visit of the Emperor Constantius II to the site in AD 357 is
given by Ammianus Marcellinus:

> But when he came to the Forum of Trajan, a structure
> which, in my opinion, is unique under the heavens, and a
> marvel which even wins the acceptance of the divine
> powers, he stopped in his tracks, astonished, while his
> mind tried to grasp the gigantic complex, which cannot
> be described by words and could never again be
> attempted by mortal men.[41]

A century later, Cassiodorus also found it 'a wonder to look
upon, even after continual viewing'.[42] In our own times,
Trajan's market deserves recognition as an early forerunner of
the twentieth-century shopping mall, but the 140-foot-high
Trajan's Column, still virtually intact, is the most visible and
impressive monument in the Imperial forums. In the extensive
literature on the column, William Wordsworth's long poem
'The Pillar of Trajan' (1837) perhaps best captures the flavour
and aftertaste of the tall, relief-covered shaft. It begins:

> Where towers are crushed, and unforbidden weeds
> O'er mutilated arches shed their seeds,
> And temples, doomed to milder change, unfold
> A new magnificence that vies with old,
> Firm in its pristine majesty hath stood
> A Votive column, spared by fire and flood;
> And, though the passions of man's fretful race
> Have never ceased to eddy round its base,
> Not injured more by touch of meddling hands
> Than a lone obelisk, mid Nubian sands
> Or aught in Syrian deserts left to save
> From death the memory of the good and brave.[43]

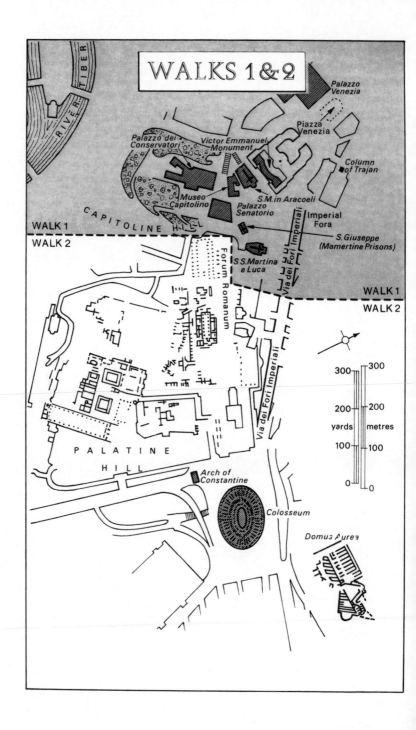

2

SECOND WALK

*The Forum Romanum, the Colosseum, and
the Arch of Constantine*

THE FORUM ROMANUM

The Forum Romanum is accessible (every day but Tuesday)
through a gate off the Via dei Fori Imperiali, opposite Largo
Ricci. If there is much to see here (the *Blue Guide* recommends
spending more than a single day), there may be even more to
think about. An anthology of visitors' printed comments
could easily fill an entire volume, for few tourists have remained unmoved by their experience. Of those that have,
James Joyce, resident in Rome in 1906, was virtually unique in
putting his apathy into words. In a letter to his brother
Stanislaus, he admitted:

> I must be a very insensible person. Yesterday I went to see
> the Forum. I sat down on a stone bench overlooking the
> ruins. It was hot and sunny. Carriages full of tourists,
> postcard sellers, medal sellers, photograph sellers. I was
> so moved that I almost fell asleep and had to rise
> brusquely. I looked at the stone bench ruefully but it was
> too hard and the grass near the Colosseum was too
> far. So I went home sadly. Rome reminds me of a man
> who lives by exhibiting to travellers his grandmother's
> corpse.[1]

Most visitors to the Forum were more stirred by their experience, even if on occasion they were surprised by what they saw. Gabriel Fauré voiced a widely held opinion in his guidebook *Rome* (1926) when he said that, at first sight,

> Your head is turned by a gust of Roman greatness, made up of confused memories, reminiscences of school, and readings of the classics. Flowing periods of orators, sonorous lines of poets, concise sentences of historians, all rise up suddenly from oblivion, as the ruins themselves have risen up from under the soil.[2]

In his autobiography, Edward Gibbon recalls the 'several days of intoxification' he enjoyed when, in 1764 he first 'trod with a lofty step [into] the ruins of the Forum; each memorable spot where Romulus *stood*, or Tully spoke, or Caesar fell, was at once present to my eye'.[3] Inspired by what he beheld, later in the same year Gibbon set himself to the task of writing *The Decline and Fall*.

For a surprisingly large number of people, however, the reality of the extant ruins failed to match their expectations, and the initial impression was one of disappointment. This was almost always the result of being unprepared for the neglected state into which their dream site had fallen. George Stillman Hillard, author of the immensely popular *Six Months in Italy* warned his readers:

> No one, unless forewarned by books and engravings, can have any conception of the change and desolation which have come over this neglected spot. An unsightly piece of ground, disfeatured with filth and neglect, with a few ruins scattered over it, and two formal rows of trees running through it, is all that we see. . . . A few peasants wrapped in their mud-colored cloaks, a donkey or two, a yoke of the fine gray oxen of Italy, or, perhaps, a solitary wild-eyed buffalo, are the only living forms in a scene once peopled with wisdom, valor, and eloquence. Nothing gives a stronger impression of the shattering blows which have fallen upon the Eternal City than the present condition of the Forum.[4]

Ever since the Middle Ages, the local name for the Forum was the Campo Vaccino (Field of Cows), yet those whose expectations were founded on classical literature and history were not prepared to find, as William Dean Howells did, a 'dirty cowfield, wandered over by evil-eyed buffaloes and obscenely defiled by wild beasts', where even the remaining classical monuments were sometimes 'half-gorged by the façade of a hideous Renaissance church'.[5]

Percy Shelley went even farther when in a letter to Thomas Love Peacock of 1818 he wrote the memorable lines:

> Behold the wrecks of what a great nation once dedicated to the abstractions of the mind! Rome is a city, as it were, of the dead, or rather of those who cannot die, and who survive the puny generations which inhabit and pass over the spot which they have made sacred to eternity.[6]

The modern visitor, on the other hand, is often beset by lethargy or an inability to recapture the spirit of the past. The fictional Phillip Warren in Gore Vidal's novel *The Judgement of Paris* (1952) stood among the ruins and tried to imagine what the site had been like: 'He failed completely, as he always did'.[7] In real life, Barbara Grizzuti Harrison confesses in *Italian Days* (1989) that her imagination

> can't reconstruct the Forum as it once was, nor can it disregard the mutilation that is there. . . . The statues are forever fallen, the columns smashed, the roofs ungilded, the narrow streets peopled not by hundreds of men in tunics and togas, smelling of garlic and pomade – they have all stepped over the brink into the great chasm – but by enervated tourists with guidebooks . . . at a loss to know if they are looking at a prison, a theatre, or a temple. There is no consolation to be derived here from the transitoriness of things. The silence of the distant world is deafening.[8]

General reflection upon the ruins of the Forum at times led to closer inspection of individual monuments. 'They require study and investigation to excite a very deep interest', wrote James Fenimore Cooper, but only a handful of structures –

usually the better preserved examples – stand out in written accounts.[9] The two more or less intact triumphal arches that stand at opposite ends of the Forum have probably provoked the most comment. The Arch of Septimius Severus, at the west end (adjacent to the Capitoline Hill) was erected in AD 203 to honour the tenth anniversary of the reign of this peripatetic emperor who was born in Leptis Magna and died in Britain. Given the arch's position below the modern street level, its squat proportions, and modest claim to artistic excellence, it has often been subject to criticism. The President De Brosses found it 'a little shabby and jumbled' in 1740,[10] and even after it was excavated in the early years of the nineteenth century, Olave Potter was still moved to write that 'its tastelessness can only be explained by the fact that Septimius Severus was an African possessed of colossal vanity, a *parvenu* even among the emperors of Rome'. 'In form', she goes on to say, 'it is the least beautiful and the most arrestive of all the monuments in the Forum; but its marbles are stained and bronzed to such glowing colours that the decadence of its art can well be forgiven'.[11]

The three stalwart and well-proportioned columns that survive from the Temple of Castor and Pollux have almost always been popular with tourists. In *Roman Mosaics* (1888), the Scottish clergyman Hugh MacMillan captured the poetry of their fragmentary remains which

> at once arrest the eye by their matchless symmetry and grace. Time had dealt very hardly with them, battering their shapely columns and rich Corinthian capitals, and discolouring their pure white Pentelic marble. But it has not succeeded in destroying their wonderful beauty; and the russet hues with which they have been stained by the long lapse of the ages have rather added to them the charm of antique picturesqueness. They rest upon a huge mound of broken masonry, in the interstices of which Nature has sown her seeds of minute life, which spread over it a tender pall of bright vegetation.[12]

Near the Temple of Castor and Pollux are the Temple of Vesta and the adjoining *Atrium Vestae*. This site has been as

evocative as any within the Forum proper. Even today, the
blasé Barbara Harrison responded to it, although she would be
the first to agree that her account in *Italian Days* has less in
common with encomiums of the past than with modern-day
feminist criticism. Tired of the 'taciturn' nature of the Forum
and wanting to

> find something to love, or to quicken my imagination
> . . . I found my way to the Temple of Vesta, where Vestal
> Virgins kept alive the Sacred Flame. The circular foun-
> dations alone remain. If a Vestal allowed the fire to go
> out, she was stripped, and beaten in the dark by the
> Pontifex Maximus. If a Virgin broke her vow of chastity,
> she was buried alive. This building is said to have been the
> prettiest little temple in Rome – 'a gay, delightful circle of
> marble and white columns around it connected with
> lattice work' (H. V. Morton), conferring such dignity
> upon its surroundings as to make them 'the most fashion-
> able neighborhood in Rome'. I think it is a horrid place
> of leprous sadness and decay, unhallowed littered
> ground. . . .
>   It saddens and alarms me to think that men are a little
> thrilled by this.[13]

From here, Emile Zola, in his novel *Rome* (1896), suggests
that

> if the eye seeks a sensation of extraordinary vastness, it
> must travel beyond the three columns of the temple of
> Castor and Pollux, beyond the vestiges of the house of the
> Vestals, beyond the temple of Faustina . . . and even
> beyond the round temple of Romulus, to light upon the
> Basilica of Constantine with its three colossal, gaping
> archways. From the Palatine they look like porches built
> for a nation of giants, so massive that a fallen fragment
> resembles some huge rock hurled by a whirlwind from a
> mountain summit.[14]

Indeed the Basilica of Maxentius and Constantine is the
grandest monument in the Roman Forum. Unlike the earlier
basilicas Aemilia and Julia, which were timber-roofed, this

structure was vaulted in concrete, the most impressive and daring innovation of Roman engineering. The very size of the building – it is nearly 1,000 feet long, over 200 feet wide, and over 100 feet high – has simply overwhelmed some visitors who were accustomed to less imposing surroundings. Like Zola, many were inclined to view it a few steps removed, from the overlooking perspective of the adjacent Palatine Hill.

Traditionally, another extremely popular monument in the Forum was the Arch of Titus, constructed by Domitian after AD 81 to celebrate the victories of Titus and his father Vespasian in the Judean War. Nearly all accounts praise the well-proportioned elegance of this arch even if, for some, like Shelley, the political message was troubling:

> On the inner compartment of the Arch of Titus, is sculptured, in deep relief, the desolation of a city. . . . The foreground is occupied by a procession of the victors, bearing in their profane hands the holy candlesticks and the tables of shewbread, and the sacred instruments of the eternal worship of the Jews. On the opposite side, the reverse of this sad picture, Titus is represented standing in a chariot drawn by four horses, crowned with laurel, and surrounded by the tumultuous numbers of his triumphant army, and the magistrates, and priests, and generals, and philosophers, dragged in chains beside his wheels. Behind him stands a Victory eagle-winged.[15]

Shelley, who probably wrote his account in the spring of 1819, concluded his remarks by saying that 'the arch is now mouldering into ruins, and the imagery almost erased by the lapse of fifty generations'. Two years later, a major reconstruction of the arch was undertaken by the celebrated Neo-Classical architect Giuseppe Valadier. Shortly after that, Stendhal noted in his *Roman Journal* for May 1828:

> This pretty little triumphal arch . . . was the most elegant up to the time when it was redone by M. Valadier. . . . Instead of supporting Titus's arch, which was falling into ruin, by steel reinforcements, or by an arched buttress of brick, quite distinct from the monument itself, the poor man rebuilt it. He had the nerve to hew blocks of traver-

tino after the form of the antique stones and to substitute
them for these, which were carted away I know not
where. What remains to us is therefore but a *copy* of
Titus's arch.[16]

Touring the site just a year or so after Stendhal, the American painter Rembrandt Peale put the matter in some perspective when, in his *Notes on Italy* (1831), he gave the assessment
that 'this little arch is renovated with modern additions which
restore its entire form, and will preserve the old portions,
much to the displeasure of the lovers of ruins, who preferred it
in its crumbling state, covered with ivy, and overwhelmed
with an ancient massive wall'.[17] The contrast between these
attitudes of course also reflects broader strains of sensibility at
this point in the nineteenth century. The Romantic Frenchman's attachment to ruins, the 'sensible' American's reasoned
response, and even Shelley's English political accent were all
part of the cultural diversity of their time.

The Palatine Hill

The path to the right of the Arch of Titus – the *Clivus Palatinus*
– ascends to the Palatine Hill, the site of the Imperial residential
quarter. This is one of Rome's loveliest parts, and its luxuriant
flora have made indelible impressions on countless visitors
from the north. The Danish author of fairy tales, Hans
Christian Andersen, was enchanted to find himself in

 a garden, so green and sweet-smelling that we cannot
 believe it is winter, that we are in the middle of January.
 Beds of mignonettes, stocks and roses are all in scented
 flower. Oranges and lemons shine on the trees amid their
 dark leaves. We stroll through an avenue of laurels to the
 natural balcony which the wall makes, looking out towards the *campagna*. Below us we can see solitary burial
 monuments, the yellow curving Tiber and, far out to the
 horizon, a glass-clear strip – the Mediterranean. . . . Up
 here, the roses are in bloom, the warm rays of the sun kiss
 the green leaves of the laurel-bush, and the foreigner

drinks in a picture of the loveliness of the South that will
never fade from his thoughts.[18]

For others, the beauty of the place was simply enervating.
Edward Lear was a most industrious artist, but on 29 Decem-
ber 1861, he wrote from the Palatine Hill to a patron in
England, 'here I sit amid vast masses of antique brickwork . . .
I wish I could say I draw . . . [too] extreme is my lizardish
enjoyment of the hot sun'.[19]

In *Rome in the Nineteenth Century*, Charlotte Eaton discovered the natural source of the Corinthian order while
strolling on the Palatine:

> On this spot, I found to my great delight, some leaves of
> the acanthus growing wild; and contrasting their native
> luxuriance with their sculptured forms clustering round
> the fallen Corinthian capitals at my feet, I scarcely knew
> whether most to admire the perfection of art in the
> imitation, or the taste which first adopted it as an
> architectural ornament.[20]

Tourists today can have this same experience for themselves, for healthy clumps of acanthus continue to grow along
the *Clivus Palatinus* and throughout the Forum. The interplay
between art and life was likewise the theme of a poem which
Thomas Hardy wrote after wandering round the Imperial
palace complex in the spring of 1887:

> We walked where Victor Jove was shrined awhile,
> And passed Livia's rich red mural show,
> Whence, thridding cave and Criptoportico,
> We gained Caligula's dissolving pile.
>
> And each ranked ruin tended to beguile
> The outer sense, and shape itself as though
> It wore its marble gleams, its pristine glow
> Of scenic frieze and pompous peristyle.
>
> When lo, swift hands, on swings nigh overhead,
> Began to melodize a waltz by Strauss:
> It stirred me as I stood, in Caesar's house,
> Raised the old routs Imperial lyres had led,

And blended pulsing life with lives long done,
Till Time seemed fiction, Past and Present one.[21]

More than a century earlier, James Boswell was also moved
by the commingling of past and present. Struck by 'the
grandeur of this imperial mansion', he wrote in his journal of
March 1765, 'I was seized with enthusiasm. I began to speak
Latin'.[22]

While savouring the vista from the Palatine, visitors about
to conclude their tour of the Forum and end their personal
reverie, may wish to ask the practical question of just what
went on in that vast ensemble lying below? The Roman comic
playwright Plautus provides a colourful, if irreverent account
in his *Curculio* (2nd century BC):

> If a man wants to meet a perjurer, let him go to the
> *Comitium*, and if he wants to meet a liar or a braggart, he
> should go to the temple of Venus *Cloacina*; for married
> men who waste their money let him ask at the Basilica
> [Aemilia]. There too he will find 'mature' prostitutes and
> men who are accustomed to quoting a price, while at the
> Forum fishmarket he'll find those who are devotees of
> public feasts. In the lower Forum good and well-to-do
> men stroll up and down; in the middle Forum near the
> [Cloaca Maxima] the mere show-offs; above the [Lacus
> Curtius] are those insolent, garrulous, and nasty types
> who audaciously slander others for no reason and who
> themselves have plenty that one could quite truthfully
> criticize. Beneath the Old Shops are those who loan and
> borrow money at interest. Behind the temple of Castor,
> there you will find those whom you shouldn't believe too
> quickly.[23]

Some reveries perhaps are best left intact, and not everyone
found the visual and historical illumination of modern archaeological discovery to their liking. Elihu Vedder, the expatriate
American painter, personally witnessed the excavations and
remained sceptical. 'The Roman Forum was infinitely more
poetic buried than it is disinterred', he wrote in his *Digressions*
(1911), 'and the sight of its skeleton is more painful than
poetic'.[24]

THE COLOSSEUM

The Colosseum has featured in literature more than any other monument in Rome, if not in all of Europe. Few visitors before the twentieth century, however, were able to view this stupendous structure for its classical harmony and solemn beauty without succumbing to the temptation to engage in all manner of moral and philosophical ruminations about its ignominious past and dilapidated present.

For most visitors, the associations of the place distracted them from any real appreciation of the building's artistic excellence. First among these associations was the fact that the great amphitheatre – constructed by the emperors Vespasian and Titus between AD 70 and 80 – was the site of the spectacular *munera*, or blood sports, of which the Romans were so fond. It was here that thousands of wild beasts, criminals, prisoners of war, and eventually Christians met their deaths before cheering crowds of as many as 50,000 spectators. Seneca, the Roman moralist and tutor of Nero, captures the spirit of the bloody spectacle:

I chanced to stop in at a midday show, expecting fun, wit, and some relaxation, when men's eyes take respite from the slaughter of their fellow men. It was just the reverse. The preceding combats were merciful by comparison; now all trifling is put aside and it is pure murder. The men have no protective covering. Their entire bodies are exposed to the blows, and no blow is ever struck in vain. . . . In the morning men are thrown to the lions and bears, at noon they are thrown to their spectators. The spectators call for the slayer to be thrown to those who in turn will slay him, and they detain the victim for another butchering. . . . 'Kill him! Lash him! Why does he meet the sword so timidly? Why doesn't he kill boldly? Why doesn't he die game? Whip him to meet his wounds! Let them trade blow for blow, chests bare and within reach!' And when the show stops for intermission, 'Let's have men killed meanwhile! Let's not have nothing going on!'[25]

Florence Nightingale perhaps best expresses the humanitarian concern of later viewers to this alfresco chamber of horrors. In a letter written from Rome in 1847, the young woman who had yet to commit herself to the medical vocation for which she was to become so well known, declared, 'I am afraid its picturesque beauty will never make up to me for its sentimental ugliness – and the contrast between the blue sky, the type of the goodness of God, shining through the rents of that type of ugliness of man, made it still more striking'.[26] Her compassion may have exceeded that of most tourists, but her basic response was not all that unusual. In *Corinne*, Madame de Staël condensed her comment even further, calling the Colosseum 'strange scourge of humanity! to decide beforehand the life or death of man, for mere pastime'.[27] Such reactions seem to have been more common among female than male visitors.

Of course there were also those for whom the spectacle of death in the afternoon held some positive fascination. The Romans' own affection for the *munera* is exemplified by Martial's lavish praise of the gladiator Carpophorus, a specialist in combat with the most ferocious beasts:

He plunged his hunter's spear into a headlong-rushing bear, the king of beasts beneath the cope of Arctic skies; and he laid low a lion, magnificent, of bulk unknown before, one worthy of Hercules' might; and with a far-dealt wound stretched in death a rushing leopard.[28]

The Marquis de Sade, whose very name is synonymous with cruel and savage practices, was no less enthralled when, centuries later, he stepped into the ancient amphitheatre. In his *Voyage* of 1775–6, he wrote:

What a difference between the spectacles of today and those given [at the Colosseum], where more than 100,000 people could enjoy the same spectacle at the same time! Cruelty, I confess, characterized the bloody scenes that took place, but at least those games didn't weaken one's courage like those of today where an actor's simple pantomime suicide brings an audience to tears. More

hardened and war-like customs conditioned these univer-
sal heroes to witness the death of others with *sang-froid*.
They were ferocious, you say. So it was. But they were
great, and we ourselves, I confess, are more humane but
smaller.[29]

By the age of the Grand Tour, the Colosseum had fallen into
a ruinous state, and it was the dilapidated condition of the
structure (Plate 3) that made the greatest impression on later
visitors. Some were content to view the gaunt remains as
emblematic of the passage of time, but Father Time was not
alone responsible for the wreck we see today. Dr John Moore,
writing of 'this horrid piece of magnificence' in his travel
account of 1781, reminds readers that 'this amphitheatre in
particular might have stood entire for two thousand years to
come: For what are the slow corrosions of time, in comparison
of the rapid destruction from the fury of the Barbarians, the
zeal of Bigots, and the avarice of Popes and Cardinals?'[30]

Sir George Head, author of *Rome: A Tour of Many Days*
(1849), gives a list of the buildings constructed since the
Renaissance from materials plundered from the Colosseum:
the Palazzo Venezia, the Palazzo della Cancelleria, the Palazzo
Farnese, the Villa Farnesina and the (now-destroyed) Porto di
Ripetta.[31] Only in 1744 did Benedict XIV, the first pope of the
Enlightenment, order the quarrying to stop. He in turn consecrated the arena in memory of the Christian martyrs who lost
their lives there, and placed a large cross in the centre of the
then unexcavated floor. This occurred just as countless Englishmen and other *forestieri* were about to set out on the Grand
Tour.

While a few visitors were plainly offended by the subsequent intrusion of Catholic iconography into the ancient
precinct – William Beckford was seized in 1780 by a 'vehement
desire . . . to break down and pulverize the whole circle of
saints' nests and chapels, which disgrace the arena' – most
eighteenth and nineteenth-century travellers were more toler-
ant of, if not actually enthusiastic about, the metamorphoses
that had taken place.[32] The earliest appreciative rendering of
the monument in verse appears in John Dyer's *The Ruins of
Rome* (1740):

Amid the tow'ry Ruins, huge supreme,
Th' enormous *Amphitheatre* behold,
Mountainous Pile! o'er whose capacious Womb
Pours the broad Firmament its varied Light . . .[33]

This short fragment from Dyer's long poem sets the tone
for much of the Romantic sentiment to come. His reaction to
its very size is echoed by any number of later authors. Goethe's
remarks on first viewing the structure in 1786 are limited to
just this very feature. 'Once one has seen it', he wrote,
'everything else seems small. It is so huge that the mind cannot
retain its image; one remembers it as smaller than it is, so that
every time one returns to it, one is again astounded by its
size'.[34]

Dyer also introduces a second topos to the literature of the
Colosseum, that of its affinities to authentic works of nature.
This, in a sense, was to become an American speciality.
For Thomas Cole, the Hudson River School painter, the
Colosseum

opens beneath the eye more like some awful dream than
an earthly reality, – a vision of the valley and shadow of
death, rather than the substantial work of man. As I
mused upon its great circumference, I seemed to be
sounding the depths of some volcanic crater, whose fires,
long extinguished, had left the ribbed and blasted rocks to
the wildflower and the ivy.[35]

For Henry James, stepping into the Colosseum made him

always . . . feel as if I were seated in the depths of some
Alpine valley. The upper portions of the side towards the
Esquiline look as remote and lonely as an Alpine ridge,
and you raise your eyes to their rugged sky-line, drinking
in the sun and silvered by the blue air, with much the
same feeling with which you would take in a grey cliff on
which an eagle might lodge.[36]

Hans Christian Andersen was more original when in 1840
he observed that 'in what we can still see here, there is a
greatness and grandeur such as one finds in the Pyramids
and in the rock temples of India'.[37] Only rarely are such

comparisons made between the Colosseum and other man-made structures. Far more common are those who evoke the grandeur of the monument on its own terms. The most memorable and often-quoted of such expressions is certainly the long stanza in Lord Byron's *Manfred* (1817):

> When I was wandering, – upon such a night
> I stood within the Coliseum's wall,
> Midst the chief relics of almighty Rome;
> The trees which grew along the broken arches
> Waved dark in the blue midnight, and the stars
> Shone through the rents of ruin; from afar
> The watchdog bay'd beyond the Tiber; and
> More near from out the Caesar's palace came
> The owl's long cry, and, interruptedly,
> Of distant sentinels the fitful song
> Begun and died upon the gentle wind.
> Some cypresses beyond the time-worn breach
> Appear'd to skirt the horizon, yet they stood
> Within a bowshot – Where the Caesars dwelt,
> And dwell the tuneless birds of night, amidst
> A grove which springs through levell'd battlements,
> And twines its roots with the imperial hearths,
> Ivy usurps the laurel's place of growth; –
> But the gladiators' bloody Circus stands,
> A noble wreck in ruinous perfection![38]

Another Romantic poet, Edgar Allan Poe, went even farther in his search for religious meaning, actually kneeling in the Colosseum's ample shadow:

> Type of the antique Rome! Rich reliquary
> Of lofty contemplation left to Time
> By buried centuries of pomp and power!
> At length – at length – after so many days
> Of weary pilgrimage and burning thirst,
> (Thirst for the springs of lore that in thee lie,)
> I kneel, an altered and an humble man,
> Amid thy shadows, and so drink within
> My very soul thy grandeur, gloom, and glory![39]

Such effusions of spirit are of course literary conventions of the period, a fact made clear by the news that Poe had never been to Rome and Byron's stay in the city was extremely brief. Nevertheless, it was during the nineteenth century that some of the most compelling utterances about the building were made. For many visitors, the experience left them saddened. In Chateaubriand's *Recollections* (1803), the author was 'constantly reminded of our nothingness. Man searches around him for objects to convince his reason. He meditates on the remains of edifices and empires; forgetting that he himself is a ruin still more unstable, and that he will perish even before these'.[40]

In an increasingly secular age, the Colosseum became the perfect vehicle for solemn meditation. 'It is best to be alone in the Colosseum', wrote Stendhal in 1827 in *A Roman Journal*, and most agreed that it was an intensely private experience, best accomplished without the distraction of others.[41] The goal, in the words of Emile Zola, was to enter 'a world where one loses oneself amidst death-like silence and solitude'.[42] Charles Dickens achieved that magical state on his first full day in Rome in 1845. In *Pictures from Italy* he wrote, 'its solitude, its awful beauty, and its utter desolation, strike upon the stranger . . . like a softened sorrow; and never in his life, perhaps, will he be so moved and overcome by any sight, not immediately connected with his own affections and afflictions'.[43]

George Stillman Hillard, the Boston lawyer who wrote the best-selling *Six Months in Italy*, was less enraptured but more analytical about what it was that made the monument so uniquely appealing:

If as a building the Colosseum was open to criticism, as a ruin it is perfect. The work of decay has stopped short at the exact point required by taste and sentiment. The monotonous ring at the outer wall is broken and, instead of formal curves and perpendicular lines, the eye rests upon those interruptions and unexpected turns which are the essential elements of the picturesque, as distinguished from the beautiful and the sublime. . . . Not by rule and measure have the huge stones been clipped and broken.

No contriving mind has told what masses should be
loosened from the wall, or where they should lie when
fallen. No hand of man has trained the climbing plants in
the way they should go. All has been left to the will of
time and chance. [44]

Mark Twain was also fascinated by the sight of natural
forms making their home in this 'monarch of all European
ruins'. In *The Innocents Abroad* (1869) he observed that 'The
butterflies have taken the place of the queens of fashion of
eighteen centuries ago and the lizards sun themselves in the
sacred seat of the emperor'. [45]

For botanists and dedicated naturalists, the flora of the
Colosseum had by then become a legitimate subject of study
in its own right. As early as 1813, the Italian Antonio Sebas-
tiani published a book entitled *Flora Colisea* which listed 261
species, and in 1855 the Englishman Richard Deakin added to
that number in his own *Flora of the Colosseum*, identifying
more than 420. The usefulness of Deakin's volume was short-
lived however. In 1871 the new Unification government
stripped the ruins of their greenery (and shortly thereafter
removed the religious appurtenances as well). This led Henry
James to observe in 1873 that 'beauty of detail has pretty well
vanished, especially since the high-growing wild-flowers
have been plucked away by the new government, whose
functionaries, surely, at certain points of their task, must have
felt as if they shared the dreadful fate of those who gather
samphire'. [46]

Today's visitors can take delight in the fact that some
unintended growth has returned to take the place of what had
been stripped away. The principal plant is now the caper
shrub, noted for its lovely white and purple spring flowers
whose buds add a savoury complement to many Italian dishes.

Early travellers were especially beguiled by visits to the
Colosseum at night when the monument was bathed in
moonlight. Among the first to record his impressions of
having done so was Goethe, who in 1787 wrote:

Nobody who has not taken one can imagine the beauty of
a walk through Rome by full moon. All details are

swallowed up by the huge masses of light and shadow, and only the biggest and most general outlines are visible. We have just enjoyed three clear and glorious nights. The Colosseum looked especially beautiful. It is closed at night. A hermit lives in a small chapel and some beggars have made themselves at home in the crumbling vaults. These had built a fire on the ground level and a gentle breeze had driven the smoke into the arena, so that the lower parts of the ruins were veiled and only the huge masses above loomed out of the darkness. We stood at the railing and watched, while over our heads the moon stood high and serene. By degrees the smoke escaped through holes and crannies and in the moonlight it looked like fog. It was a marvellous sight.[47]

But it was Lord Byron, more than anyone else, who fixed this nocturnal vision in our poetic consciousness. He did so in the just-quoted lines from *Manfred*, set 'in the blue midnight', and again in *Childe Harold's Pilgrimage* (1818):

But when the rising moon begins to climb
Its topmost arch, and gently pauses there;
When the stars twinkle through the loops of time,
And the low night-breeze waves along the air
The garland-forest, which the grey walls wear,
Like laurels on the bald first Caesar's head;
When the light shines serene but doth not glare,
Then in this magic circle raise the dead:
Heroes have trod this spot – 'tis on their dust ye tread.[48]

Night visits to the Colosseum thereafter became *de rigueur* for all sensitive souls. Some occasionally got carried away, as did the Englishwoman Frances Elliot, author of *Diary of an Idle Woman in Italy* (1871):

The Colosseum rose before us, serenely, calmly beautiful in the mournful moonlight, breathing a solemn monumental melancholy which was absolutely pathetic. . . . As we strolled about the moonlight arcades, unspeakable hope and peace came into my soul. Angels seemed to look down from the star-sown heavens, and the spirits of slaughtered saints to sanctify the scene of their martyr-dom. Looking at the moon, clear and argentine as a silver mirror, the ills and troubles of this life faded away like a vain and troubled dream.[49]

It was just this sort of exaggeration that prompted Nathaniel Hawthorne in *The Marble Faun* (1860) to satirize 'a party of English or Americans paying the inevitable visit [to the Colosseum] by moonlight, and exalting themselves with raptures that were Byron's, not their own'.[50] Byron, in fact, was the author of two expressions that were to become the most commonplace of tourist clichés. Mark Twain was proud to point out one of them. After devoting half the previous chapter of *The Innocents Abroad* to the Colosseum, he begins a new chapter saying:

> So far, good. If any man has a right to feel proud of himself and satisfied, surely it is I. For I have written about the Coliseum and the gladiators, the martyrs and the lions, and have never once used the phrase 'butchered to make a Roman holiday'. I am the only free white man of mature age who has accomplished this since Byron originated the expression.[51]

But Byron's most famous passage concerning the Colos-seum was doubtless his translation of those memorable lines uttered more than a millennium earlier by the Venerable Bede, the so-called 'Father of English History'. They first appear in *Childe Harold's Pilgrimage*:

> While stands the Coliseum, Rome shall stand;
> When falls the Coliseum, Rome shall fall;
> And when Rome falls – the World.[52]

Like Twain forty years before him, James Joyce had a fine ear for the moronic repetitions of Byronic verse. In a letter to his brother written in 1906, the 24-year-old Irishman told of his recent visit to the Colosseum:

> The neighbourhood of the Colisseum is like an old cemetery with broken columns of temples and slabs. You

know the Colisseum from pictures. While we were in the middle of it, looking at it all round gravely from a sense of duty, I heard a voice from London on one of the lowest gallery [sic] say:

– The Colisseum –

Almost at once two young men in serge suits and straw hats appeared in an embrasure. They leaned on the parapet and then a second voice from the same city clove the calm evening, saying:

– Whowail stands the Colisseum Rawhm shall stand
When falls the Colisseum Rawhm sh'll fall
And when Rawhm falls the world sh'll fall –

but added cheerfully:

– Kemlong, 'ere's the way aht –[53]

The Colosseum had frequently appeared as a backdrop in a number of works of fiction, although only in a few cases has it played an important role in the narrative. This is more common in American novels, with their portentous tendency to moralize, than in those of other countries. One literary critic has even called the Colosseum 'the Moby Dick of architecture'.[54] Most fictional renderings are just as well left forgotten, but one major figure, Henry James, made the Colosseum the leitmotif in no fewer than four novels and one early short story. *Daisy Miller* (1878) stands out among them all, the heroine a fragile figure overcome by the 'villainous miasma' of her own romanticism. In one of the last lines she speaks, Daisy says, 'Well, I *have* seen the Colosseum by moonlight! . . . That's one thing I can rave about!'[55] But once having broken the code of social convention by meeting her new Italian boyfriend in the dusky arena, Daisy simply had to be punished. A week later she died from the 'Roman Fever'.

THE ARCH OF CONSTANTINE

Just to the south-west of the Colosseum lies the triumphal Arch of Constantine, built in the fourth century to celebrate Constantine's victory over Maxentius at the Milvian Bridge. The recent excavation of the adjacent Meta Sudans,

Domitian's strange conical fountain, has now turned the
whole area into a relatively peaceful pedestrian zone. The
Meta Sudans, for its part, looks no better than it did in the
seventeenth century when Richard Lassels described it as an
'old round rubbage of brick'.[56]

One of the earliest descriptions of the arch was written at the
beginning of the fifteenth century by a visiting Byzantine
humanist and diplomat, Manuel Chrysoloras. So taken was he
with the general aura of the city that he wrote a letter home
saying:

> Can you believe of me that I am wandering about this city
> of Rome, swivelling my eyes this way and that like some
> boorish gallant, clambering up palace walls, even up to
> their windows, on the chance of seeing something of the
> beauties inside? I never used to do this sort of thing when I
> was young, as you know, and had a poor opinion of those
> who did. Yet here I am, getting on in years, and I scarcely
> know how I have been brought to this point.

He went on to comment on the sculptural decoration of the
arch itself:

> Truly, the skill of these representations equals and rivals
> Nature herself, so that one seems to see a real man, horse,
> city, or army, breastplate, sword, or armour, and real
> people captured or fleeing, laughing, weeping, excited or
> angry.[57]

Chrysoloras missed by little more than a decade, however,
the dawn of the Italian Renaissance, with its mania for pictorial
unity and its revival of classical form. Later viewers steeped in
such values were usually offended that this was, in fact, an
eclectic work that combined weak Constantinian carvings
with sculpture plundered from a variety of earlier monuments. Dr John Moore, writing in 1781 at the height of the
Neo-Classical era, praised the quality of the arch itself, but felt
obliged to add:

> its chief beauties are not genuine, nor, properly speaking,
> its own; they consist of some admirable basso relievos
> stolen from the Forum of Trajan, and representing that

Emperor's victories over the Dacians. This theft might, perhaps, not have been so notorious to posterity, if the artists of Constantine's time had not added some figures, which make the fraud apparent, and, by their great inferiority, evince the degeneracy of the arts in the interval between the reigns of these two Emperors.[58]

This was to be the standard response for the next two centuries. Efforts to focus solely on the architecture of the arch have been more courageous. Stendhal, for example, may have confused the arch's chronology, but he did note perceptively in his 1828 *Roman Journal* that 'it is singular that so useless a thing should give such great pleasure; the style of the triumphal arch is an architectural conquest'.[59]

The Domus Aurea

To the north-east of the Colosseum lies the Oppian Hill, one of the four summits of the Esquiline. It is on this hill that one of the most stunning monuments of Roman antiquity – the Domus Aurea or Golden House of Nero – once stood. The site is described in *The Lives of the Caesars* by the second-century author Suetonius:

> There was nothing, however, in which he [Nero] was more ruinously prodigal than in building. He made a palace extending all the way from the Palatine to the Esquiline . . . [whose] size and splendour will be sufficiently indicated by the following details. Its vestibule was large enough to contain a colossal statue of the emperor 120 feet high; and it was so extensive that it had a triple colonnade a mile long. There was a pond too, like a sea, surrounded by buildings to represent cities, besides tracts of country, varied by tilled fields, vineyards, pastures and woods, with great numbers of wild and domestic animals. In the rest of the house all parts were overlaid with gold and adorned with gems and mother-of-pearl. There were dining rooms with fretted ceilings of ivory, whose panels could turn and shower down flowers and

were fitted with pipes for sprinkling guests with per-
fumes. The main banquet hall was circular and constantly
revolved all day and night, like the heavens. He had baths
supplied with sea water and sulphur water. When the
edifice was finished in this style and he dedicated it, he
deigned to say nothing more in the way of approval than
he was at last beginning to be housed like a human
being.[60]

'Calumnies stuck to Nero like sackfuls of feathers to a tarred
man', wrote Elizabeth Bowen in *A Time in Rome* (1960).[61] His
Flavian successors almost totally demolished the sybaritic
complex, a gesture that was destined to please those later
generations who saw all of Roman antiquity as a *vanitas*
anyway. 'Today', continues Miss Bowen, 'you enter the
Domus Aurea through the horrible little forefront of rusti-
cation, as you might a cave-dwelling'. The park that houses
these pathetic remains would depress the Irish writer even
more now than it did in 1960, for today it is the home of a
community of gypsies, beggars, drug addicts, and other
unsavoury characters. Better than anyone else, though, Elizabeth Bowen captured the flavour of what authentic ruins do
remain on the site, while not hesitating to give her opinion of
the motives of those responsible for its destruction:

> Irretrievably damaged by hatred, shorn, voided, made
> phantom and rendered null, the Domus Aurea has not
> even power to stir up regret for a silenced rhapsody (of
> whatever quality). Stains blotch the surrounds of
> paintings themselves to be guessed at rather than seen;
> calcinated appear the alcoved chambers into which arc-
> lamps protrude their glare; the halls, dank, are over you
> like great soiled tents. Where there are gashes of sickly
> daylight, they fall on floors which, deadened under one's
> foot, are glossed by a perpetual sweat. War or time could
> have accomplished this same work – but it happens that
> neither *was* the enemy. I could choke with anger against
> censoriousness, its cautious vengeances, its ungodly
> claim to the right to judge.[62]

The Domus Aurea, despite its former Xanadu-like opu-
lence, is not a popular tourist attraction. For some time now
the authorities have closed it for what they call 'restoration'.

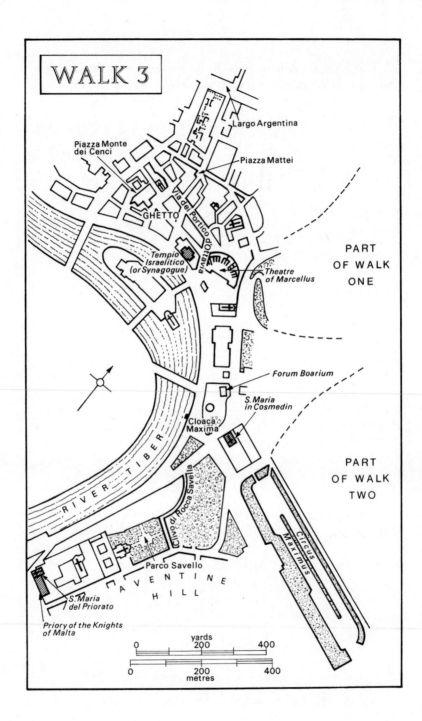

WALK 3

Largo Argentina

Piazza Monte
dei Cenci

Piazza Mattei

GHETTO

Via dei Portico d'Ottavia

Tempio
Israelitico
(or Synagogue)

Theatre
of Marcellus

PART
OF WALK
ONE

Forum Boarium

S.Maria
in Cosmedin

Cloaca
Maxima

PART
OF WALK
TWO

RIVER TIBER

Clivo di Rocca Savella

Circus Maximus

Parco Savello

AVENTINE
HILL

S.Maria
del Priorato

Priory of the Knights
of Malta

yards
0   200   400

0   200   400
metres

3

THIRD WALK

*From the Largo Argentina to the Ghetto and along the Tiber
to the Aventine Hill*

THE LARGO ARGENTINA

The Largo Argentina is one of Rome's least alluring piazzas,
but more than any other it introduces visitors to the timeless-
ness of the city. On the south side of the rectangular square is
a precinct of Republican temples; one block to the west is a
Renaissance *palazzetto* designed by Raphael; to the east is a
church from the Baroque period and drab nineteenth-century
façades define the square itself. Michael Mewshaw captured
the spirit of this charmless piazza in his recent book *Playing
Away* (1988):

> At Largo di Torre Argentina, a major crossroads for
> buses and a blaring chaos of converging traffic of all
> types, the air is so fouled by exhaust fumes it stings the
> eyes and grates the throat. Yet the crowds keep coming,
> staring off toward the eye of the storm, where there
> stand the ruins of four temples, a tall brick tower and its
> handsome loggia, several truncated pillars and fluted
> columns, and a copse of cypress and pine trees that have
> somehow survived the pollution, sinking their roots deep
> into stone.
>   When the sun is out, brightening the colors, warming
> the cats sleeping on marble slabs, this spot strikes me as a

reassuring symbol of the city's long history, and the local
people and tourists who congregate at the square are like
solemn witnesses of what has endured and will always
endure in Rome. But on overcast days, when the air
closes over it like a heavy lid, Largo di Torre Argentina
seems a fitting scene for a stoic to contemplate. Cars,
buses, and motor-cycles careen around the classical remains with all the brutal indifference of scavengers scut-
tling past meatless bones. *Tempus fugit*, and the tourists,
dressed in the flashy plumage of birds of paradise, appear
poised to fly with it.[1]

The four Republican temples, now sunk below the modern
street level, do not play much of a role in the city's literary
bibliography. They came to light only in the twentieth century as Eleanor Clark teasingly explains in *Rome and a Villa*
(1952):

The little republican temples were excavated behind a
high fence during fascism, and a story popular at the time
was that Mussolini wanted some ruins there and had a lot
of old stones dragged together to make them, but this was
carrying the natural suspicion too far. It seems they are
real, more or less.[2]

Mussolini in fact did have a hand in preserving the temples
from the schemes of private developers intent on burying the
antiquities under new construction. Spiro Kostof explains in
The Third Rome (1973):

The temples appeared doomed when, on 28 October
1928, the anniversary of the Fascist March on Rome,
Mussolini appeared on the site, expansive of mood; heard
claims like a modern Solomon; and declared; 'I would feel
dishonoured if it is allowed to erect even one meter of
new construction on this site'. And that was that. Back
several years later to inaugurate the Foro di Largo Argentina, the Duce commented (through righteous anger and
not meaning it literally, we are assured): 'I should like to
have brought to me here those who opposed this work, to
have them shot on the spot'.[3]

As many visitors have noticed, the *Area Sacra* of the Largo Argentina has long provided a safe haven for a goodly number of Rome's many cats, estimated in 1967 at 784,000.[4] For no discernible reason, the cat population has declined markedly in recent years. Cynical Romans blame the authorities for having taken unspecified Draconian measures to bring this about, but a Yale University sociologist, Dr Steven Brint, has another explanation:

> Yes, it is true, the cat population of Rome *has* declined, but not at the rate suggested by some observers. There are two reasons for this: the adaptability of cat society and new forms of cat provisioning in human society. We see a lot of self-help in the cat community: cats staying up extra hours – moonlighting, if you will – to supplement the food they have managed to obtain during the day: a measurable increase in the degree of stealth and material cupidity among the feline; and paradoxically, also a greater willingness to double up on rations and a decrease in the size of territories that are defended against interlopers. We also see a slow process of suburbanization as cats move out from the *centro* seeking new food supplies. The Largo di Torre Argentina and the Forum may be relatively depopulated, but the cat population in Monteverde and other outlying areas is booming.
>
> On the human side, the demise of the *gattare* [the old women who feed cats] seems to have brought out a latent . . . love of cats in the rest of the Roman population. People have taken up the slack by picking up strays and feeding them for a few weeks or months before letting them shift for themselves again. I like to think that we have moved from a system of oligarchical control in cat provisioning to a sort of foster care system.[5]

THE PIAZZA MATTEI

From the Largo Argentina one may wish to turn south and wander in the direction of the more colourful Jewish Ghetto.

Starting down the cacophonous Via Arenula, it is best to take
the first left, turning into the narrower Via dei Falegnami
which leads into the Piazza Mattei. In the centre of this small
square stands one of Rome's loveliest Renaissance fountains,
the Fountain of the Tortoises. In *The Fountains of Rome* (1966),
H. V. Morton describes the work in its setting:

> The piazza is small and distinctly grim. Shutting out the
> sunlight, ancient palaces stand round it, now divided into
> flats, the ground floors devoted to shops and storerooms.
> The pavement slopes downwards towards the centre
> where the gayest public monument in the city stands,
> murmuring softly with the sound of falling water. Four
> life-sized bronze youths, naked and pagan, lean against
> the stem of the fountain and, with uplifted arms, push
> four bronze tortoises over the rim of the marble bowl
> above them. The effect is enchanting, no matter how
> many times you may see [it].[6]

The ancient palaces that face this gracious fountain are the
Palazzi Costaguti and Mattei. Today's visitor coming from
the Largo Argentina and the Via Arenula may find them less
grim than they appeared in the past. In 1820 Charlotte Eaton
found that

> The Palazzo Costaguti is a most dismal, dirty, miserable
> place. Words cannot give you an idea of its utter
> wretchedness, and I could scarcely believe these forlorn,
> filthy chambers were the residence of the Marchesa I had
> seen blazing in diamonds at the ***** ambassador's ball,
> the night before.[7]

But both palaces house exceptional private art collections
that can be tempting to art-lovers weary of the bigger public
museums. The ancient statuary in the courtyard of the Palazzo
Mattei is relatively accessible, but Mrs Eaton's efforts to see
what lay behind its closed doors led to an experience which
remains all too common in Rome today:

> We have been several times at the Palazzo Mattei, if
> possible a still more deplorable place than the Palazzo

Costaguti. . . . Our attempts have been all fruitless; either we thundered for half a hour at the door and got no answer, or, if we obtained admittance, the Cardinal Mattei was in bed or at dinner; or else he had gone out with the key in his pocket, even when a time had been fixed; so that we have given it up in despair.[8]

THE GHETTO

From the Piazza Mattei it is but a short walk down the Via della Reginella or the Via di S. Ambrogio to the heart of the old Ghetto. It was here that from 1556 to 1870 the Jewish population of Rome was segregated and subjected to various abuses. Confined within gates and living under a curfew, Jews were forbidden to own land and officially could earn a living only by operating open markets, although in fact they often pursued astrology, usury, and other arcane practices on the side. Most early sightseers, Christian and Jew alike, found the Ghetto an exotic place to visit. In 1645 John Evelyn went there to witness a circumcision, a 'slovenly ceremony' that he describes at great length in his diary.[9] Others came to eat *carciofi alla Giudia*, or simply to look at 'these poor Hebrews [who] are a dwarfish race with large heads and rickety legs'.[10] Mrs Anna Jameson in her *Diary of an Ennuyée* (1826) describes her visit there in 1822, years before the zone was liberated by Pope Pius IX:

Today we drove through the quarter of the Jews, called the Ghetto degli Ebrei. It is a long street enclosed at each end with a strong iron gate, which is locked by the police at a certain hour every evening; (I believe at 10 o'clock;) and any Jew found without its precincts after that time, is liable to punishment and a heavy fine. The street is narrow and dirty, the houses wretched and ruinous, and the appearance of the inhabitants squalid, filthy, and miserable – on the whole, it was a painful scene, and one I should have avoided, had I followed my own inclinations.[11]

At the end of the Ghetto's main street, the Via del Portico d'Ottavia, are the remains of the great *porticus* that the Emperor Augustus reconstructed in 23 BC in honour of his sister Octavia, the virtuous and neglected wife of Anthony. This *porticus*, which originally consisted of three hundred columns, enclosed the twin temples of Jupiter and Juno, but almost all that survives of the complex today is the south entrance with its clumsy medieval restorations. For centuries, this structure housed Rome's main fish market. A Renaissance inscription still visible on the front wall mandates 'the heads, as far as the first fin, of all fish longer than this sign [93 cm.] shall be the property of the conservators'.[12] Artists as diverse as Albert Bierstadt (Plate 4), Samuel Prout, and E. Roesler Franz were among those who captured the spirit of this now defunct but once bustling market-place.

But visitors who came here in search of local colour were forced to confront their deepest feelings about dirt and cleanliness. Some, like Charlotte Eaton, were quick to point out that 'the remains of the Portico of Octavia stand in what I am convinced is the filthiest spot upon the whole face of the globe',[13] but others took the matter under more thoughtful consideration. Although he was not directly referring to the Octavian fish-market, the American sculptor, author, and long-time Roman resident William Wetmore Story was rather more circumspect when in *Roba di Roma* (1862) he wrote:

> It was dirty, but it was Rome; and to anyone who has long lived in Rome even its very dirt has a charm which the neatness of no other place ever had. All depends, of course, on what we call dirt. No one would defend the condition of some of the streets or some of the habits of the people. But the soil and stain which many call dirt I call color, and the cleanliness of Amsterdam would ruin Rome for the artist. Thrift and exceeding cleanliness are sadly at war with the picturesque.[14]

Undoubtedly it was to Story that Henry James was alluding in a likeable passage in *Transatlantic Sketches* (1875):

> The squalor of Rome is certainly a stubborn fact, and there is no denying that it is a dirty place. 'Don't talk to

me of liking Rome', an old sojourner lately said to me;
'you don't really like it till you like the dirt.' This state-
ment was a shock to my nascent passion; but – I blush to
write it – I am growing to think there is something in it.

'What you call dirt', an excellent authority has affirmed, 'I call color;' and it is certain that, if cleanliness is
next to godliness, it is a very distant neighbor to
chiaroscuro. That I have came to relish dirt as dirt, I
hesitate yet to affirm; but I admit as I walk about the
streets and glance under black archways into dim old
courts and up mouldering palace façades at the colored
rags that flap over the twisted balustrades of balconies, I
find I very much enjoy their 'tone'.[15]

After the Ghetto was liberated and Jews restored their rights
in 1870, the zone took on a brighter, less gloomy tone.
Barbara Grizzuti Harrison walks through it in *Italian Days*
(1989) and finds it, despite the sadness of its history,

a delightful place. It is lively; it is a gorgeous architectural
jumble: Renaissance buildings next to medieval houses,
Corinthian columns on sidewalks, in courtyards, even on
staircases. And medieval houses gussied up with discreet
and beautiful windows . . . and narrow streets hung with
laundry that debouch into sunny small piazzas, some little
more than cul-de-sacs; houses draped in ivy, courtyards
adorned with succulents and fountains. . . . To walk here
is a tactile experience – sun and shadow on your skin as
you walk down dark, narrow streets crowded with tall,
narrow houses and exit into intimate piazzas. Architecture feels like your skin's skin and this makes a kind of
moral sense.

Here there are pomegranates among the ruins. Life is
within us.[16]

Tourists have always taken pleasure in shopping and dining
out in Rome and the Ghetto has long catered to each of these
desires. For shopping, Augustus Hare's *Walks in Rome* (first
edition, 1871) informed its readers that

Everything may be obtained in the Ghetto; precious
stones, lace, furniture of all kinds, rich embroidery from
Algiers and Constantinople, striped stuffs from Spain –
but all is concealed and under cover. '*Cosa cercate*', the Jew
shopkeepers hiss at you as you thread their narrow alleys,
and try to entice you in to bargain with them. The same
article is often passed on by a mutual arrangement from
shop to shop, and meets you wherever you go.[17]

For dining in the Ghetto, there are few records before the
late nineteenth century and it was not something that most
early guidebooks were apt to recommend. Nonetheless, the
American artist Elihu Vedder, who lived in Rome on and off
after 1856, informs us in his *Digressions* (1911) that

It was once the fashion and still holds, to go in the season
of the artichoke (carcioffoli) across the river to the Ghetto
to eat 'carcioffoli alla Giudea' – that is, cooked in the
Jewish manner. And they are very good, too, when
washed down with the wine of the Castelli, and eaten
in good company. The place now in vogue is Father
Abraham's in the Ghetto.[18]

Located in Piazza Monte dei Cenci, Padre Abram's, as it was
then more commonly called, was taken over in 1860 by the
Piperno family whose name it continues to carry. On the
current menu, it is claimed of the house speciality that

They cheer the peevish and are the gourmet's delight,
They are the cook's pride and glory,
They make peace between husband and wife,
And can soften the shrewest mother-in-law.
For dinner or supper, at home or eating out,
Crunchy gold, the joy of every gourmet –
These are our artichokes Jewish style.

The Piazza Monte dei Cenci is also the ancestral home of the
infamous Cenci family, one of whose members, the lovely
young Beatrice, became a legend after she was executed for
parricide in 1599. A charming painting long believed to be her
portrait once hung in the Barberini Gallery where it enthralled

Browning, Dumas, Shelley, Stendhal and countless others (the painting and the legend will be inspected on the eighth walk).

The modern Tempio Israelitico, or Synagogue, literally casts its shadow over the Ghetto. This was built between 1889 and 1904, and though a natural source of pride to Rome's Jewish residents and visitors, from an architectural historian's point of view, 'the composition does not depart far from the usual Beaux-Arts practice at the time, and the details, though exotic, are at a distance easily taken to be conventional ones. It is a building which lacks distinction'.[19]

THE THEATRE OF MARCELLUS

Just to the east of the Synagogue is the great Theatre of Marcellus, begun by Julius Caesar and completed by Augustus. Were it anywhere but in Rome, it would be far better known, but its reputation has been completely eclipsed by that of the Colosseum. Not only is it smaller than the Colosseum, but as a theatre – not an amphitheatre – it never hosted the gladiatorial contests that aroused such strong passions. Moreover, since it never was allowed to decay into as ruinous a state as the Colosseum, it never achieved that state of 'natural' picturesqueness which so appealed to the Romantic sensibility.

Perhaps because of its smaller size, the Theatre of Marcellus was easily and repeatedly adapted to the practical needs of the Middle Ages and the Renaissance. Its later transformations were cheerfully recounted by the Reverend T. H. White in his *Fragments of Italy* (1841):

> After much research, I discovered, the other day, that . . . this lordly fabric has experienced various metamorphoses. From a Temple of the Tragic Muse, it became the stage for tragedies of real life, when converted into a Feudal Fortress, by the Savelli family, during the domestic wars of the Dark Ages; and subsequently, it received the more pleasing attributes of an Italian palace,

at the command of the Massini, from the hands of
Balthasar Peruzzi. It now belongs to Prince Orsini, the
solitary 'Senator', and is still adorned with bassi rilievi,
and other valuable remains of its original structure.[20]

It takes imagination to be touched by a monument of such
eclectic character. One of the few who took inspiration from it
was Olave Potter, author of *The Colour of Rome* (1909):

> It is impossible to look upon the blackened shell of the
> Theatre of Marcellus without being moved to something
> more than a mere antiquarian's interest or an architect's
> enthusiasm. For this ruin more than any other in Rome is
> associated with the tragedy of the greatest Roman, and
> the personal ambitions and disappointments of his suc-
> cessor. Julius Caesar chose the site and planned the great
> theatre which was to be capable of holding fourteen or
> fifteen hundred people. He was murdered long before its
> completion, and Augustus continued it in honour of
> Marcellus, the beautiful and beloved son of Octavia. Poor
> young Marcellus died when he was still a boy, and the
> vast theatre which the Emperor had opened with such
> pomp in his honour must have seemed to him the
> mausoleum of his hopes and ambitions.
>
> The immense circular ruin, with its three tiers of
> arcades and its ragged blocks of travertine, with frag-
> ments of a cornice showing here and there, has withstood
> the many fires that have swept across Rome like the anger
> of Jove, but its blackened stones have a sombre, tragic
> aspect. They frown down upon the cheerful piazza be-
> low, where contadini with their gaily-painted carts
> lounge through the sunny day. The dark mouths of
> habitations gape on the narrow road; windows are cut in
> every arch; the upper tier has been entirely rebuilt for
> modern apartments; and within its old walls stands the
> Orsini Palace with its zigzag drive, its fountains and
> orange trees, and the bears of the family juggling on the
> pillars of the gate.[21]

The juggling bears of the Orsini may seem a frivolous
emblem for a family so prominent in the drama of the city's

history. Able to trace their patrician lineage to Roman times,
over the centuries they sent three of their own to the papal
throne and engaged in numerous political intrigues of which
only the most recent was Felice Orsini's failed assassination
attempt on Napoleon III in 1858.

THE FORUM BOARIUM

Walking in a southerly direction along the modern Via del
Teatro di Marcello towards the Forum Boarium, one will pass
on the right a charming little medieval house known as the
Casa dei Crescenzi. Built from ancient spoils and medieval
recreations thereof, it is now known to date from around the
year 1100. It originally belonged to a patrician family named
Crescenzi, then passed to the tribune Cola di Rienzi, a charis-
matic religious reformer of the fourteenth century (whereupon it came to be called the Casa di Rienzi). However, the
most appealing chapter in its history turns out to be pure
medieval fabrication. In *Rome: A Tour of Many Days* (1849),
Sir George Head informed his readers that

> According to other accounts the building is identified
> with a much earlier period, coeval with the commence-
> ment of the Christian era, being supposed to have be-
> longed to Pontius Pilate. Among the common people it is
> accordingly called the 'House of Pilate' as often as the
> 'House of Rienzi', though no reason that I ever heard of,
> otherwise than mere tradition, is assigned for concluding
> that Pontius Pilate ever visited the metropolis of the
> Roman empire or had a house there.[22]

Sir George was right, but the legend gave the house a special
aura nonetheless. In his picaresque 'novel' *The Unfortunate
Traveller* (1594), Thomas Nashe has his adventurous hero Jack
Wilton pay a quick visit: 'I was at Pontius Pilate's house and
pist against it'.[23] Nashe may have done so himself when he
visited Rome in 1587, and other (male) travellers may have
favoured Roman monuments in a like manner, but young

Wilton's gesture seems never to have been repeated in respectable works of literature.

The Forum Boarium is so named because it was the site of the cattle market in antiquity. Two very fine Republican temples, one rectangular and the other circular, have stood there since the second century BC. During the Middle Ages and the Renaissance both were adapted to Christian use and infelicitously transformed by structural additions. Mussolini again played a key role in their restoration. In 1925 he made a speech saying 'the millennial monuments of our history must loom gigantic in their necessary solitude', and within a few years they were deconsecrated and freed of their parasitic attachments.[24]

Of the two temples, the round, so-called Temple of Vesta was by far the more popular and photogenic. The modest size of the building has prompted every imaginable simile. Seeing it for the first time in 1825, William Hazlitt found it to be 'not unlike an hour-glass – or a toadstool; it is small, but exceedingly beautiful, and has a look of great antiquity'.[25] In 1858 Nathaniel Hawthorne also found it 'very beautiful, though so small that, in a suitable locality, one would take it rather for a garden-house than an ancient temple'.[26] Hawthorne's friend and fellow New Englander George Stillman Hillard described it as 'a pretty toy of a building; too small – to borrow an expression of Horace Walpole's – to live in, and too large to hang at one's watch-chain'.[27]

Very near the Temple of Vesta, but far less pretty, is another ancient construction that stirred souls in the past. This is the Cloaca Maxima, the massive sewer that ran from the Argiletum through the Roman Forum and emptied here into the Tiber. Although it is hard for modern tourists to muster much enthusiasm for the mouth of a common sewer, it is still visible encased in the new embankment on the west bank of the river (the side nearest the Forum Boarium), just south of the Ponte Palatino. Livy, Strabo, and Pliny all expressed great admiration for it in antiquity, and in modern times Henry James, following the advice of his *Murray's Handbook*, visited the famed site. In a letter to his mother from 1869 he wrote:

A man sallied forth from the neighboring shades with an enormous key and whispered the soul-stirring name of the *Cloaca Maxima*. I joyfully assented and he led me apart under a series of half-buried arches into a deeper hollow, where the great mouth of a tunnel seemed to brood over the scene and thence introduced me into a little covered enclosure, whence we might survey a small section of the ancient sewer. It gave me the deepest and grimmest impression of antiquity I have ever received. He lit a long torch and plunged it down into the blackness. It threw a red glare on a mass of dead black travertine and I was assured that I was gazing upon the masonry of Tarquinius Prisens [sic]. If it wasn't I'm sure it ought to have been.[28]

Not every visitor was similarly impressed. Perhaps it helped to have once been a boy, for few female sightseers have been as enraptured by the prospect of exploring the damp, dark hole. Frances Elliot, author of *Diary of an Idle Woman in Italy*, published her account of a visit to the Cloaca in 1871, just two years after James had been there:

The place swarmed with washerwomen, who scrub perpetually at small reservoirs in the thickness of the wall, under the massive vaults once the pride of Rome.

I was infinitely disappointed, and could only marvel at the high trumpetings conveyed in the sound and fame of a name – nothing but a name – which leads half Europe to gaze on an impure ditch! It is all very well for books and antiquarians to tell us that those blocks of stone are Etruscan architecture, and were hewn and constructed in the time of Tarquinius Priscus, fifth king of Rome; but these details do not alter the fact that the much-extolled Cloaca, through which Strabo says a waggon loaded with hay might once pass, must now be classed as one of the many disagreeable objects from which one turns disgusted away.[29]

S. Maria in Cosmedin and the Bocca della Verita

Standing opposite the Temple of Vesta and the ebullient Baroque Fountain of the Tritons is the early medieval church of S. Maria in Cosmedin. This had its origins as a *diaconia*, or Christian welfare centre, around the year 600, was enlarged in the eighth century, rebuilt in the twelfth century, and 're-stored' in the last years of the nineteenth century. 'This church is a gem of beauty which Time and the Tiber and the vandals of the sixteenth and seventeenth centuries have been unable to rob of its glory', wrote Olave Potter in the early years of the twentieth century.[30] Bernard Berenson, on the other hand, was distressed by the over-enthusiasm of the restorers. In 1947 he wrote in his diary, 'the worst about these restored basilicas is their emptiness, [they] look as if they served to show off the restorer's skill rather than to impress as temple of the Lord'.[31] The ever-sensible H. V. Morton put the matter in some perspective when he wrote, 'some people think that restorers have done too much to this church, but the less critical viewer will be grateful to them. They have brought back a great deal of its queer half-oriental beauty'.[32] It is still an extremely handsome little church even without its formerly pretty Rococo façade, lost in the 1890s restoration.

S. Maria in Cosmedin's greatest attraction, however, has nothing to do with art or architecture. It is the Bocca della Verità, or Mouth of Truth, a large, flat, stone face set into the left wall of the porch. In the Middle Ages it was believed that if someone told a lie while placing his hand in the mouth, the jaws would snap shut and sever the hand. According to one local legend, occasionally in judicial cases where the accused was presumed guilty, a policeman wielding a sword would hide behind the mouth and administer the proper justice.[33] Another story has it that an English tourist swore falsely with his hand in the mouth and was bitten by a scorpion.[34] Richard Lassels may have been more sceptical than most when, in *The Voyage of Italy* (1670) he wrote, 'but this not being affirmed by the *Mouth of Truth*, I dare not beleeve it. I rather beleeve it served in some old building for a gutter spout: I know *Truth* may speake lowd, and have a *Wide Mouth*, but he that takes every wide mouth for the mouth of *Truth*, is much mistaken'.[35]

But even today, Roman parents remind their children of the Bocca della Verità when they suspect they may not be hearing the truth. H. V. Morton recalls being in the church when a party of Italian schoolgirls was inspecting the Bocca: 'I watched with amusement the alarm of the girls as they dared each other to thrust their hands into the dark gash, and the dismay of the little nun in charge as she cried, *"Silenzio! Silenzio!"* and waved an umbrella in a vain attempt to keep order'.[36]

THE CIRCUS MAXIMUS

The fragmentary remains of ancient Rome's largest stadium, the Circus Maximus, lie directly behind S. Maria in Cosmedin. Positioned in the natural valley formed by the Palatine and the Aventine, this stadium is said to have held three to four hundred thousand people, many times the number accommodated at the modern Stadio Olimpico. The entertainment consisted of horse races, water battles, athletic contests, and wild-beast fights. It was the latter, of course, that were the most memorable. One account, said to be based on Pliny, claimed that

> in the second Punic War, Scylla, when he was Praetor, sent into the circus one hundred lions, one hundred elephants, and one hundred bears, which were turned loose together to devour one another. Pompey, who desired to have a nearer view of these sports, had seventeen elephants and hundreds of panthers and other wild animals brought into his theatre, which amused the people for five days. Hadrian had one thousand beasts slaughtered on his birthday, and Commodus killed several thousands with his own hands.[37]

For gentler souls, there were other entertainments to be had at the Circus Maximus. In the *Ars Amatoria*, Ovid recommends

Nor should you neglect the horse races. Many are the opportunities that await you in the spacious circus. No call here for the secret language of fingers; nor need you depend upon a furtive nod. Nobody will prevent you sitting next to a girl. Sit as closely as you like. That's easy enough; the seating compels it. . . . Now find an excuse to start a pleasant conversation, and begin by saying things that you can say quite audibly. Be sure you ask her whose horses are entering the ring; and, whatever her fancy may be, hasten to approve her choice. . . . If, as may well happen, a speck of dust falls in your lady's lap, brush it gently away; but should none fall, still persist in brushing. . . . If her cloak hangs low and trails on the ground, gather it up and lift it carefully from the dirt. As a reward, she won't hesitate to allow you a glimpse of her leg. At the same time, look to the row behind and see that a stranger's knees are not pressed into her tender back. Light natures are won by little attentions. The clever arrangements of a cushion has often done a lover service. . . . Such are the advantages that the circus offers you when you are set upon a new affair.[38]

THE AVENTINE HILL

Rising to the south-west of the Circus Maximus, the Aventine Hill offers the weary sightseer a peaceful respite from the clamour of the city below. The most pleasant approach is up the Clivo di Rocca Savella, a lovely wide footpath diverging from the Via di S. Maria in Cosmedin a short distance to the right of the church. The hill itself has changed hardly at all since Edward Hutton described it in 1909:

Of all the hills of Rome the Aventine alone, precipitous and almost uninhabited as it is, still impresses us with its own beauty and serenity. It is as though the ancient curse of the Patricians were still heavy upon it. Something certainly of those far-off days seems to linger even yet about its shadowy, deserted ways, among the gardens there, where in the spring the almond trees are so strangely lovely and in summer the *cicala* wearies us with its song; where many an ancient church still counts the Ave Mary through the centuries, half-forgotten in a world of silence and flowers.[39]

The public garden – the Parco Savello – affords breathtaking views of the city from its broad parapet. Elizabeth Bowen was especially fond of this park, associating it 'with singing birds, aisles of slender trees, and reposefulness – here in so green a space, at so great a height, above Rome'.[40] An old legend has it that in the adjacent cloister garden of S. Sabina is the first orange tree planted in Italy. Its trunk now protected by a formidable cement encasement, this tough old tree is said to have been planted by St Dominic more than seven centuries ago.

Nearby is the Priorato, or Priory, of the Knights of Malta. Securing these grounds is the gate whose famous keyhole allows a glimpse of the artfully framed cupola of St Peter's in the distance. Eleanor Clark grappled with the underlying aesthetic of this perspective, concluding that

It is good Easter-egg magic, always a hit, and for good reason; the trickery is basic. The Dome, which has a way of following you around the town, proclaiming Michelangelo and the center of the world – happens not to be visible from anywhere else on that street, and looks, through the keyhole, more like an image abstracted from the real thing and placed there by some feat of physics, so that you are surprised not to find some other basilica in the second keyhole in the same door. It is both real and not real, there and not there; and so an object in space clearly illustrates for you the trickery of all Rome, which has to do, as Pirandello was trying to say, with time.[41]

The piazza, gateway, and enclosed church of S. Maria del Priorato were all designed by the celebrated printmaker G. B. Piranesi in the middle of the eighteenth century. The late Mario Praz, a connoisseur of Neo-Classical taste, described the architecture as 'romantic, morbid, and hallucinated', while

Carroll Meeks found it 'profoundly disturbing'.[42] But most early visitors were more taken with the splendid views through the keyhole and from the garden. Stendhal in 1827 enthused in his *Journal*:

> What view could be more singular than the one from the Priory of Malta, built on the western summit of Mount Aventine which, on the Tiber side, ends in a precipice! What a deep impression the tomb of Cecilia Metella, the Appian Way and the Campagna of Rome produce when seen from this height![43]

Stendhal's claim that the Appian Way and the Tomb of Cecilia Metella are visible from the heights of the Priory may strike today's visitor to Rome as a bit odd. Admittedly, nearly all the buildings that now block the view to the south were constructed later, but there is reason to suspect that Stendhal may have based his remarks on a topographical print rather than on what he saw with his own eyes. To be sure, his working method was unconventional. Haakon Chevalier, in the introduction to his translation of *A Roman Journal* (*Promenades dans Rome*), lets us down easily:

> Will it spoil the pleasure of the present-day reader to know that the whole *machinery* of this journal is sheer fabrication . . . that the entire book was written in a hotel room in [Paris] . . . almost directly opposite the Bibliothèque Nationale? I think not. In fact, this and other circumstances connected with this book – of which his contemporaries had no knowledge and which would have meant less to them than to us – give it added spice.

As our shock at discovering Stendhal's fraud slowly sinks in, Chevalier twists the knife further:

> He actually knew Rome far less well than he seems to. He claims – and the illusion is created – that everything that he sets down he has freshly seen and heard. In actual fact, many of the things he describes in such loving detail he has never seen, or has seen hurriedly or so long ago that he can have no clear recollection of them.[44]

A more credible but no less romantic witness was Mrs Frances Elliot whose own *Diary* of 1871 gives a more accurate impression of the view from the Priory garden:

> Rome was invisible, but the windings of the Tiber through the leafy groves . . . and the desolate Monte Testaccio, surmounted by a single cross, occupied the foreground. Below lay the low, marshy Campagna towards Ostia, broken by the magnificent basilica of San Paolo fuori le mura, surrounded by vineyards and gardens, the trees just bursting into snowy blossoms. All save this bright spot was indescribably melancholy. In the surrounding plain, malaria, ruin, decay, and pestilence unite to form a wilderness noxious in summer both to man and beast. The wind sighed gently as it rose from the plain, fanning the deep woods of the garden, like the voice of Nature mourning over the desolation of this once rich and pleasant land.[45]

The plaintive Mrs Elliot would undoubtedly be even more melancholy if she could visit this lovely spot today and discover the extent to which car fumes have followed malarial 'vapours', and suburban sprawl has replaced ruin and decay.

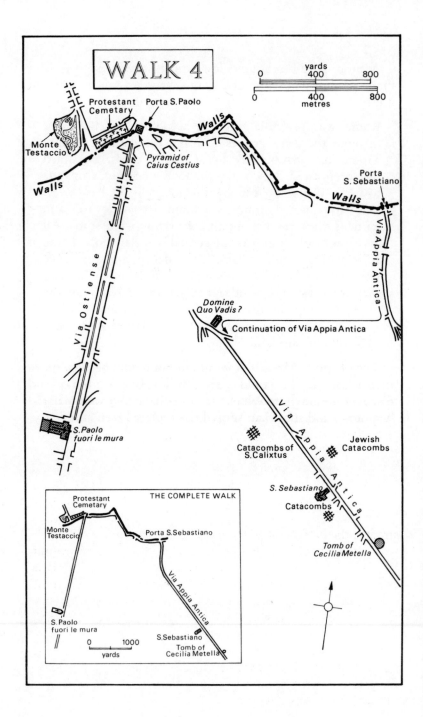

WALK 4

yards
0   400   800

0   400   800
metres

Monte
Testaccio

Protestant
Cemetary

Porta S. Paolo

Walls

Walls

Pyramid of
Caius Cestius

Porta
S. Sebastiano

Walls

Via Appia Antica

Via Ostiense

Domine
Quo Vadis?

Continuation of Via Appia Antica

Via Appia Antica

S. Paolo
fuori le mura

Catacombs of
S. Calixtus

Jewish
Catacombs

S. Sebastiano

Catacombs

Tomb of
Cecilia Metella

THE COMPLETE WALK

Protestant
Cemetary

Monte
Testaccio

Porta S. Sebastiano

Via Appia Antica

S. Paolo
fuori le mura

S. Sebastiano

Tomb of
Cecilia Metella

0   1000
yards

4

FOURTH WALK

*From the Basilica of S. Paolo, past the Pyramid and Protestant
Cemetery, to the Via Appia and the Catacombs*

S. PAOLO FUORI LE MURA

Early travellers coming from the seaport at Ostia, or modern
tourists arriving at Fiumicino Airport have always entered
Rome along the Via Ostiense. In 1581 Michel de Montaigne
remarked that this road 'abounds in vestiges of its ancient
splendour', despite having an otherwise 'barren and unculti-
vated look'.[1] The view from the window of the airport bus
reveals little more than a dreary panorama of grimy modern
blocks of flats, congested traffic, and an assortment of public
utilities.

The single important monument to be seen on this lengthy
street is the basilica of S. Paolo fuori le mura, one of the four
patriarchal churches of Rome. Before it burned to the ground
in 1823, the original basilica of the fourth century surpassed
even St Peter's in grandeur and lavish decoration. In 1645 John
Evelyn was greatly impressed by its 'incomparable architecture . . . precious oriental marbles', and 'excellent' paintings
and sculpture.[2] The present basilica is a heartless nineteenth-
century recreation of the lost original. Possessed of 'a cold
splendour', and 'great propriety', its limited appeal was most
forthrightly interpreted by William Dean Howells in *Roman
Holidays and Others* (1908):

It far surpasses St Peter's [in so much as] the antic touch of the baroque is scarcely present in it, for being newly rebuilt . . . its faults are not those of sixteenth-century excess. It would be a very bold or a very young connoisseur who should venture to appraise its merits beyond this negative evaluation.[3]

Henry James may have been just such a person as Howells had in mind. Years earlier, at the age of thirty, James wrote in 'From a Roman Note-Book' (1873):

The restored Basilica is incredibly splendid. It seems a last pompous effort of formal Catholicism, and there are few more striking emblems of later Rome. . . . It rises there, gorgeous and useless, on its miasmic site, with an air of conscious bravado – a florid advertisement of the superabundance of faith. Within it's magnificent, and its magnificence has no shabby spots – a rare thing in Rome.[4]

About the same time, the 63-year-old Franz Liszt also had a positive response to the newly rebuilt basilica. In a letter of 1874, the Hungarian composer revealed that 'notwithstanding the widely accepted criticisms levelled against the reconstruction of this church, it harmonizes more with my own personal feelings of worship than any other in Rome . . .'[5]

THE PYRAMID AND THE PROTESTANT CEMETERY

The Via Ostiense culminates in a shapeless piazza surrounding the Porta San Paolo gateway of the ancient city wall. To one side of this banal, large square stands Rome's most unusual public monument, the Pyramid of Caius Cestius. Built as the tomb of a minor Roman bureaucrat who died in 12 BC, this anomalous structure commands considerable attention both for its size – it is 88 feet high – and for its excellent state of preservation. Historically, it is of far less importance. Madame de Staël was admirably succinct when she noted that 'the massive pyramid that enclosed [Cestius] defends his death from the oblivion which had utterly effaced his life'.[6]

The Pyramid abuts the Protestant Cemetery whose proximity has ensured greater notoriety for each. The juxtaposition of ancient and modern tombs had a special appeal for non-Catholic visitors who sought solace in its unconsecrated ground. Samuel Rogers expressed some of the sentiments involved in an essay appended to his *Italy, A Poem* (1830):

> It is a quiet and sheltered nook, covered in the winter with violets; and the Pyramid, that overshadows it, gives a classical and singularly solemn air. You feel an interest there, a sympathy you were not prepared for. You are yourself in a foreign land; and they are for the most part your countrymen. They call upon you in your mother-tongue – in English – in words unknown to a native, known only to yourselves: and the tomb of CESTIUS, that old majestic pile, has this also in common with them. It is itself a stranger, among strangers. It has stood there till the language spoken round it has changed; and the shepherd, born at the foot, can read its inscription no longer.[7]

Years later, Henry James also responded to the commingling of epochs, finding an ambiguous atmosphere there:

> I recently spent an afternoon hour at the little Protestant cemetery where the ancient and modern world are insidiously contrasted. They make between them one of the solemn places of Rome – although indeed when funereal things are so interfused it seems ungrateful to call them sad. Here is a mixture of tears and smiles, of stones and flowers, of mourning cypresses and radiant sky, which gives us the impression of our looking back at death from the brighter side of the grave.[8]

One experiences instant serenity as one passes through the portal marked RESURRECTURIS and steps into the verdant and perfectly manicured grounds. 'It might make one in love with death, to be buried in so sweet a place', wrote Shelley, whose own tomb was later to become one of the site's major attractions.[9] H. V. Morton thought 'this must be the most beautiful cemetery in the world and is certainly the best tended. . . . The cypress trees cast their long shadows upon the most extraordinary collection of exiles ever assembled in one place'.[10]

The first to be buried there was a 25-year-old Englishman

named George Langton. Since then nearly 4,000 departed
souls have been interred, the most celebrated being Keats and
Shelley. Keats died at the age of twenty-five just four months
after he came to Rome in the autumn of 1820 seeking relief
from tuberculosis. As he realized that his life was drawing to a
close, he asked his faithful companion Joseph Severn to go and
inspect his intended gravesite. When Severn returned and told
him that white and blue violets, daisies, and anemones grew
wild over the graves, Keats rejoiced and said that he 'already
seemed to feel the flowers growing over him'.[11]

Keats's tomb (next to that of Severn) is in the oldest part of
the cemetery (Plate 5) and is visible, even when the grounds
are closed, through a small wall grating in the Via Caio Cestio.
The epitaph on his gravestone reads:

> This Grave
> contains all that was Mortal
> of a
> YOUNG ENGLISH POET
> Who,
> on his Death Bed,
> in the Bitterness of his Heart,
> at the malicious Power of his Enemies,
> Desired
> these Words to be engraven on his Tomb Stone
>
> Here lies One
> Whose Name was writ in Water
> Feb 24th 1821

The middle lines of the inscription were composed by his
friend Charles Brown, while the final couplet, derived from
Shakespeare's *Henry VIII* ('Men's evil manners live in brass;
their virtues We write in water'), was requested by Keats
himself.[12] Brown came to regret his invective against the
poet's English critics, and years later, in a letter to Severn,
even requested that it be erased from the epitaph. Severn, for
his part, found the inscription an 'eye-sore', and the same lines
have long bothered others as well.[13] George Hillard probably
spoke for many when he stated his opinion that 'the epitaph

upon the monument . . . is not in good taste . . . for a tombstone . . . should contain nothing transient or impassioned, but only simple statements and solemn truths'.[14]

News of Keats's death took two months to reach Shelley who was then living in Pisa. In the space of another two months, Shelley composed the elegy *Adonais* (1821) to his deceased friend. The preface to this poem contains a vituperative attack on those reviewers that Shelley (and Brown) held responsible for hastening Keats's death. The poem itself is among Shelley's best, and beyond being a memorial to Keats, it portrays Rome as a city of romantic destiny. To mourners he suggests:

> Go thou to Rome, at once the Paradise,
> The grave, the city and the wilderness;
> And where its wrecks like shattered mountains rise,
> And flowering weeds and fragrant copses dress
> The bones of Desolation's nakedness
> Pass, till the spirit of the spot shall lead
> Thy footsteps to a slope of green access
> Where, like an infant's smile, over the dead
> A light of laughing flowers along the grass is spread.[15]

The next year, 1822, Shelley himself died in a mysterious boating accident off the coast of Viareggio. When his body eventually washed ashore, it was supposedly identified by a copy of Keats's poems that was still in his pocket. The body was cremated on the beach and the ashes sent to Rome for burial, but his heart was snatched from the pyre and later given to his wife, wrapped in one of the sheets from *Adonais*. Shelley's tombstone in the newer part of the Protestant Cemetery, near the ancient wall, bears the inscription COR CORDIUM (Heart of Hearts) followed by three lines from the 'Song of Ariel' in Shakespeare's *The Tempest*:

> Nothing of him that doth fade,
> But doth suffer a sea-change
> Into something rich and strange[16]

The sight of Shelley's grave surprised John Ruskin 'into tears almost', touched George Eliot 'deeply', impressed

Henry James as 'a happy grave every way', and moved Oscar
Wilde to write sonnets on the graves of both Shelley and
Keats.[17] Wilde visited the Protestant Cemetery on the very
day in 1877 that he had been granted an audience with Pope
Pius IX. Prostrating himself on the grass in humbler obeisance
than he had offered the pope, Wilde considered Keats's grave
'the holiest place in Rome', even finding religious significance
in the poet's death. The most memorable lines in his sonnet to
Keats read:

> The youngest of the martyrs here is lain,
> Fair as Sebastian, and as early slain.[18]

His poem 'The Grave of Shelley' employs a more conventional iconography, but is probably the more successful of the
two sonnets in capturing the sense of place. It begins:

> Like burnt-out torches by a sick man's bed
>   Gaunt cypress-trees stand round the sun-bleached
>   stone;
>   Here doth the little night-owl make her throne,
> And the slight lizard show his jewelled head.
> And where the chaliced poppies flame to red,
>   In the still chamber of yon pyramid
>   Surely some Old-World Sphinx lurks darkly hid,
> Grim warder of this pleasuance of the dead.[19]

Today's visitor to the cemetery will find dozens of other
tombstones that mark the graves of less eminent but still
familiar figures who made lasting contributions to the worlds
of art, letters, and diplomacy. But there is one tomb the visitor
will not find, although it is reported to be, like Shelley's, 'in an
angle of the wall of imperial Rome, beneath the cypresses and
thick spring-flowers'.[20] This is the grave of Miss Daisy Miller
whose mortal remains the fictional Rome has claimed as one of
its own.

Just to the west of the Protestant Cemetery lies one of
Rome's most unusual cultural attractions, the ancient dump-
ing ground known as Monte Testaccio. In *Sights in Italy*
(1847), William Gardiner provides a brief description of the
site:

[It] is a remarkable hill . . . one hundred and sixty feet
high, and one-third of a mile in circumference, entirely
composed of fragments of pottery. It seems difficult to
account for so vast an accumulation of rubbish. Dig
where you will it is all the same. The use of earthenware
in vases to contain wine, oil, ashes of the dead, lamps,
ornaments, and vessels for various purposes, was general
among the Romans. There must have been a law to
prevent these fragments being thrown into the river or
into the streets, or else such an accumulation, as large as
Primrose Hill, never could have been heaped together.[21]

In the past, Monte Testaccio enjoyed a reputation as a
setting for Bacchic revelries. Caverns excavated in its sides
housed rowdy wine bars but by the mid-twentieth century,
according to Eleanor Clark, 'there is no great carousing any
more at the foot of Monte Testaccio, only a few gypsy wagons
halted there from time to time as a base for begging oper-
ations, and the district around . . . the pyramid is a screeching
turmoil of traffic'.[22]

Appreciating that Monte Testaccio 'shares with the catacombs the distinction of being the only memory in Rome of
the ordinary life of common people', H. V. Morton, recalls a
visit he made to the site in the 1950s:

I climbed all over the hill . . . and I thought it one of the
most curious and fascinating relics in Rome. Vegetation
can obtain no foothold, and at every step I dislodged a
shower of pottery, and when I thrust a stick into the side
of the hill I disturbed and pulled out fragments of pots and
the handles of *amphorae* which had been buried and
hidden for centuries. . . . Some of the potters stamped
the handles of the *amphorae* with their initials, and in
scrambling about I dislodged two or three of these. The
discovery aroused my fervour, and I went hunting about
until my pockets bulged with potters' stamps. Two small
boys who were playing on the hill thought it might be
greater fun to assist me, and in fifteen minutes we had
assembled such a large pile that I begged them to seek no
more.[23]

Along the Wall from Porta San Paolo to the Via Appia Antica

Walls have always played a part in Roman city planning and
the first was reportedly built by Romulus. The present walls,
begun by Aurelian in 271, circle the city with an irregular
circumference of some 12 miles. They were originally 12 feet
thick, 25 feet high, and were defended by 381 towers and 18
fortified gateways.

Building the wall, according to Gibbon, 'was a great melancholy labour, since the defence of the Capital betrayed the
decline of the monarchy'.[24] It also proved to be a useless labour
for when the barbarians came, they ignored the wall and
took the more expedient measure of cutting the aqueducts.
Because it lacks a heroic history, Elizabeth Bowen suggests
'the Aurelian wall is played down by guide-books, whose
references to it are hurried, oblique, and grudging'.[25]

Literary accounts of the wall are rarely occasioned by the
same sentiments aroused by monuments with a prouder past.
But if the wall's history was undistinguished, some later
travellers did find it moderately picturesque. In 'Roman Rides'
(1873), Henry James recalls the pleasure he took in riding his
horse round the walls and out into the Campagna. 'If you are a
person of taste, don't grumble at the occasional need of
following the walls of the city', he advises, for

> even to idle eyes the prodigious, the continuous thing
> bristles with eloquent passages. In some places where the
> huge brickwork is black with time and certain strange
> square towers look down at you with still blue eyes, the
> Roman sky peering through lidless loopholes, and there
> is nothing but white dust in the road and solitude in the
> air, I might take myself for a wandering Tartar touching
> on the confines of the Celestial Empire. . . . The colour
> of the Roman ramparts is everywhere fine, and their rug-
> ged patchwork has been subdued by time and weather into
> a mellow harmony that the brush only asks to take up.[26]

Following the wall from the Porta San Paolo in an easterly
direction for about a mile, one comes to the Porta San Sebas-

tiano, or Porta Appia, which in turn leads directly to the famed Appian Way.

The Appian Way and the Campagna

The Appian Way, or Via Appia Antica (Plates 6 and 7), was built by Appius Claudius in 312 BC and originally ran as far as Capua before it was extended a century later to Benevento and Brindisi. From the beginning, the road was paved with stone, and Horace found it 'For to quick Trav'lers, 'tis a tedious Road / But if you walk but slow, 'tis pretty good'.[27]

It is a narrow road – 'no wider than a pool table' according to John Gunther; 'not like Milton's [wide] way [to hell]' according to Herman Melville.[28] At times it is sunk below ground level and for the first several miles it is lined with ancient tombs. Six thousand of Spartacus's troops were crucified along its southern reaches in 71 BC. In more recent years it has been viewed as desolate or inspiring depending on one's romantic imagination and one's view of progress. Towards the end of the *Marble Faun* (1860), Nathaniel Hawthorne describes what Kenyon, the American art student, sees as he takes a solitary walk along the road:

> For the space of a mile or two beyond the gate, this ancient and famous road is as desolate and disagreeable as most other Roman avenues. It extends over small, un-comfortable paving-stones, between brick and plastered walls, which are very solidly constructed, and so high as almost to exclude a view of the surrounding country. The houses are of most uninviting aspect, neither picturesque, nor homelike and social; they have seldom or never a door opening on the wayside, but are accessible only from the rear, and frown inhospitably upon the traveller through iron-grated windows. Here and there appears a dreary inn, or a wine-shop, designated by the withered bush beside the entrance, within which you discern a stone-built and sepulchral interior, where guests refresh themselves with sour bread and goats' milk cheese, washed down with wine of dolorous acerbity.[29]

Just a decade earlier, Charles Dickens took the same walk. In *Pictures from Italy* (1846), he too was left with the taste of dolorous acerbity:

> We wandered out upon the Appian Way, and then went on, through miles of ruined tombs and broken walls, with here and there a desolate and uninhabited house. . . .Except where the distant Apennines bound the view upon the left, the whole wide prospect is one field of ruin. Broken aqueducts, left in the most picturesque and beautiful clusters of arches; broken temples; broken tombs. A desert of decay, sombre and desolate beyond all expression; and with a history in every stone that strews the ground.[30]

Despite its modern asphalt resurfacing, it is hard to disagree with Elizabeth Bowen's prescription that 'the Via Appia Antica should not be travelled any way but on foot'.[31] Strolling along, and temporarily foregoing a detour into the beckoning catacombs, one encounters on the rise of a hill just before the third milestone the celebrated tomb of Cecilia Metella. This massive cylindrical tomb of the Augustan era was, according to Charlotte Eaton in *Rome in the Nineteenth Century* (1820), 'generally acknowledged to be the most beautiful sepulchral monument in the world'.[32]

As a monument, the austere tomb is not in itself a thing of compelling beauty. Like the Pyramid, it houses the remains of a person of little historical consequence. Cecilia Metella was the wife of the consul Marcus Crassus, an extravagant *nouveau riche* whose very name suggests dubious taste. All that is known of her is comprised in Byron's apostrophe:

> Thus much alone we know, – Metella died,
> The wealthiest Roman's wife; Behold his love or pride![33]

Visitors with a social conscience were often critical of this ostentatious display of personal vanity. James Fenimore Cooper, the American author of the *Leatherstocking Tales*, viewed the tomb caustically in his *Gleanings in Europe: Italy* (1829–30), noting that the interred was the wife of a mere triumvir, a *millionnaire* of his day. This tomb is, therefore, the Demidoff of the Via Appia. It is probably the noblest mausoleum now standing in Europe. There is no uncertainty about its history; and yet, while one looks at it with wonder as a specimen of Roman luxury and magnificence, it fails to excite one half the interest that is felt when we linger around a spot that is celebrated, by even questionable tradition, for any other sort of greatness.[34]

More tender temperaments at times romanticized the couple's lives. In this *Travels through Italy* (1788), the President of the Bordeaux Parliament Charles Dupaty suggests that

Cecilia Metella . . . perhaps was beautiful and possessed of the tenderest sensibility, and . . . most certainly was unfortunate; the memory of Crassus, the image of a distracted [husband], who strives, by piling up stones, to immortalize his sorrow . . . gradually plunged my soul into a delicious reverie, and it was with difficulty I could leave the place.[35]

Naturally it was Byron who did the most to fix Cecilia in the minds of countless later visitors. 'Byron's description of this tomb in the fourth canto of "Childe Harold" is one of those eloquent bursts of feeling which appeal irresistibly to the heart', advised *Murray's Handbook*.[36] Of the six stanzas of the poem devoted to Cecilia and her tomb, the most irresistible to nineteenth-century romantics was undoubtedly the fourth (stanza CII), with its intimations of premature death:

> Perchance she died in youth; it may be, bowed
> With woes far heavier than the ponderous tomb
> That weigh'd upon her gentle dust, a cloud
> Might gather o'er her beauty, and a gloom
> In her dark eye, prophetic of the doom
> Heaven gives her favourites – early death; yet shed
> A sunset charm around her, and illume
> With hectic light the Hesperus of the dead,
> Of her consuming cheek the autumnal leaf-life red.[37]

Most musings over the tomb were strongly affected by its location at the edge of the peaceful Roman Campagna, a setting that inspired many an Arcadian reverie. Even the seemingly unsentimental Henrik Ibsen, working productively in Rome in 1864, admitted:

> How glorious nature is down here! Both in form and colour there is an indescribable harmony. I often lie for half a day among the tombs on . . . the old Appian Way; and I do not think this idling can be called waste of time.[38]

The Campagna is the vast undulating plain that surrounds Rome from the Tyrrhenian coast to the inland hills. A fertile area but one that for centuries harboured malarial marshes, it long discouraged human habitation and, lying fallow, only generated, in the words of Mrs Trollope, 'an annual harvest of death'.[39] Dickens, as might be expected, found this district – which he was obliged to pass through on his way to Rome – 'so sad, so quiet, so sullen . . . [with] nothing to relieve its terrible monotony and gloom'.[40] Yet even before the marshes were drained a little more than a century ago, a sizeable number of tourists were attracted to 'this strange tract of land, untilled, fever-haunted, yet full of a weird and individual enchantment'.[41]

In antiquity, Horace sang the praises of rural life in the region where he was himself a resident. The second ode in his *Book of Epodes* is in effect a renunciation of city life in favour of the charm of the Campagna. He fails to mention, however, the pre-eminent man-made features of the Campagna, the graceful aqueducts which brought water from various springs, a river, and a lake into the city. In his *Natural History* (first century), Pliny the Elder dryly comments:

> If one were to reckon accurately the plentiful amount of water in public buildings, baths, pools, channels, private houses, gardens, suburban villas, and if he were to consider the distance traversed by the water, the arches raised to support it, the mountains which had to be tunnelled through, the valleys which had to be traversed with level courses, he would have to admit that there is no work more worthy of admiration in the whole world.[42]

The barbarian invasions of the Middle Ages combined with the slower effects of time to reduce this magnificent system to what Henry James eventually called a 'long gaunt file of arches . . . their jagged ridge stretching away like the vertebral column of some monstrous mouldering skeleton'.[43] The interplay of rural tranquility with such sublime relics of the classical past made a powerful impression on foreign visitors. No one captured the sense of place better than the American historian and man of letters Henry Adams. Elsewhere so harsh, in a letter of 1860 he is effusive in his praise for the beauty of the Campagna:

> Of all glorious things here I think a ride on the Campagna in the morning or the evening is the most beautiful. There one has Rome and Italy, the past and the present, all to oneself. There the old poetic mountains breathe inspiration around. There one sees the aqueducts in their grandeur and beauty, and the ruins stand out on the landscape without being wedged in by a dozen dirty houses, or guarded by a chorus of filthy beggars. The whole country lies open, unfenced and uncultivated, and as one rides from hill to hill, the scene changes with the ground and St Peter's or the Lateran, an aqueduct or a tomb, Mount Albano and Frascati or Soracte and Tivoli almost bewilder one with their different charm. The Campagna is now green and fresh, the flowers are blooming on it and the poppies are redder than blood: the little lizards fly about with their green backs that glitter in the sun, and when one is glowing with the heat after a quick gallop, there's always a pleasant breeze to comfort one. This is the Rome that delights me, and in all Europe as yet I've seen nothing so beautiful and so pleasant.[44]

It is almost impossible to view the Campagna without being reminded of the pastoral canvases of Claude Lorrain. His nostalgic evocations of the golden age of ancient innocence are almost always set in this region. In his *Recollections* (1815), Chateaubriand recalls being particularly struck by the area's 'Claudian' light:

A peculiar vapour is spread over distant objects, which takes off their harshness and rounds them. The shadows are never black and heavy; for there are no masses so obscure, even among the rocks and foliage, but that a little light may always insinuate itself. A singular tint and most peculiar harmony unite the earth, the sky, and the waters. All the surfaces unite at their extremities by means of an insensible gradation of colours, and without the possibility of ascertaining the point at which one ends, or another begins. You have doubtless admired this sort of light in Claude Lorrain's landscapes. It appears ideal and still more beautiful than nature; but it is the light of Rome.[45]

After finding 'Claudes' everywhere in the Campagna, Henry James sought the real paintings in a Roman museum in order

to enjoy to the utmost their delightful air of reference to something that had become a part of my personal experience. Delightful it certainly is to feel the common element in one's own sensibility and those of a genius whom that element has helped to do great things. Claude must have haunted the very places of one's personal preference and adjusted their divine undulations to his splendid scheme of romance, his view of the poetry of life.[46]

Another nineteenth-century traveller, John Ruskin, was less captivated by the Campagna's gentle Claudian complexion than by its occasional meteorological transformation into a Turneresque melodrama. In the first volume of *Modern Painters* (1843), Ruskin recalls his most memorable impression of the place:

It had been wild weather when I left Rome, and all across the Campagna the clouds were sweeping in sulphurous blue, with a clap of thunder or two, and breaking gleams of sun along the Claudian aqueduct lighting up the infinity of its arches like the bridge of chaos. But as I climbed the long slope of the Alban mount, the storm swept finally to the north, and the noble outline of the

domes of Albano and [the] graceful darkness of its olive
grove rose against pure streaks of alternate blue and
amber, the upper sky gradually flushing through the last
fragments of rain-cloud in deep, palpitating azure, half
ether and half dew. The noon-day sun came slanting
down the rocky slopes of [Ariccia], and its masses of
entangled and tall foliage, whose autumnal tints were
mixed with the wet verdure of a thousand evergreens,
were penetrated with it as with rain. I cannot call it
colour, it was conflagration. Purple, and crimson, and
scarlet, like the curtain of God's tabernacle, the rejoicing
trees sank into the valley in showers of light, every
separate leaf quivering with buoyant and burning life;
each, as it turned to reflect or to transmit the sunbeam,
first a torch and then an emerald.[47]

Ruskin's description evokes the same sense of 'Vital Beauty'
that he most keenly praises in works of art, particularly those
of the early Turner. While the imagination of many visitors to
the Campagna has been awakened by their recollection of
various landscape paintings, one of Ruskin's contemporaries,
George Stillman Hillard, thought only of music. In *Six Months
in Italy* (1853), the author realized after a walk in the
Campagna that

the grace and grandeur of the scenes we had just left were
in perfect unison with the deep-hearted and impassioned
strains of Beethoven or Schubert; and the language they
addressed to the ear renewed and deepened the impressions which the eye had brought home. We seemed to
hear again the breezes sighing among the pines of the
Campagna, or sweeping across the broken arches of the
Claudian aqueduct. The melancholy beauty of the region
we had traversed appeared to live again in the composer's
dreamy and ideal chords, and, like that, they seemed
darkened with the shadow of vanished hopes, and
strewed with the fragments of shattered ideals.[48]

Those inclined to seek musical counterparts to the Roman
landscape might now think of the 'symphonic poems' of the

Roman composer Ottorino Respighi (1879–1936). The fourth part of his *Pines of Rome* is in fact an evocation of 'The Pines of the Appian Way'. In the foreword to the score of this piece, Respighi suggests exactly what he had in mind:

> Misty dawn on the Appian Way; solitary pines guarding the magic landscape; the muffled, ceaseless rhythm of unending footsteps. The poet has a fantastic vision of by-gone glories: trumpets sound and, in the brilliance of the newly risen sun, the army of the Consul surges along the Sacred Way, mounting in triumph the Capitoline Hill.[49]

Among twentieth-century commentators on the Campagna landscape, one of the most sensitive is also the most unexpected. Virginia Woolf was in Rome with her husband Leonard Woolf in the spring of 1927 when she wrote to her sister saying 'I only wish to be allowed to stay here – for ever and ever – never to see a soul'. In the same letter, she tells Vanessa:

> We rambled over the Campagna on Sunday. I suppose France is all right, and England is all right, but I have never seen anything as beautiful as this is. Figure us sitting in hot sunshine on the doorstep of a Roman ruin in a field with hawk-coloured archways against a clear grape-coloured sky, silvery with mountains in the background. Then on the other side nothing but the Campagna, blue and green, with an almond-coloured farm, with oxen and sheep, and more ruined arches, and blocks of marble fallen on the grass, and immense sword-like aloes, and lovers curled up among the broken pots.[50]

The Catacombs

Four different sets of catacombs lie off the Appian Way between the second and third milestones. These labyrinthine, subterranean chambers and galleries served as Early Christian cemeteries, not as secret meeting places as has sometimes been erroneously maintained. By the seventh century, guidebooks for literate pilgrims pointed out the resting places of the most famous Christian martyrs. The *De Locis Sanctis Martyrum* kept readers moving at a fast pace:

> then on the Appian Way you come to Saint Sebastian, the martyr whose body rests in a place farther down and there are [also] the graves of the Apostles Peter and Paul where they lay for forty years; and in the western part of the church you go down to where Saint Quirinus lies. . . . And on the same road farther north [you reach] the holy martyrs Tiburtius, Valerian and Maximus.[51]

The first account of the catacombs to offer more than a mere recitation of the relics was written in 1450 by the English Augustinian prior John Capgrave. In *Ye Solace of Pilgrimes*, Capgrave described what it was like to enter one of these subterranean burial chambers. 'Ye must undirstande', he writes, 'that the cymyteries at rome be grete voutes and mynes undir the erde in wheech seyntis dwellid but now be thei desolate for horrible derknesse and disuse'.[52]

With the Reformation and the ensuing dispute over the efficacy of relics and religious art in general, Protestant visitors could not resist pointing out the foibles and superstitions attached to the catacombs. Anthony Munday, an English Protestant who was in Rome in 1578–9 posing as a candidate for the priesthood, claims in his book *The English Romayne Lyfe* (1582) that:

> if they chaunce to finde a bone . . . whether it be a Dog, a Hog, a Sheepe, or any Beast, they can tell presentlie what Saints bone it was . . . Then must no body touch it, without he be a Priest, and it must be brought home for an especiall Relique: and thus . . . encreaseth the genealogie of the holy Reliques in Roome.[53]

This clearly was the stuff of Protestant polemic which often wore the ill-fitting disguise of the personal travel account. But even travellers who came to Italy without strong anti-Catholic convictions were often given to ruminate on the mysteries of Catholic iconography. In *Pictures from Italy*, Charles Dickens' visit to the catacombs of St Sebastian called to mind, in 'spots and patches', images of pictures, bad and wonderful, and impious, and ridiculous; of kneeling people, curling incense, tinkling bells, and sometimes (but not often) of a swelling organ; of Madonne, with their breasts stuck full of swords, arranged in a half-circle like a modern fan; of actual skeletons of dead saints hideously attired in gaudy satins, silks, and velvets trimmed with gold: their withered crust of skull adorned with precious jewels, or with chaplets of crushed flowers . . .[54]

By the 1860s church authorities had begun to move the valued relics from the catacombs to various churches for safekeeping. As a consequence, a tour of the underground passages became less of a religious pilgrimage and more of what it had always been for many, a secular adventure. To be sure, before the days of electric illumination and guard rails, this was no place for the faint of heart. Goethe's experience in 1788 was probably not uncommon. In his *Italian Journey* he admits that

My visit to the Catacombs was not much of a success. I had hardly taken a step into that airless place before I began to feel uncomfortable, and I immediately returned to the light of day and the fresh air and waited, in that unknown and remote quarter of the city, for the return of the other visitors who were more daring and less sensitive than I was.[55]

During his visit, Dickens was somewhat braver but still discomforted by the experience of 'this profound and dreadful place'. Guided by 'a gaunt Franciscan friar, with a wild bright eye', he quickly lost his bearings and could not help thinking 'Good Heaven, if, in a sudden fit of madness, he should dash the torches out, or if he should be seized with a fit, what would become of us?'[56]

For many, a visit to the catacombs undoubtedly satisfied the same craving for pleasurable terror that one might find in a good Gothic novel. This was certainly the case, at least in retrospect, for Lady Anna Miller who became lost in the catacombs in 1770. In her *Letter from Italy* (1776), she tells of becoming separated from her party, and pausing to relight her candle:

> figure to yourself the horror that seized me, when, upon attempting to move, I perceived myself forcibly held by my clothes from behind, and all the efforts I made to free myself proved ineffectual. My heart, I believe, ceased to beat for a moment, and it was as much as I could do to sustain myself from falling down upon the ground in a swoon.[57]

As it turned out, she had merely got herself caught on an iron spike, but her guide cheerfully used this as an excuse to regale her with stories of visitors like herself being robbed and thrown into bottomless pits. There may have been some truth in what he said, but corroborating texts are few and far between. In Castiglione's *The Book of the Courtier* (1528), there is a horrible account of a virtuous woman being strangled by a spurned suitor in the catacomb of St Sebastian.[58] Years later, De Blainville's *Travels* of 1707 further contributed to the mythic terror of the place by providing a 'Tragical Account' of the disappearance of 'seven or eight Germans . . . together with a guide and several servants'.[59]

Of those fictional accounts of misadventure in the catacombs, the most memorable probably occurs at the beginning of Hans Christian Andersen's early novel, *The Improvisatore* (1833). Here the child-narrator tells of being set upon by a pederastic foreigner who has first terrified him with the false report that they have lost their way. But young Antonio is a resilient lad, and having been given a silver pocket watch for his troubles, 'quite forgot all that happened'.[60]

Today's tourists have little to fear in visiting the catacombs. Tours are conducted in groups by well-informed guides and there is ample (and dependable) illumination. After an excursion along the Via Appia on a hot summer day, the sun-drenched sightseer will even find the dark subterranean corridors refreshingly cool and inviting. Foot-weary after all of that, it may seem just as inviting to disregard Elizabeth Bowen's advice and board one of the two minibuses that travel along the Appian Way back to the city.

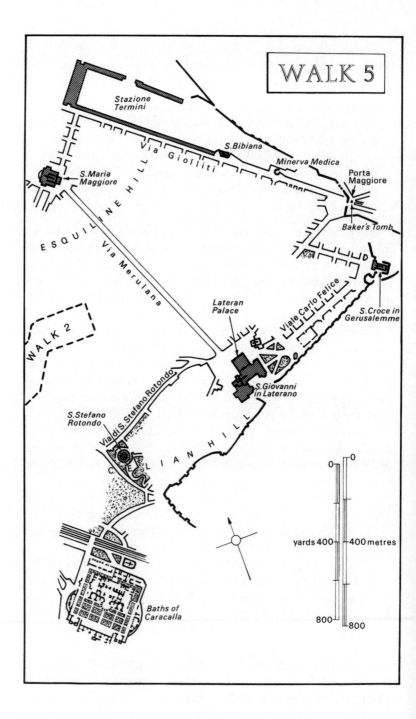

5

FIFTH WALK

From the Stazione Termini to three major basilicas and the Baths of Caracalla

THE STAZIONE TERMINI

The Stazione Termini is the destination of most visitors who arrive in Rome by public conveyance. Trains, airport coaches, inter-city buses, and the metro all deliver their expectant passengers to this ultra-modern station whose name denotes not its role as a terminus but its proximity to the *Terme* (Baths) of Diocletian. Abutting the station proper, and inspirational for its design, is an expanse of the 2,300-year-old Servian Wall. The juxtaposition of slick modernism and crumbling antiquity inspired the American poet Richard Wilbur to write 'For the New Railway Station in Rome' (1954–5). The first stanzas read:

> Those who said God is praised
> By hurt pillars, who loved to see our brazen lust
> Lie down in rubble, and our vaunting arches
> Conduce to dust;
> Those who with short shadows
> Poked through the stubbled forum pondering on decline,
> And would not take the sun standing at noon
> For a good sign;

> Those pilgrims of defeat
> Who bring their injured wills as to a soldier's home;
>   Dig them all up now, tell them there's something new
>   To see in Rome.
>
>   See, from the travertine
> Face of the office block, the roof of the booking-hall
>   Sails out into the air beside the ruined
>   Servian Wall,
>
>   Echoing in its light
> And cantilevered swoop of reinforced concrete
>   The broken profile of these stones, defeating
>   That defeat[1]

Since the new station was opened in the late 1940s, first-time visitors to Rome have had a very different experience from those who entered by more scenic routes in the past. Sean O'Faolain underscored the point in his *A Summer in Italy* (1949) when he noted that:

> There is no 'Ecco Roma!' on this route, no distant heart-lifting outline, no rising excitement and gradual satisfaction, and when you are at last spilled out into the raucous street you might, if it were not for the great Baths of Diocletian mounting before you in the square, be in London or Birmingham. What is more, you hardly care. You do not cry out 'Ave Roma Immortalis!' You cry out for a taxi, a bath and breakfast.[2]

But the station, at least in its early years, was not completely devoid of romance. Vittorio de Sica filmed his *Stazione Termini [Indiscretion of an American Housewife]* (1953) exclusively on the site. The love affair between Montgomery Clift and Jennifer Jones is made to seem all the more unsettling and transitory in the sequences set in the station's public spaces. The underlying theme of the film is a familiar one: an innocent foreign woman is befriended by a charming Italian. When he later asks why she agreed to an affair, she replies, 'It was you; it was Rome; and I'm a housewife from Philadelphia'.[3]

In recent years, the Stazione Termini has become far less

conducive to romance than to the harsher aspects of urban life. Pickpockets, con artists, drug pushers, gypsies, and scoundrels of all types work in concert to unnerve the unwary. It would not be fair to say, however, that criminal and antisocial behaviour is the exclusive product of contemporary Roman society. More than three-quarters of a century ago, Richard Bagot claimed in *My Italian Year* (1912) that 'the stereo-typed British idea that every Italian carries a knife in his pocket which he will use on the slightest provocation is an enormously exaggerated one'.[4] *Enormously* exaggerated perhaps, but some foreign visitors had for good reason taken to carrying their own knives for protection. Hector Berlioz recalls in his *Autobiography* an incident that occurred across town late one evening in 1831:

> As we ascended the steps of the Trinità del Monte, we had to draw our big Roman knives. Some wretches lurking in the shadow demanded our money or our lives; but as there were two of us and only three of them, and as they caught the gleam of our knives in the moonlight, they lapsed temporarily into the path of virtue.[5]

Around the same time, James Fenimore Cooper also had a scare on the road just outside Rome. Arriving from Naples, he he had been warned of the dangers and even saw the skull of a thief mounted on a gate as a warning to evil-doers. With nerves already on edge, Cooper and his wife were sitting in their carriage when

> A league beyond the tavern, [Mrs Cooper] had a good fright. I was reading, when she drew my attention to a group of three men in the road, who were evidently awaiting our arrival. I did not believe that three banditti would dare attack five men, – and such, including our postilions, was our force, – and felt no uneasiness until I heard an exclamation of alarm from [Mrs Cooper]. These men had actually stopped the carriage, and one of them poked the end of a pistol (as she fancied) within a foot of her face. As the three men were all armed, I looked about me; but the pistol proved to be a wild duck, and the

summons to 'deliver', an invitation to buy. I believe the
rogues saw the alarm they had created, for they withdrew
laughing when I declined the duck.[6]

Accounts of tourists being set upon by real criminals are
anything but rare in accounts of the past. One particularly
amusing anecdote of a failed robbery in the papal city is told by
Nathaniel Hawthorne in his *French and Italian Note-Books*
(1858):

> My wife, some time ago, came in contact with a pick-
> pocket at the entrance of a church; and failing in his
> enterprise upon her purse, he passed in, dipped his thiev-
> ing fingers in the holy water, and paid his devotions at a
> shrine. Missing the purse, he said his prayers, in the hope,
> perhaps, that the saint would send him better luck next
> time . . .[7]

S. Maria Maggiore

S. Maria Maggiore sits on the highest swell of the Esquiline
Hill, commanding long perspectives to the front and rear.
'Here I am and here I'll stay' it seems to say.[8] Closer inspection
reveals that both exterior elevations of this early medieval
church are products of the Baroque period, a fact that curried
little favour for the majority of visitors. Most ignored
Rainaldi's apse and Fuga's façade and headed straight for the
interior which, except for two prominent chapels, remained
more or less untainted by the excesses of post-Reformation
papal patronage. Simple and spare, the nave is lined with forty
Ionic columns of ancient origin that are worthy of interest in
their own right. With its splendid early mosaics and glittering
ceiling fashioned from the first gold brought by Columbus
from the New World, Stendhal thought it 'magnificent',
Hawthorne 'of noble simplicity', George Eliot 'exquisitely
beautiful', and Bernard Berenson 'gorgeous'.[9] But as was
often the case, it was Henry James who found just the right
words to describe what it was like to enter 'the singularly

perfect nave of that most delightful of churches' for the first time:

> I remember my coming uninformed and unprepared into [S. Maria Maggiore and sitting] for half an hour on the edge of the base of one of the marble columns of the beautiful nave and enjoyed a perfect revel of – what shall I call it? – taste, intelligence, fancy, perceptive emotion? . . . The obvious charm of the church is the elegant grandeur of the nave – its perfect shapeliness and its rich simplicity, its long double row of white marble columns and its high flat roof, embossed with intricate gildings and mouldings. . . . The deeper charm . . . however, is the social or historic note or tone or atmosphere of the church – I fumble, you see, for my right expression; the sense it gives you, in common with most of the Roman churches, and more than any of them, of having been prayed in for several centuries by an endlessly curious and complex society.[10]

Olave Potter, in *The Colour of Rome* (1909), was struck by the sensation that 'there is always a dim rich light in S. Maria Maggiore, and a little mist, as though clouds of incense were hanging in the dark aisles'. But like James, she too responded to the social 'tone' of the place, observing that

> Peasants kneel on the marble pavement and tell their rosaries with eyes clouded with introspection; and nuns in blue robes and flat Dutch collars bend their heads reverently till only the enormous snowy wings of their caps are to be seen. The voices of the invisible choir thrill through the church, and clouds of incense float up between the purple columns of the High Altar and the purple-clad priests who stand before it. Contadini [peasants] come in at the east door and advance towards the High Altar one after another, when they have dipped their toil-worn hands in the holy water. Their skirts are full, and often blue, of the colour which is to be found in a hundred faded frescoes. They wear their green or red velvet stays outside their bodices, and their ear-rings

glisten under their snowy *tovagliette* [head-cloths].
Thrown into relief against the dark group of worshippers
near the chancel rails, they are like a chain of the gaily-
coloured stones found in the tombs of dead Etruscans.[11]

Potter fails to mention another important ingredient in the
social mix: the foreign tourists. Moreover, where there are
tourists there are souvenir sellers. In *Roman Holidays and Others*
(1908), William Dean Howells laments that S. Maria
Maggiore 'seems more densely fringed than most other
[churches] with pedlars of post-cards and mosaic pins. On
going in you can plunge through their ranks, but in coming
out you do not so easily escape'. Howells had to admit,
however, that his encounter with a particular young vendor
brought him some amusement:

> One boy pursued me quite to my cab, in spite of my
> denials of hand and tongue. There he stayed the driver
> while he made a last, a humorous appeal. 'Skiddoo?' he
> asked in my native speech. 'Yes', I sullenly replied,
> 'skiddoo!' But it is now one of my regrets which I shall
> always feel for my wasted opportunities in Rome that I
> did not buy all his post-cards. Patient gayety like his
> merited as much.[12]

The modern Via Merulana leads directly to another Early
Christian church, the Basilica of S. Giovanni in Laterano. If
one temporarily foregoes a visit to this famous site and instead
slants back to the farther flanks of the train station, one will
discover the lovely small church of S. Bibiana which was
rebuilt by Bernini, and the remains of a magnificent ancient
nymphaeum. Although inside the city wall, both monuments
before modern times were surrounded by farmland, but the
vigorous development of this area after the Risorgimento of
1870 has left it in a sorry state. The Via Giolitti, which skirts
both the church and the nymphaeum, runs alongside the train
tracks and echoes with the screeching of trains. But it would
be ungrateful to complain of its gracelessness, for nowhere but
in Rome would such historic monuments have even survived
in the path of progress.

Kate Simon offers a realistic view of what it is like to follow this route:

> Southward on the Via Giolitti, beyond the airport buses, the snack bars, fruit stalls and vendors of packed lunches for railroad trips, the vivacious tone of the area slows, dulls, begins to smell of poverty and abandonment. . . . At a point where the street seems to have lost all life and meaning, except for the flinty highlights on railroad tracks, one comes to a small church said to contain 10,000 martyrs' bones, S. Bibiana, whose reconstruction was the earliest architectural work of Bernini. Should the church be open, you might see the statue of the saint, the first such commission for the young Bernini, and frescoes of her martyrdom . . . by Pietro da Cortona.[13]

Bernini's demure and decorous statue of the historically obscure S. Bibiana was admired by French visitors in the eighteenth century who may have been especially attracted by its coy charm. Montesquieu, the Marquis de Sade, and the President De Brosses sang its praises, with the latter even finding it a 'stupendous statue . . . one of the four most famous in Rome, and the most beautiful of them all'.[14]

Simon goes on to describe what lies farther down the Via Giolitti:

> The faceless street drags along decayed tenements and endless railroad tracks and springs the surprise of a round temple, as misplaced and lonely as its neighbor church. The denuded structure, which must have been imposing when it was dressed in marbles, was built in the fourth century. It then housed a statue of Minerva holding a serpent, a combination that had medical significance and therefore left the temple (an inspiration for many Roman painters before it fell almost completely apart 150 years ago) the name of Minerva Medica.[15]

The nymphaeum or 'Temple' of Minerva Medica originally stood in a rural setting that captured the imagination of artists throughout the eighteenth and nineteenth centuries. Stendhal even remarked that this 'picturesque ruin . . . looks as if

it had been arranged expressly to serve as a subject for one
of those beautiful English prints that would represent Italy and
in which everything is wrong, except the lines of the
monuments'.[16]

THE PORTA MAGGIORE AND THE BAKER'S TOMB

Just beyond the nymphaeum of Minerva Medica lies the
monumental gate known as the Porta Maggiore. This imposing structure was built by the emperor Claudius at the juncture
where the graceful arcades of the aqueduct bearing his name
traverse the city wall. While most guidebooks, old and new,
cite it as the finest surviving Roman gate, virtually no one was
inspired to write poetically about it. Even Henry James rode
his horse past it without comment. Doubtless, it was the
'barbaric', unfinished character of its rusticated columns and
walls that put off those with more refined tastes or those who
mistakenly believed that in ancient times the classical orders
were always handled with inviolable purity.

Immediately adjacent to the Porta Maggiore is the even
more idiosyncratic ancient structure known as the Baker's
Tomb. 'One of the most curious things I have seen', is the way
Mrs Trollope described this first-century BC monument, an
assessment with which, even today, few would disagree.[17] It
is in fact the tomb of the baker Marcus Vergilius Eursaces and
it is shaped just like an ancient baking oven, topped with the
kitchen mortars that were the tools of his trade.

Despite its prominent location, this 'uncouth-looking
structure', as Sir George Head described it, provoked little
response from artists or authors, even in the 1960s when it
might well have served as an early icon of kitsch and popular
culture.[18]

S. CROCE IN GERUSALEMME AND S. GIOVANNI IN LATERANO

From the Piazza di Porta Maggiore, it is a short walk to S.
Croce in Gerusalemme, another major Early Christian basilica

and one of the 'Seven Churches' on the Roman pilgrim's itinerary. The surrounding site was once rather captivating. Henry James confesses in 'A Roman Holiday' (1873) that 'I lost my heart to this idle tract, and wasted much time in sitting on the steps of the church and watching certain white-cowled friars who were sure to be passing there for the delight of my eyes'.[19] Mrs Anna Jameson, in her *Diary of an Ennuyée* (1826), describes in more detail the views to be had in this peaceful setting, yet unspoiled by modern urban development:

> To the right were the ruins of the stupendous Claudian Aqueduct with its gigantic arches, stretching away in one unbroken series far into the Campagna . . . to the left, other ruins . . . and thence the view extended to the foot of the Apennines. All this part of Rome is a scene of magnificent desolation, and of melancholy yet sublime interest; its wildness, its vastness, its waste and solitary openness, add to its effect upon the imagination.[20]

Urban development has permanently altered the character of its surroundings, but S. Croce in Gerusalemme remains the venerable church reportedly founded by St Helena, the mother of Constantine. Tradition has it that she went all the way to Jerusalem to find the True Cross and brought it back to Rome where a portion of it is still displayed here. It is this relic that has earned major indulgences for pilgrims from all parts of the world. Cloaked in the late Baroque finery of an eighteenth-century restoration, S. Croce has otherwise not been a major attraction for those in Rome for more secular reasons.

S. Giovanni in Laterano, just a few blocks to the south-west, was the first Christian basilica to be constructed in the city and it still remains the Cathedral of Rome, as well as one of the 'Seven Churches' on the Roman pilgrimage route. Since its consecration by Constantine in the fourth century, it has suffered the indignity of having been sacked by Vandals, damaged in an earthquake, burned (twice), and fallen prey to the natural ravages of time. It has been rebuilt and repaired so many times that its character is purely hybrid. Dante saw it before the two fires and was stupefied by its majesty. In Rome

for the Jubilee of 1300, he recorded his impressions of it in the
Paradiso of *The Divine Comedy:*

> If Barbarians . . .
>
>   . . .
>
> Were wonder-struck at such a spectacle,
> Imagine with what wonder I was filled,
> Who came from earthly things to things divine,
> From time unto eternity itself –
> From Florence, to a people just and sane!
> In truth, between my wonder and my joy,
> I felt no wish to listen or to speak.[21]

Five centuries later, after the disastrous fires and much
rebuilding, Lady Sydney Morgan found that the church 'now
wears a character of antique splendour, of barbarous magnificence, and Gothic gloom, infinitely more imposing to the
imagination, than all the light and lustre of St Peter's'.[22] She
evidently did not lack imagination, nor did she seem bothered
by the seventeenth- and eighteenth-century restorations
which give to the basilica its dominant personality. What she
calls 'barbarous magnificence' has struck most modern visitors, even the customarily fair-minded H. V. Morton as
'disappointing', for so little of the original structure remains to
be seen.[23]

From any approach – from S. Croce to the east, S. Maria
Maggiore to the north, or the Colosseum to the west – S.
Giovanni and its dependencies are an impressive sight. But the
principal façade faces east, and it is the approach from S.
Croce, particularly in the morning light, that best reveals the
basilica in all of its grandeur.

The façade was designed in 1732 by Alessandro Galilei, a
Florentine architect who previously had worked for an extended period in England. Architectural connoisseurs find
reflections of English architecture – of works by Wren,
Hawksmoor, and Aldrich – in the façade, but even less
knowledgeable viewers will recognize that Galilei's frontispiece signals the beginning of a new trend away from the
exuberant Baroque towards rational order and restraint in
Italian architecture. For this reason, the façade did not offend

visitors like Sir George Head who admitted to finding it 'noble
and imposing', or Nathaniel Hawthorne who thought it 'very
lofty and grand'.[24] For the majority of foreign visitors,
however, the associations with the post-Reformation papacy
were enough to dampen any subliminal sympathy for Galilei's
creation.

Before entering the Lateran basilica, visitors past and present usually will have first undergone a test of their charitable
nature. The sentiments of Tryphosa Batcheller will be familiar
to many from the account of her visit in 1905:

> After giving some pennies to a poor old man at the door,
> which I suppose was not at all the right thing to do, but he
> looked so miserable that my feelings got the better of my
> judgement, we went inside.[25]

The beggars of Rome have always presented something of a
dilemma to foreigners, for determining the right amount of
compassion is not easy. Many, 'with rented children smeared
up for the job', as Eleanor Clark put it, are outright charlatans,
but sometimes the opposite is also true.[26] Henry Wadsworth
Longfellow in *Outre-Mer* (1833–5) recounts the tale of having
tossed his coins into the hat of a 'piteous' man with 'a woe-
begone face, and a thread-bare coat', whereupon the old gent

> Showered upon me the most sonorous maledictions of
> his native tongue, and, emptying his greasy hat upon the
> pavement, drew it down over his ears with both hands,
> and stalked away with all the dignity of a Roman senator
> in the best days of the Republic, – to the infinite amuse-
> ment of a green-grocer, who stood at his shop-door
> bursting with laughter. No time was given me for an
> apology; but I resolved to be for the future more discrimi-
> nating in my charities, and not to take for a beggar every
> poor gentleman who chose to stand in the shade with his
> hat in his hand on a hot summer's day.[27]

To enter the portals of the Lateran basilica is to step into a
less ambiguous realm of churchly splendour. Italian guides
have always taken this in their stride, but non-Catholics or
those cynical of the pious intentions of the post-Reformation

papacy have often resisted the material attractions of the place. 'Here is the wretched taste of the seventeenth century, neither pagan nor Christian, or rather both', is the way Hippolyte Taine viewed Borromini's refurbished interior.[28] To Lady Morgan, 'the sumptuous, but dismal chapels look as if they were decked with the plunder, and raised by the taste, of new-converted Huns'.[29]

In truth, what offended most visitors was actually not the architectural revestment of the nave, but the twelve over-lifesize sculptures of the Apostles that early in the eighteenth century were carved and set in niches between the nave pilasters. By the time these robustly Baroque figures were put in place, the vagaries of taste were about to change and classicizing sentiments were becoming widespread. Religious attitudes aside, the sculptures then became vulnerable to artistic criticism as well. In one of his *Discourses* at the Royal Academy in London, Joshua Reynolds singled out the Apostles for dishonesty to their medium.

The distrust of virtuosity for its own sake, a by-product of the Enlightenment, persisted well after the Age of Reason had drawn to a close. By the middle of the nineteenth century, George Stillman Hillard spoke for many, and influenced scores more when, in *Six Months in Italy*, he pronounced the Lateran Apostles to be

> characterized by flutter and extravagance. The draperies look as if the wearers had been out in a high wind and suddenly stiffened into stone: and their attitudes are painful to the eye, for they seem to be maintained by muscular effort. But they show great skill and mechanical cleverness. They are in art what Darwin's Botanic Garden is in poetry; and in making this comparison, I recognize the merits of both the statues and the poem.[30]

The interior of the Lateran might seem an unlikely setting for a murder set to music, but according to legend, this almost occurred in the late seventeenth century. The intended victim was the composer Alessandro Stradella, a forerunner of Purcell and Scarlatti. Operas and novels have embellished the tale, but the purportedly factual account is related by the nineteenth-century music critic William Gardiner:

> It was in this Church that Stradella, who ran away with a Roman lady, Hortensia, was found singing in the service, by the assassins sent for their destruction by a Venetian nobleman. Scarcely had they listened for a few moments to the delightful voice of Stradella than they began to soften. They were seized with remorse – they were melted into tears; and their last consideration was how to save the lovers whose destruction they had sworn. They waited for Stradella at the door of the church and saw him coming out with Hortensia. They approached, thanked him for the pleasure they had just received, and informed him that he owed his life to the impression which his voice had made upon them. They then explained to them the horrible object of their journey, and advised him to leave Rome immediately in order to give them the opportunity of making the Venetians believe that they had arrived too late.[31]

Exiting from the front of the basilica and dodging the traffic in the square, one comes upon the modest building that houses the Scala Santa, or Holy Stairway. These twenty-eight marble steps are said to have been those which Christ ascended after his condemnation by Pilate. They were supposedly brought from Jerusalem to Rome by Constantine's mother Helena, and they remain an object of intense veneration (covered up now by wooden boards) even for Catholics today. The steps may be ascended only on one's knees, and to see them attended by the faithful is still a sight to behold. William Evill, a Protestant who was in Rome for the opening of the Ecumenical Council in 1870, recorded his impressions of this ageless ritual in *A Winter Journey to Rome and Back*:

> Through slits in the [wooden] risers . . . a sight of the sacred marble is vouchsafed. About every fourth or fifth step, there is a brass plate with a glass centre, through which dark stains are seen, believed to be the Saviour's blood. This plate the devout reverently kiss. For every

step that is thus ascended you get nine years' indulgences if you are active enough to reach the top. Now this is worth climbing for, and no wonder the stairs require their coverings to be so frequently renewed.

It was a strange and suggestive, ludicrous, and yet painful and depressing sight. There were reverend ecclesiastics, elderly ladies, beggars, and educated gentle-men, all shuffling up together. It looked like a game – a kind of race in sacks – and one insensibly picked out a penitent to back as the winner.[32]

Non-Catholic visitors who have written of the Scala Santa often gleefully report the different sort of spiritual experience that one man experienced years ago while ascending the steps. It was here that Martin Luther, having gone part way on his knees, suddenly stood up and walked back down after hearing a voice that directed him to seek another path to grace.

At the top of the Sacred Steps is the Sancta Sanctorum, the medieval chapel renowned as the 'Holiest of Holies' because of the important relics preserved there. Inaccessible to the public, it is visible through a metal grating. Italian guidebooks like Panciroli and Posterla's *Roma Sacra, e Moderna* (1725) inform their readers that the most precious relic contained here, the large portrait of the Saviour, 'was begun by St Luke and finished by the hands of angels, hence its reputation as the *picture made without hands*'.[33] Of this, the seventeenth-century painter Carlo Maratta is said to have remarked that the Evan-gelist should have had a few more lessons before he turned portrait painter.[34] Non-Italians and especially Protestants viewed the picture with the usual sceptical cynicism. Few of their comments, however, are as memorable or original as those of Henry James who, looking through the gilt lattice grating found that

it is very sombre and splendid, and conveys the im-pression of a very holy place. And yet somehow it sug-gested irreverent thoughts; it had to my fancy – perhaps on account of the lattice – an Oriental, a Mahometan note. I expected every moment to see a sultana appear in a

1. The Capitoline Hill in the eighteenth century

2. The Roman Forum in the nineteenth century

3. Interior of the Colosseum by an artist in the circle of Hubert Robert

4. *The Portico of Octavia* by Albert Bierstadt

5. The Protestant Cemetery today

6. *View of the Roman Campagna* by Benjamin Champney

7. The interior of a sepulchral vault on the Via Appia in the nineteenth century

8. *Shelley in the Baths of Caracalla* by Joseph Severn (detail)

9. Horse-racing on the Via del Corso in the nineteenth century

10. *Goethe at the Window of his House in the Via del Corso* by J.H.W. Tischbein

11. The Piazza del Popolo in the eighteenth century

12. The Spanish Steps today

13. Interior of the Caffè Greco today

14. The Trevi Fountain in the nineteenth century

15. The Piazza del Pantheon in the nineteenth century

16. The interior of the Pantheon in the nineteenth century

17. The Piazza Navona in the eighteenth century

18. *The Castel Sant'Angelo, Rome* by J.B.C. Corot

19. St Peter's Square in the eighteenth century

20. The interior of St Peter's in the eighteenth century

silver veil and silken trouers and sit down on the crimson carpet.[35]

Leaving the Scala Santa and recrossing the piazza, one passes on the right flank of the basilica the stern and unremarkable Lateran Palace. Behind this rises a great Egyptian obelisk which, according to the turn-of-the-century archaeologist Rodolfo Lanciani, has a shaft 105 feet high that weighs 455 tons. This monolith, he goes on to explain

> was brought from Heliopolis to Alexandria by Constantine, and was transferred to Rome in the year 357 by Constantius, on a vessel or raft manned by three hundred oarsmen, which landed at the Vicus Alexandri, three miles below Rome. The hieroglyphic inscription commemorates King Thothmes III of the Eighteenth Dynasty.[36]

It was discovered sunk in mud at the Circus Maximus in 1587 and was re-erected by Domenico Fontana, architect of the Lateran Palace, at its present location. Fontana was not inexperienced in such undertakings for the year before he had designed the equipment necessary for moving and re-erecting the great obelisk in St Peter's Square. His papal patron Sixtus V was so keen on this idea that during his short reign (1585–90), he had Fontana re-erect obelisks behind S. Maria Maggiore and in the Piazza del Popolo as well. Each was topped with Sixtus's coat of arms surmounted by a cross, a clever Counter-Reformation conceit.

S. STEFANO ROTONDO

A short way down the Via di S. Stefano Rotondo, one comes upon a remarkable fifth-century church of the same name. S. Stefano is unusual among early Roman churches in having a circular groundplan. It is further renowned for its interior decoration, having frescoes that depict in a most grisly manner the tortured deaths of a number of Early Christian martyrs. These scenes were painted in the late sixteenth century during the darkest days of the Counter-Reformation, and they have rarely failed to provoke poignant comment from those who dared to seek them out. Charlotte Eaton admitted that these 'horrible frescoes of horrible martyrdoms . . . is almost martyrdom to look at',[37] while Stendhal relates that the ladies in his company were unable to endure the sight and were moved to wait outside. Although he attributes the fame of these paintings to 'vulgar men whom chance brings through Rome', Stendhal cannot resist describing 'a saint whose head is crushed between two millstones; the eye is wrenched from its orbit and . . . the rest is too frightful for me to set down'.[38]

Even the Marquis de Sade confessed in his *Voyage d'Italie* (1775) that he found some of the scenes 'neither edifying or *bien placés*.[39] In *Pictures from Italy* (1846), Charles Dickens went farther than most in actually describing the frescoes and admitting what a powerful impression they made on him:

> To single out details from the great dream of Roman churches would be the wildest occupation in the world. But San Stefano Rotondo, a damp mildewed vault of an old church in the outskirts of Rome, will always struggle uppermost in my mind, by reason of the hideous paintings with which its walls are covered. These represent . . . such a panorama of horror and butchery no man could imagine in his sleep, though he were to eat a whole pig, raw, for supper. Grey-bearded men being boiled, fried, grilled, crimped, singed, eaten by wild beasts, worried by dogs, buried alive, torn asunder by horses, chopped up small with hatchets; women having their breasts torn with iron pincers, their tongues cut out, their ears screwed off, their jaws broken, their bodies stretched upon the rack, or skinned upon the stake, or crackled up and melted in the fire – these are among the mildest subjects.[40]

THE BATHS OF CARACALLA

From S. Stefano, it is an easy walk down the Celian Hill to the Baths of Caracalla. Built in the third century, the Terme di

Caracalla is the largest bath and indeed the largest single structure that survives from antiquity. Bath halls with their massive vaults and awesome spaces were the most daring inventions of Roman architecture, and if they spawned no progeny in succeeding eras, their very uniqueness made them objects of immense curiosity. Later visitors, accustomed to private ablutionary practices, were often perplexed by the functioning of these public sanitary establishments. Few general travellers have felt comfortable commenting on such utilitarian matters. Florence Nightingale, in a mood of misinformed cynicism even thought the *palaestrae* or exercise yards were stages for gladiatorial combat. In a letter of 1847 addressed to her Aunt Jenny in London, she wrote:

> The ruins of the Baths of Caracalla are something so enormous that one would have thought that they were barracks for a whole species. There are immense halls for the Gladiator's fights, but when I found that I could not be in my bath and look on at the murders all in one, which would have been the beauty of luxury, or the 'luxury of beauty', I thought the whole concern contemptible.[41]

Apart from the occasional remark that the Baths provided 'another fertile school for vice and luxury',[42] most visitors were content to limit their comments to an appraisal of the building's prodigious size. In *Rome*, the second part of his trilogy *Three Cities* (1894–8), Emile Zola describes

> the baths of Caracalla, standing there like relics of a race of giants long since vanquished from the world: halls extravagantly and inexplicably spacious and lofty; vestibules large enough for an entire population; a *frigidarium* where five hundred people could swim together; a *tepidarium* and a *calidarium* on the same proportions, born of a wild craving for the huge; and then the terrific massiveness of the structures, the thickness of the piles of brick-work, such as no feudal castle ever knew; and, in addition, the general immensity which makes passing visitors look like lost ants; such an extraordinary riot of the great and mighty that one wonders for what men, for

what multitudes, this monstrous edifice was reared. Today, you would say a mass of rocks in the rough, thrown
from some height for building the abode of Titans.[43]

As was the case with the Colosseum, with which it was
frequently compared, discourses about the dimensions of the
structure often led to imaginative reflections upon its current
state of disintegration. Hippolyte Taine was reminded of
broken-down man-made structures like bridges and cities as
well as of natural forms like 'stones encrusted with deposits of
the sea'.[44] For Henry James, who at the Colosseum was
reminded of 'an Alpine ridge', the Baths likewise suggested
geological grandeur. In a letter to his sister, James wrote:

> Even more than the Colosseum I think they give you a
> notion of Roman *scale*. Imagine a good second-class
> mountain in reduced circumstances – perforated and
> honeycombed by some terrestrial cataclysm – and you'll
> have an idea of these terrific ruins.[45]

Accounts of the Baths of Caracalla differ from those of the
Colosseum in their greater freshness and freedom from literary convention. Since Byron neglected to gild them with his
lyrical brush, later romantics were left to their own devices. It
was here that Shelley composed his lyrical drama *Prometheus
Unbound* in 1818–19. In his preface, the poet explains:

> This poem was chiefly written upon the mountainous
> ruins of the Baths of Caracalla, among the flowery glades
> and thickets of odoriferous blossoming trees, which are
> extended in ever-winding labyrinths upon its immense
> platforms and dizzy arches suspended in the air.[46]

But the four-act mythical/political drama is not set in Rome
and as a consequence made but a modest impression on
vulnerable Rome-bound travellers. Herman Melville was
among the few visitors to the Baths whose thoughts of Shelley
may actually have affected what he saw. In his *Journal* of 1857,
the author of the recently published *Moby Dick* noted:

> Went to Baths of Caracalla. – Wonderful. Massive. There
> are glades, & thickets among the ruins – high up. –

Thought of Shelley. Truly, he got his inspiration here.
Corresponds with his drama & mind. Still magestic &
desolate grandure.[47]

Shelley's presence in the Baths is best imagined through the
charming posthumous portrait Joseph Severn painted of him,
now hanging in the Keats-Shelley House in the Piazza di
Spagna (Plate 8). Done more than two decades after the poet's
death, it captures the insouciant tone of his youth, at ease in
just the setting he describes in the preface to Prometheus.

In recent times, the Baths of Caracalla, like the Colosseum,
have been stripped of their colourful vegetation and very tidily
groomed in conformity to the needs of today's visitors.
Outdoor opera performances are staged there on summer
evenings, and the memory of Aïda probably outweighs all
other recollections in the minds of most visitors. It is to
Bernard Berenson, the connoisseur of Renaissance painting,
that we owe the sharpest of twentieth-century appraisals. In
November 1953, he jotted in his dairy:

> After many years returned to the Baths of Caracalla, now
> bereft of all picturesqueness, of every effort of nature to
> absorb into its bosom what man has done in competition
> with her. Now the ruin stands out bare and stark, but
> how bold, how sublime and still overpoweringly im-
> pressive. Those colossal masses of brick . . . how were
> they finished, stuccoed, decorated? Was the effect better
> . . . than interiors of the classical style put up in the last
> century and that still can be enjoyed in Italian Atlantic
> liners? Ruins have the advantage of suggesting romantic
> wishful reconstructions, free from disturbing detail and
> probably bad taste.[48]

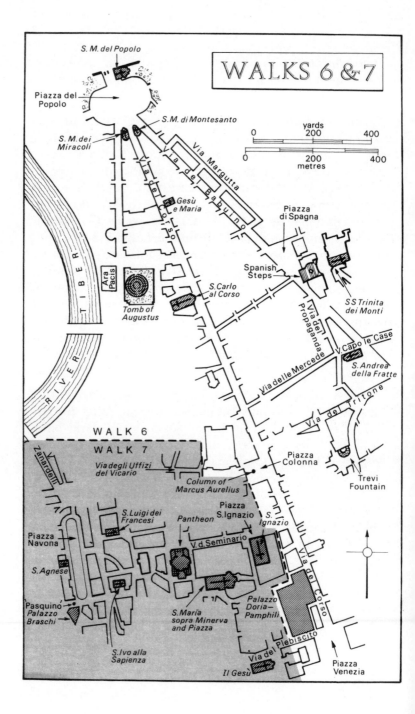

WALKS 6 & 7

S. M. del Popolo

Piazza del
Popolo

S.M. di Montesanto

S. M. dei
Miracoli

Via Margutta

yards
0   200   400

0   200   400
metres

Gesù
e Maria

Via del Babuino

Via del Corso

Ara
Pacis

Tomb of
Augustus

S.Carlo
al Corso

Piazza
di Spagna

Spanish
Steps

SS Trinita
dei Monti

Via di Propaganda

V. Capo le Case

S. Andrea
della Fratte

Via delle Mercede

Via del Tritone

WALK 6

WALK 7

Zanardelli

Via degli Uffizi
del Vicario

Piazza
Colonna

Trevi
Fountain

Column of
Marcus Aurelius

S. Luigi dei
Francesi

Pantheon

Piazza
S.Ignazio

S.
Ignazio

Piazza
Navona

V. d. Seminario

S. Agnese

Via del Corso

Pasquino
Palazzo
Braschi

S. Maria
sopra Minerva
and Piazza

Palazzo
Doria—
Pamphili

S.Ivo alla
Sapienza

Via del Plebiscito

Il Gesù

Piazza
Venezia

TIBER

RIVER

6

SIXTH WALK

*From the Piazza Venezia to the Piazza del Popolo, the Piazza
di Spagna, and the Trevi Fountain*

THE VIA DEL CORSO

The Via del Corso is the longest and straightest street in Old
Rome. It is also among the oldest streets in the city, but it was
given its present name only after the Carnival races, or *corse*,
were instituted there in 1466 by Paul II. Visitors have frequently commented on the time it takes newcomers to appreciate its subtler virtues. Stendhal, in an oft-quoted line from
his *Roman Journal*, confessed that 'the Corso, which I judged
unfairly for two years because of its smell of rotten cabbages
and the rags glimpsed in the apartments through windows, is
perhaps the most beautiful street in the universe'.[1] For
Stendhal, the source of its beauty lay in the fact that 'the
palaces that edge this street have a great deal of *style*'. At the
end of the nineteenth century, Emile Zola, in his novel *Rome*,
has Pierre, a priest visiting from the suburbs of Paris, also
exclaim his initial disappointment with the crowded and
stifling street, but gradually he too comes to appreciate its
special flavour. Unlike Stendhal, however, he was won
over not by its architectural distinction but by its social
anthropology:

> Perpetually going up and coming down the Corso,
> people scrutinized and jostled one another. It was

open-air promiscuity, all Rome gathered together in the smallest possible space, the folks who knew one another and who met here as in a friendly drawing-room, and the folks belonging to adverse parties who did not speak together but elbowed each other, and whose glances penetrated to each other's soul. Then a revelation came to Pierre, and he suddenly understood the Corso, the ancient custom, the passion and the glory of the city. Its pleasure lay precisely in the very narrowness of the street, in that forced elbowing which facilitated not only desired meetings but the satisfaction of curiosity, the display of vanity, and the garnering of endless tittle-tattle.[2]

Since the fifteenth century, the Corso has provided the setting for Rome's most festive public occasion, the Carnival celebrations held just prior to the Lenten season, which included a series of races held in the narrow street. Montaigne's *Journal* for 1581 gives an account of races which were 'now of children, now of Jews, and now of old men naked, who ran from one end of the street to the other'. There were also, he goes on to explain, races of horses, and of asses and buffaloes.[3] John Evelyn was in Rome for the 'impertinences' of the Carnival in 1645 and found the area 'swarming with whores, buffoones & all matter of rabble'.[4] Shortly afterwards. in 1688, Clement IX ended the 200-year-old practice of Jew races, but the horse racing continued until the end of the nineteenth century (Plate 9).

Goethe, himself a resident of the Corso, gives a long account in his *Italian Journey* of the 'overcrowded and torrential merriment' of the 1788 Carnival which he found, like life itself, 'unpredictable, unsatisfactory, and problematic'.[5] Dickens' *Pictures from Italy* (1846) also offers keen observations of Carnival activities on the Corso. His eye for detail led him to remark upon the costumes of the party-goers:

Every sort of bewitching madness of dress was there. Little preposterous scarlet jackets; quaint old stomachers, more wicked than the smartest bodices; Polish pelisses, strained and tight as ripe gooseberries; tiny Greek caps, all awry, and clinging to the dark hair, Heaven knows how;

every wild, quaint, bold, shy, pettish, madcap fancy had
its illustration in a dress . . .[6]

Dickens was just as impressed with the temporary viewing
boxes that sprouted for this occasion on the sides of dwellings
along the Corso:

> There are verandas and balconies, of all shapes and sizes,
> to almost every house – not on one storey alone, but often
> to one room or another on every storey – put there in
> general with so little order or regularity, that if, year after
> year, and season after season, it had rained balconies,
> hailed balconies, snowed balconies, blown balconies,
> they could scarcely have come into existence in a more
> disorderly manner.[7]

Hardened confetti was thrown from these balconies, forc-
ing pedestrians, according to the author of *Ave Roma Immortalis* (1898) 'to wear a shield of thin wire netting to guard the
face, and thick gloves to shield the hands; or in older times, a
mask, black, white, or red, or modelled and painted with
extravagant features, like evil beings in a dream'.[8]

By the beginning of the twentieth century, the Carnival
festivities had lost most of their lustre. 'The Carnival is dead,
as far as Society is concerned', wrote Mary Waddington in
Italian Letters of a Diplomat's Wife (1905).[9] Golf and automobile
rides in the country became the new vogue and the Carnival
celebrations came to an end with the First World War.

Strolling down the Corso from Piazza Venezia to Piazza del
Popolo, one quickly comes to the Palazzo Doria-Pamphili on
one's left (visible in Plate 9). Nathaniel Hawthorne described
the palace in his *Note-Books* (1858):

> all the rooms, halls, and galleries of beautiful propor-
> tions, with vaulted roofs, some of which glow with
> frescoes; and all are colder and more comfortless than can
> possibly be imagined without having been in them.[10]

In this century, sections of the palace have been subdivided
into rented flats, one of which was occupied for a time by John
Cheever. 'It was all built for giants', Cheever recalled of his
residence, while his biographer adds that

There was only one chair in the salon where he could sit and have his feet touch the floor. The room was drafty and magnificent, with a marble floor and a golden ceiling two stories high. It would make a splendid place for signing treaties, he thought, provided that the kings and generals were tall and did not have to go to the bathroom.[11]

It is the Doria-Pamphili picture gallery which has traditionally attracted most visitors. John Ruskin found this 'a dull, blue devilish, dirty hole though handsome outside, All the pictures, it seemed to me, copies; but I could not see one, all in direct front lights or no lights at all – dirty and stained and neglected'.[12]

Since Ruskin's visit in 1840, conditions have improved somewhat, but attitudes towards the pictures have brightened considerably. Herman Melville, amusingly, found the so-called Veronese portrait of Lucrezia Borgia a 'good-looking dame – rather fleshy', and the purported Del Sarto likeness of Machiavelli to have an 'ugly profile'.[13] No one before the mid-twentieth century bothered to take note of the two works by Caravaggio, the artist now considered to be the most important Italian painter since Raphael. The naturalism of his *Mary Magdalen* and his *Rest on the Flight to Egypt* seemed too ordinary to the majority of early viewers, Italian and foreign alike. Before our own secular and informal age, decorum and rhetorical convention were prerequisites for good taste.

One painting in the Doria-Pamphili collection has always been held in high esteem by visitors from every background. This is Velazquez's portrait of the Pamphili pope, Innocent X, executed while the Spanish painter was in Rome in 1649–50. While not everyone admired the subject, the painter's skill transformed his sitter in an almost magical way, as Hippolyte Taine appreciated: 'the masterpiece of all the portraits is that of Pope Innocent X by Velazquez; on a red chair before a red curtain under a red hat and above a red mantle is a red face, that of a miserable fool and pedant; make a picture out of this which is never forgotten!'[14]

Englishmen as different as Sir Joshua Reynolds and Oscar

Wilde agreed that the portrait was extraordinarily fine. An avowed papist, Wilde was especially enthusiastic. In a letter of 1900 he wrote, 'I have been three times to see the great Velazquez of the Pamphili Pope: it is quite the grandest portrait in the world. The entire man is there'.[15]

Farther down the Corso, in the charmless Piazza Colonna, stands the newly-cleaned Column of Marcus Aurelius. The reliefs that wind round this column celebrate the emperor's victories over the Marcomanni, Quadi, and Sarmatian tribes in AD 169–76. The latter, a fierce Slavic people whose women joined in battle, were a favoured target for Marcus Aurelius. In his *Memoirs*, he wrote:

> A spider prides itself on capturing a fly; one man on catching a hare, another on netting a sprat, another on taking wild boars, another bears, another Sarmatians.[16]

The shaft of this gigantic column is 97 feet (100 Roman feet) tall and its relief carvings depict the emperor no fewer than fifty-nine times, although never in battle. 'No one but the tourist notices this gigantic milestone of history', observes Olave Potter in *The Colour of Rome* (1909), 'its marble is stained and mellowed by time, and the twisted script is being slowly obliterated; the bronze saint on its summit stretches his arms in unheeded blessing over the gay and busy life of the Corso'.[17]

Much of the Piazza Colonna was built only after the Risorgimento. The mall-like galleria was opened in 1923 and the Rinascente department store across the street in 1899. The Corso briefly widens at this point and becomes even more densely thronged with shoppers, pavement artists, and gypsies. Barbara Grizzuti Harrison conjectures in *Italian Days* (1989) that the gypsies may outlive us all:

> Sometimes I think the ragged Gypsy girl curled up, somnolent, in the doorway of the Alemagna pastry shop on the Corso will be there forever, she will never grow and never move, she belongs to Rome, as permanent as rock.[18]

At Via del Corso 372–6, formerly the Palazzo Verospi and now a modern bank, a wall plaque reminds passers-by that Shelley resided there in 1819 while writing *The Cenci* and *Prometheus Unbound*. It is here that one enters Rome's chic shopping district, where even the most unworldly souls have been known to go on shopping sprees. The prudent young Bostonian Henry Adams, in Rome in 1860, wrote to his mother:

> I am dreadfully tempted in every direction. Roman jewelry, mosaics, cameos, silk scarfs, bronzes, to say nothing of photographs, engravings and now and then a pretty picture, and all dear as one's life-blood.[19]

Some years later, in 1891, Anton Chekhov thought even the prices were tempting. Writing to a friend in Moscow, he declared that 'neckties are amazingly cheap here, so terribly cheap that I may even take to eating them'.[20] This part of the city is a natural mecca for dandyism. Already in the second century, Juvenal commented on how 'in Rome men dress in a showy style beyond their means', an observation that still seems true today.[21] Foreign tourists and residents, no matter how hard they try to impersonate the sartorial style of the native population, are destined to feel shabby, physically uncomfortable, or both. For most, it is best not even to try.

It is in this neighbourhood that the true events underlying Browning's tragic epic *The Ring and the Book* (1868–9) occurred. A book of seventeenth-century documents that Browning chanced to purchase in a Florentine bookstall provided him with the plot and the setting. Pompilia and the evil count Guido Franceschini were married in S. Lorenzo in Lucina (just off the Corso, opposite Via Frattina), she and her family were murdered in a house a few blocks away on the Via Vittoria, and the count was later executed in the Piazza del Popolo. When he was in Rome in 1854, Browning himself lived in a house in the same neighbourhood, at Via Bocca di Leone, 43.[22]

Behind the ponderous front of S. Carlo al Corso lies the Mausoleum of Augustus and the Ara Pacis. The circular mausoleum once housed the ashes of five Roman emperors, but no trace remains of the magnificent colonnaded tholos that topped the burial mound. H. V. Morton does not embroider the truth when in *A Traveller in Rome* (1957) he describes its present condition:

> The Mausoleum of Augustus stands near the Tiber and is one of those miserable ruins which refuses to disintegrate. It has been a stronghold, a bull-ring, a circus, and a concert hall. Now it is a locked-up ruin where lame cats seek refuge from small boys.[23]

The Ara Pacis Augustae, or Altar of the Augustan Peace, lies between the mausoleum and the river. In his auto-biographical *Monumentum Ancyranum*, Augustus relates:

> When I returned to Rome from Spain and Gaul after having successfully attended to affairs in the provinces, during the consulship of Tiberius Nero and Publius Quintilius, the Senate, in honour of my return, decreed that an altar of the Augustan Peace be consecrated in the *Campus Martius*, and ordered that the magistrates, priests, and Vestal Virgins should perform annual sacrifices on it . . .[24]

Fully excavated only in our own century, the Ara Pacis was reassembled and housed in its present glass and concrete box in 1937–8. H. V. Morton, who found this modern structure 'hideous', goes on to describe the altar which is universally acknowledged as one of the great works of Roman sculpture:

> A frieze of life-sized figures runs round the walls, show-ing a grave and solemn assembly of men and women walking in procession to the consecration of the altar; and among them we see Augustus himself, his toga drawn over his head; his successor Tiberius, Livia, the wife of Augustus, and his daughter Julia. These beautiful por-traits were made during the lifetime of these persons by the finest sculptor of the day. It is astonishing to see how little damaged are those portions which have been lying for centuries under the Corso: saved from barbarians and Barberini, they confront us with the startling freshness of their resurrection.[25]

Both of the famous Alfredo restaurants are found in this neighbourhood. The closer one, Alfredo all'Augusteo, was opened in 1950 by the owner of the original Alfredo alla Scrofa, still operating on the nearby Via della Scrofa. Each serves the world-famous *fettucine all'Alfredo*, each proudly displays autograph books and autographed pictures of celebrities who have dined there and each, puzzlingly, possesses the gold fork and spoon presented to the original owner in 1927 by Douglas Fairbanks Sr. and Mary Pickford.[26] Alfredo alla Scrofa, in business since 1914, naturally has played host to more literary legends. In Sinclair Lewis's novel *Babbitt* (1922), the protagonist George Babbitt is seated at a dull dinner party next to a woman named Lucille McKelvey who is described elsewhere in the book as 'red-haired, creamy, discontented, exquisite, rude, and honest':

> He concentrated on Lucille McKelvey, carefully not looking at her blanched lovely shoulder and the tawny silken band which supported her frock.
> 'I suppose you'll be going to Europe pretty soon again, won't you?' he invited.
> 'I'd like to run over to Rome for a few weeks.'
> 'I suppose you see a lot of pictures and music and curios and everything there.'
> 'No, what I really go for is: there's a little *trattoria* on the Via della Scrofa where you get the best *fettucine* in the world.'[27]

A decade later, in 1932, Lewis was himself in Rome. He had won the Nobel Prize for Literature two years earlier and was now somewhat of a celebrity. But finding that his old Roman haunt had become more fashionable and crowded, his biographer tells us:

> He sat in a corner, eyeing a little wistfully the elegant crowd, and toying with the menu, on which the passage from *Babbitt* was proudly quoted. You could order other dishes there, but *fettucine al burro* was what the waiters expected you to take. . . . So Sinclair Lewis ordered some. . . . As he lingered over the meal and the restaurant emptied, the proprietor came to chat with the tall

stranger who sat alone. He referred casually to the number of Americans who always visited him, boasted of having been written about by one of the most famous novelists in the world, and tried to impress the visitor. . . . 'Perhaps the Signore would like to put his name [in the guest-book] among the famous ones?' It was a kindly gesture to a lonely stranger. Sinclair Lewis drew out his fountain pen, signed, wished the man good night and went out. He had written 'John Smith'.[28]

Farther up the Corso, one passes on one's right the church of the Gesù e Maria. This was the spiritual home of Franz Liszt who attended mass there every morning during his second stay in Rome in 1873, when he was living in the nearby Via dei Greci. The most important literary address on this stretch of the Corso, however, is the house at number 18, the residence of Wolfgang Goethe in the years 1786–8, and it was here that the great Romantic poet found the serenity and peace that so eluded him prior to his arrival in Rome. A charming and candid drawing by his friend J. H. W. Tischbein (Plate 10) gives a glimpse of Goethe looking down at the Corso streetscape from his upper-floor window.

THE PIAZZA DEL POPOLO

The Corso soon spills into the majestic Piazza del Popolo. Early visitors who entered the city from the north followed the Via Flaminia through the Porta del Popolo into this square (Plate 11) where they absorbed their first impression of historic Rome. Virtually everyone was impressed by the sight. Even the cantankerous Tobias Smollett, who found little else to praise in Rome, thought this 'noble piazza' with its 'august entrance cannot fail to impress the stranger with a sublime idea of this venerable city'.[29] A century later, Frances Elliot in *Pictures of Old Rome* (1882) captured the magic of the physical setting as well as anyone:

The Piazza del Popolo realizes all our poetic visions of Rome. It opens out with such magnificence, a mysterious

Obelisk browned by unnumbered centuries in the centre,
flashing fountains and dark groves around, while above,
towers the Pincian – the hill of Gardens. How majes-
tically that hill rises aloft – shaded by cypress and ilex
woods, and broken by sumptuous porticoes, descending
terraces, rich balustrades, graceful statues, stately
trophies; a scene such as the imagination of a poet might
call forth in a delicious day dream![30]

Mrs Elliot in her Byronic enthusiasm remained blissfully
disinterested in the human history that has unfolded in the
piazza. William Dean Howells reminds his readers in *Roman
Holidays and Others* (1908) that

it was here Sulla's funeral pyre was kindled; that Nero
was buried on the left side of it, and out of his tomb grew
a huge walnut-tree, the haunt of demoniacal crows till the
Madonna appeared to Paschal II and bade him cut it
down; that the arch-heretic Luther sojourned in the
Augustinian convent here while in Rome; that the digni-
taries of Church and State received Christina of Sweden
here when, after her conversion, she visited the city; that
Lucrezia Borgia celebrated her bethrothal in one of the
churches; that it used to be a favourite place for executing
brigands, whose wives then became artists' models, and
whose sons, if they were like Cardinal Antonelli, became
princes of the Church.[31]

S. Maria del Popolo stands next to the gate at the north end
of the square. Nearly everyone – from the Marquis de Sade to
Bernard Berenson – who has ventured through its modest
portal has been impressed by the artistic riches found within.
Even a tough critic like John Ruskin wrote in his diary that the
church struck him as 'the most perfectly finished and best
supported of any after St Peter's: the architecture is very pure,
the marbles glorious, and the tombs very striking'.[32]

Works by Raphael, Pinturicchio, Sansovino, Caravaggio
and Bernini are dispersed throughout the interior. As might be
expected, only in modern times have the Baroque artists
received anything like the praise they deserve. Kate Simon, in

Rome: Places and Pleasures (1972) writes sensitively of the two Caravaggios in the Cerasi Chapel at the end of the left side aisle:

> Painting at the very opening of the seventeenth century, he [Caravaggio] discarded the musical dreaminess, the elegance, and the sensuality of religious painting and turned to the direct impact of naturalism. The furrowed face of a peasant, the rump of a horse, St Paul lying on the ground, outstretched, reaching to and guarding the blazing light that suffuses the whole painting, force a here-and-now religious experience for a long time before lost in Italian painting.[33]

Sean O'Faolain was less enthusiastic about the Baroque works of art he encountered while walking about the church. With some wit, the Irish novelist and renegade Catholic commented in his *Summer in Italy* (1949) upon the

> horrors it contains, largely thanks to Bernini. . . . What inspiration can anybody get from the cluttered and gaudy mess of the high altar, and the two altars right and left of it, whose columned foppery suggests nothing at all but a sculptor's delight in his own virtuosity? . . . Or that weird truant from Madame Tussaud's beside the door, a yellow skeleton looking out through the bars of the vault? Or the Haberdashery monument outside the Chigi Chapel, composed of yards and yards of trailing red marble, like velvet in a draper's window, with a prowling lion below, looking like Oscar Wilde in a temper, and a snarling eagle above, and two naked cupids hanging the portrait of a long-nosed female in between, and a medley of ropes and tassels and branches and ivied lumps of rock thrown in for good measure?[34]

Life in the Piazza del Popolo is a beehive of activity. Swarms of buzzing traffic, hordes of pedestrians, and a miscellany of Rome's *jeunesse dorée* lend their colour and vitality to this stately square. In 1972 Kate Simon noted that 'progress has made of the piazza a parking lot, a taxi stand, a trial by brake for pedestrians and drivers who shoot down at roller-coaster speed from unexpected slots and, most recently, a meeting place of black-leathered motorcycle drivers with unsavory reputations, moral and political.'[35]

The most absorbing spectator events to take place in the piazza were the public executions of criminals, a ritualistic practice that ended only in the late nineteenth century. In his *Journal*, Montaigne recorded the circumstances of one such execution that occurred in 1581:

> [Here] they let precede the criminal a huge crucifix draped with black, at the foot of which went a great crowd of men wearing cloaks and masks of cloth, and these were said to be the chief gentlefolk of Rome, a confraternity sworn to accompany criminals to execution and corpses to the grave. Two of these – or two monks in similar garb – helped the condemned man into the cart and preached to him, one of them letting him kiss continually a picture of our Lord. This they did so that those in the street might not see the man's face. At the gibbet, which was a beam upon two posts, they held this picture before his face till he was thrown off the ladder. He died as criminals commonly do, without movement or cry; a dark man of thirty or thereabouts, and after he was strangled they cut his body in four quarters. It is the custom amongst these people to kill criminals without torture, and after death to subject the body to very barbarous usage.[36]

More efficient ways of killing were adopted in later eras. With the Napoleonic occupation of Rome in 1798 came the introduction of the guillotine. The Englishman Henry Matthews praised this device which he saw put to use in the Piazza del Popolo in 1818. In his *Diary of an Invalid* (1820) he wrote that it 'appears to be the best of all modes of inflicting the punishment of death; combining the greatest impression on the spectator, with the least possible suffering to the victim'.[37] Matthews did have one complaint, however: the criminal kept him waiting for five hours, 'for the execution is delayed till the culprit is brought to a due state of penitence'.

Charles Dickens was also kept waiting for several hours by the victim's delay in confessing, but this gave the author time to contemplate the guillotine itself. In *Pictures from Italy* he described it as 'an untidy, unpainted, uncouth, crazy-looking thing . . . glittering brightly in the morning sun'.[38] The young man being executed had murdered a religious pilgrim – a Bavarian countess – in the countryside outside Rome. His execution was scheduled during Lent 'so as to make an example of him at that time, when great numbers of pilgrims were coming towards Rome, from all parts, for the Holy Week'. Dickens could not resist devoting several pages to detailing every aspect of the grisly event that followed.

The entertainments in the Piazza del Popolo have become more civilized since the Unification government abolished public executions in 1870. Other spectator sports have taken their place. People-watching is a favourite activity of many foreigners, and nowadays women, like men, can play the game. In *Italian Days* Barbara Grizzuti Harrison sits in a café appraising the male population: 'The young men in the Piazza del Popolo are so fair', she writes, 'it is easy to believe that the breeze that ruffles their hair was made only to complete them. Their existence argues for a moment of sweetness before we turn to dust'.[39]

The pair of seemingly symmetrical Baroque churches at the south end of the square were intended as a dramatic frontispiece to the *trivium* of streets leading back into the heart of the city. The church on the left, S. Maria di Montesanto, has historically been the site of some of Rome's finest church music. In the eighteenth century Alessandro Scarlatti was named maestro di cappella and, while living in Rome, George Frederick Handel composed two psalm-settings, 'Laudate pueri' and 'Nisi Dominus' for a special feast held there in 1707.[40]

FROM THE VIA DEL BABUINO TO THE PIAZZA DI SPAGNA

The Via del Babuino runs through the artists' and antiquarians' quarter of the city to the Piazza di Spagna. The contemporary Roman novelist Ugo Moretti described life on this street in his book *Artists in Rome, Tales of the Babuino* (1956):

The Babuino is overpopulated, and its population con-
sists mainly of pretty girls, ugly girls, bums, painters,
sculptors, shopgirls, queers, movie people, lesbians, and
foreigners – all constantly inside or outside the bars and
shops. Or rather, they are in constant movement, cook-
ing up deals, one-man shows, confidence games, art
editions, documentary films; they sell million-dollar
ideas for ninety cents, they argue, neck, waste time, and
sponge drinks, coffee, cigarettes for themselves and their
friends.[41]

Chic galleries now line the street, but the original Bohemian
atmosphere of the neighbourhood where Rubens, Poussin and
hundreds of lesser artists resided is still to be savoured along
the nearby Via Margutta, a short street running parallel to it,
one block to the left. A visit to the artists' studios was a
favoured pastime of many tourists in the past. In a letter to his
brother of 1860, Henry Adams wrote:

> The studios are a great feature in Rome. It's delightful to
> take one's luncheon towards two o'clock and then smoke
> an hour and watch the clay take form or the sketch fill out
> into color and life, and meanwhile talk nonsense or sense
> as it happens. The range is enormous. It stretches from art
> to prize-fighting; and men talk equally well about the
> Apollo and the Dying Gladiator, or about [the fighters]
> Heenan and Pryor.[42]

Depending upon one's attitude, the Via Margutta can have
many moods. Percy Lubbock, an English literary critic who
was a friend and disciple of Henry James, relates in *Roman
Pictures* (1923) that he could not walk down this street without
thinking of the fictional characters of Hawthorne, Andersen,
Zola, and James.[43] The Italian Moretti, on the other hand, saw
his own neighbourhood in a more cynical light:

> Then there's Via Margutta, that kind of *grande dame*
> among streets, fallen on hard times through menopause
> and the opening of garages. Most of our population lives
> there: models, students, actresses (at so much per hour),

painters and sculptors with families that perhaps aren't quite all theirs.[44]

The area around the Piazza di Spagna and Spanish Steps (Plate 12) has historically been a magnet for literary figures as well. The English were particularly partial to the neighbourhood, and among those who resided in the piazza, or in streets just off the piazza, were George Eliot and Edward Lear (Via del Babuino), William Makepeace Thackeray (Via della Croce), Henry James and the Brownings (Via Bocca di Leone), and Tobias Smollett, Byron, Shelley, and Keats in various houses in the piazza itself. The chief gathering place for English Grand Tourists was the now-defunct English Coffee House, located at Piazza di Spagna, 85, opposite the present Babington's Tea Rooms. In his *Memoirs*, Thomas Jones describes going there in the winter of 1776 when his own unheated house had become too uncomfortable:

> For relief – there was no other Alternative but flying to the English Coffee House, a filthy vaulted room, the walls of which were painted with Sphinxes, Obelisks and Pyramids, from capricious designs of *Piranesi*, and fitter to adorn the inside of an Egyptian Sepulchre, than a room of social conversation – Here – seated around a brazier of hot embers placed in the Center, we endeavoured to amuse ourselves for an hour or two over a Cup of Coffee or a glass of Punch and then grope out our way home darkling, in Solitude and Silence.[45]

When Edward Lear was in Rome in 1837, he found the English Coffee House a congenial place to start his day. 'At 8:00', he wrote to his sister, 'I go to the café, where all the artists breakfast, and have two cups of coffee [and] two toasted rolls for 6½d.'[46] One didn't have to be English to go there. The young Venetian sculptor Antonio Canova, when first in Rome in 1779–80, recorded in his diary the many happy hours he spent at the café talking with friends.[47]

Most non-English speaking foreign residents preferred, however, to frequent the rival Caffè Greco, still bustling round the corner at Via Condotti, 86 (Plate 13). Among the illustrious patrons of bygone ages were Hans Christian Andersen, Charles Baudelaire, Hector Berlioz, Anatole France, Wolfgang Goethe, Nikolai Gogol, Franz Liszt, Felix Mendelssohn, Artur Schopenhauer, Stendhal, William Thackeray, Mark Twain, and Richard Wagner. The often-told tale that in 1743 the amorous Casanova was stood up by a woman at the Caffè Greco should be treated with suspicion, for even the management now acknowledges that the establishment was not founded until 1760.[48] The interior has been much remodelled over the years, but portrait medallions of Liszt, Wagner, and others still grace the walls of one back room, while in another, a small bronze statue of Mark Twain stands proudly in a niche.

There is no shortage of colourful descriptions of the place or its *habitués*. Felix Mendelssohn gave a particularly vivid account in his *Letters from Italy and Switzerland* (1830). The German composer was a prickly sort, and he wrote with some vituperation about the many Bohemian artists that frequented the café:

> I scarcely ever go there, for I dread both themselves and their favourite place of resort. It is a small dark room, about eight yards square, where you may smoke on one side, but not on the other; round this they sit on benches, with sombrero hats on their heads, and huge mastiffs beside them; their cheeks and throats, and the whole of their faces covered with hair, puffing fearful clouds of smoke . . . and saying rude things to each other, while the mastiffs provide for a due distribution of vermin. A neckcloth or a coat would be here quite innovations; spectacles hide any portion of the face left visible by the beard; and so they drink their coffee, and talk of Titian and Pordenone.[49]

By the middle of the twentieth century, the café had already become a tourist attraction. In *Europe without Baedeker* (1947), the American literary critic Edmund Wilson recounts his impressions just after the close of World War II. The place he found was still dim and dingy, but it had already begun to trade on its former reputation:

The waiter prides himself on his languages and has a humorous-familiar tinge, as if he were playing a role in some comedy of the eighteen-forties. He will show you the yellow old albums in which the great men have signed their names, if your interest is sufficiently keen and you back it with the hint of a tip.[50]

In 1953 the Caffè Greco was named a national monument. Since then, prices have risen and the clientele has changed accordingly. Most of today's stylish patrons would seem to have little in common with those authentic if unpolished talents whose fame continues to bestow cachet on the ageless café.

Round the corner at Via Mario de' Fiori, 26 is the Ristorante Ranieri, another renowned historical and literary landmark. According to Theodora Fitzgibbon, author of *A Taste of Rome* (1975),

> Its real historical interest begins, however, in 1865 when it was bought by Giuseppe Ranieri, who had been chef to Queen Victoria and then to the ill-fated Emperor Maximilian, whom he accompanied to Mexico. After the Emperor's arrest the Empress Carlotta, who had lost her reason, brought Ranieri back to Rome and tried in vain to get papal support. Ranieri stayed in Rome and took over the restaurant, which is continued in the old style today by his direct descendent, with its damask-covered walls and superb food. Many distinguished people have left their signatures in the visitors' book and the restaurant is mentioned in the books of Gide, Anatole France, Stendhal, Paul Bourget and Destree.[51]

The pre-eminent literary landmark in the area is the Keats-Shelley Memorial House, located immediately to the right of the Spanish Steps (visible in Plate 12). The name is somewhat of a misnomer for in the poets' day, the house was actually a *pensione* and Shelley never stayed there. It owes its fame principally to Keats, who came to Rome for his health in November 1820, and spent the last three months of his life there, dying at the age of twenty-five in a small room on the third floor overlooking the grand Rococo stairway. Joseph Severn, the faithful friend who attended him in his final days, left an epistolary account of his death:

> He is gone – he died with the most perfect ease – he seemed to go to sleep. On the 23rd, about 4, the approaches of death came on. 'Severn – I – lift me up – I am dying – I shall die easy – don't be frightened – be firm, and thank God it has come!' I lifted him up in my arms. The phlegm seemed boiling in his throat, and increased until 11, when he gradually sunk into death – so quiet – that I still thought he slept. I cannot say now – I am broken down from four nights' watching, and no sleep since, and my poor Keats gone. Three days since, the body was opened; the lungs were completely gone. The Doctors could not conceive by what means he had lived these two months. I followed his poor body to the grave on Monday, with many English.[52]

Severn also made a memorable drawing of Keats on his deathbed (now hanging in the very room in which he died). Years later, Rainer Maria Rilke wrote a poem, 'On the Drawing Depicting John Keats in Death' and countless others have been moved to tears since the house was opened as a public museum in 1909. One stalwart visitor, Sinclair Lewis, confessed that it was the only time he ever cried.[53]

The house is full of literary mementos. Drawings, photographs, prints, and assorted documents cover the walls and fill display cases. Keats's own drawing of a Grecian urn, Severn's posthumous portrait of Shelley at the Baths of Caracalla, Keats's life and death masks, and locks of Keats's, Shelley's, John Milton's and Elizabeth Barrett Browning's hair are among the memorabilia to be found in the three cramped rooms whose walls are otherwise lined with shelf upon shelf of books. As A. C. Sedgwick, a *New York Times* correspondent put it when the house was reopened in 1944 after the German Occupation, 'There was the smell – more of England than of Italy, or so one thinks – of leather bindings that bewitched Henry James. There was quiet, peace, pause. . . .'[54]

The view of the Spanish Steps from Keats's bedroom has

not changed since the poet's death. The great Rococo flight is grand and imposing and a good description of the 'glorious flight of stone' was given by Hugh MacMillan in *Roman Mosaics* (1888): 'This lofty staircase comprises one hundred and thirty steps, and the ascent is so gradual, and the landing-places so broad and commodious, that it is quite a pleasure, even for the most infirm persons, to mount it'.[55] The pleasure of ascending the steps has even been experienced in musical terms. A current Roman resident, Louis Inturrisi, an expatriate American teacher and travel writer, has written:

The Spanish Steps do for space what a Baroque concerto does with time. The rhythms produced by the variations of intervals, angles, directions and landings suggest the irregularities of Vivaldi or Handel. . . . Nowhere in Rome is the music of form so brilliantly illustrated architecturally.[56]

In the past, the Spanish Steps have played host to two resident populations: models, who catered to the many artists living nearby, and beggars, who set their sights on tourists. Many early accounts commented at some length on both. In *Roba di Roma* (1862), the American sculptor and author William Wetmore Story introduces the cast of colourful characters that populate countless nineteenth-century paintings made in Rome:

All day long, these steps are flooded with sunshine, in which, stretched at length, or gathered in picturesque groups, models of every age and both sexes bask away the hours when they are free from employment in the studios. Here in a rusty old coat, and long white beard and hair, is the *Padre Eterno*, so called from his constantly standing as model for the First Person of the Trinity in religious pictures. Here is the ferocious bandit, with his thick black beard and conical hat, now off duty, and sitting with his legs wide apart, munching in alternate bites an onion, which he holds in one hand, and a lump of bread, which he holds in the other. Here is the *contadina*, who spends her studio life in praying at a shrine with

upcast eyes, or lifting to the Virgin her little sick child, –
or carrying a perpetual copper vase to the fountain. . . .
Here is the invariable pilgrim, with his scallop-shell, who
has been journeying to St Peter's and reposing by the way
near aqueducts . . . who is now fast asleep on his back,
with his hat pulled over his eyes.[57]

The models have all but disappeared in the twentieth century, but the memory of them perched amidst the potted
plants remained in the minds of many who had spent earlier
days in Rome. In her autobiography *A Backward Glance*
(1934), Edith Wharton reminisced 'through the trailing clouds
of infancy, [about] the steps of the Piazza di Spagna thronged
with Thackerayan artists' models, and heaped with early
violets, daffodils and tulips'.[58]

The beggars, on the other hand, have not gone away,
although few today are truly as unfortunate as those of the
past. A century and a half ago, Hans Christian Andersen found
that 'by day the place is swarming with beggars with withered
arms and legs, some hopping like frogs, springing up and
down on their hands. Others lie on the pavement, displaying
their deformities'.[59] John Ciardi, in a poem entitled 'Rome,
1951', laughs at himself for falling prey to a woman whose
baby was probably hired. In *Rome: Places and Pleasures*, Kate
Simon has an informative chapter called 'Grace Notes' in
which she provides a thorough *catalogue raisonné* of the city's
beggars and gypsies:

> Gypsies come in a wide assortment, the lowest form a
> listless lolling on sidewalls, borrowed baby on one skinny
> arm, the other extended in dirty, begging claws. Larger,
> more vigorous gypsies, with the usual barnacles of babies
> clinging to their skirts, often have an enviable insouci-
> ance. Give one of them a coin and they march the kids
> into the nearest bar for gelati.[60]

In a commanding position atop the Spanish Steps looms the
stately two-towered façade of SS. Trinità dei Monti. Built by
the French King Charles VIII in 1494, this church houses what
was long believed to be one of the world's finest paintings,

Daniele da Volterra's fresco of the *Descent from the Cross*. Most nineteenth-century observers commented angrily on the grave damage done to this late Renaissance painting when Napoleon's troops invaded Rome. Samuel Taylor Coleridge visited the church in 1805 and found 'most of the pictures annihilated, and the famous Deposizione of Daniele da Volterra, left enough of to excite one's deepest Horror of these Wretches'.[61] The picture was subsequently restored, but its reputation is not what it used to be. Few today would concur with the widely accepted view of the eighteenth and nineteenth centuries that this Mannerist work is 'one of the three finest pictures in the world'.[62]

The view overlooking the city from the Trinità dei Monti is among Rome's most captivating sights, especially at dusk. Of the many poetic passages that describe it, one of the most beautiful appears in the novel *Jan Maria Plojhar* (1891) by the Czechoslovakian author Julius Zeyre:

The view was so marvellous that it enthralled one in mute contemplation. The Eternal City seemed in that instant more like a fantastic vision than a real thing. Under the deep blue sky, like a stream of diamonds flowing from its bed, the Via del Corso stretched across the city, gigantic, indefinite, fantastic; a sea of buildings which in that pale light took on the strangest and most bizarre forms; an undulation of cupolas, a fugue of profiled shapes thrust into the silver shadow emanating from the sky from which the moon also descended, throwing its innocent spell upon these ancient remains of the world on the Tiber. All Rome appeared of marble. Its head plunged into the glimmer of light, but shadows rose from the ground, coiling at its feet. In darkness, the long strand of gas lamps twinkled like ribbons of stars.[63]

At the very foot of the Spanish Steps, occupying a prominent place in the piazza, is the popular but unusually shaped fountain known as the Barcaccia. It stands opposite the flower vendors' stalls, and the sight, sound, and fragrance of the two together make for a lushly sensuous experience. In *The Colour of Rome*, Olave Potter writes that the 'quaint fountain' reminds Rome of a river-boat stranded in the piazza during one of her floods. It is an out-at-heel derelict; it might have drifted from fairyland down the parted waters of the cascade of steps, which are crowned by the golden towers of SS. Trinità dei Monti, and are hidden with a foam of almond-blossom as they meet the piazza in a bank of lilies, and carnations, and roses, and anemones. The mingled fragrance of the blossoms is turbulent; the gurgle of the water in the broken barge of the fountain is the music of a brook.[64]

The Barcaccia, or 'worthless boat' in fact does commemorate the arrival of a river vessel in the piazza after the Tiber overran its banks during the great flood of 1598. The authorship of the work is much disputed by art historians who do not agree if it should be assigned to Gianlorenzo Bernini or to his father Pietro, who also was a sculptor.

FROM THE PIAZZA DI SPAGNA TO THE TREVI FOUNTAIN

It is only a short if somewhat indirect walk from the Piazza di Spagna to the Piazza della Fontana di Trevi. Along the way one passes two works by Borromini, the Palazzo della Propaganda Fide and the Scottish church, S. Andrea della Fratte. Few would disagree with Charles Eliot Norton's assessment that Borromini's cupola and bell-tower at S. Andrea is 'one of the oddest and most irrational of [his] fantastic erections',[65] or Sacheverell Sitwell's claim that this is 'a sensational work that resembles nothing built before or since'.[66] Alessandro Scarlatti was married in this church and Angelica Kauffmann is buried there. Near the high altar are two splendid angels that were carved by Bernini for the Ponte Sant'Angelo and later replaced by his own copies. Eleanor Clark thought these to be 'Rome's two best sculpture angels'.[67]

The palace directly across the piazza from S. Andrea (Via della Mercede, 11) was Bernini's own residence in his mature years. A century and a half after his death in 1680, Sir Walter Scott took up lodging there. Like many others, Scott came to

Rome for his health and only got worse, returning to Scotland to die shortly thereafter. Scott's journal entry for his first day in Rome, 16 April 1832, is short and ends abruptly: 'We slept reasonably, but on the next morning –'. His contemporary biographer John Lockhart believed these to have been the last words Scott ever wrote.[68] A few decades later, in the years 1864–8, Hendrik Ibsen moved into the neighbourhood. The house he shared with his wife and young son (later demolished) was one block east at the corner of the Via Due Macelli and the Via Capo le Case. A plaque attached to the wall of the modern Hotel Cecil on the nearby Via Francesco Crispi notes a shorter residence he spent there as well.

Crossing the fearsome traffic of the grimy modern Via del Tritone hardly prepares one for the delights that lie ahead in the Piazza della Fontana di Trevi. The Fontana di Trevi (Plate 14) is the fountainhead of the Acqua Vergine whose sweet waters have been savoured by Romans since antiquity. After several projects were designed but left unexecuted in previous centuries, the present structure was built to the design of Nicola Salvi in 1732–62. While the fountain's sculpture is unabashedly Baroque, the architectural backdrop – based as it is on the Arch of Constantine – signals the restrained antiquarianism of the coming Neo-Classical era.

Visitors' reactions to the fountain have been mostly positive. Even John Ruskin, who was no enthusiast of Baroque art, found it captivating, noting in his diary of 1840:

> I got on the mimicked rocks, and among the deep pools of this most noble fountain until I fancied myself among the gushing torrents of my own Cumberland – then to raise my head, and come gradually on the crowded and rich costumes of the surrounding market, the grey portico of the opposite church [SS. Vincenzo ed Anastasio], and the white leafage of the Corinthian capitals above; it is one of the most surprising combinations and sudden changes of feeling I have yet found.[69]

Oscar Wilde, writing a letter in a café facing the fountain, gave the most succinct characterization of anyone: 'the sound of the waters is wonderful: it soothes: it has κάθαρσις'.[70]

There have been those, however, for whom the fountain did not live up to its exalted reputation, mostly as a result of its 'natural' forms and constricted setting. This occurred to Charlotte Eaton, author of *Rome in the Nineteenth Century* (1820):

> The fountain of Trevi has been renowned through the world, and so highly extolled, that my expectations were raised to the highest stretch; and great was my disappointment when I was taken to a little, dirty, confined, miserable piazza, nearly filled up with one large palace, beneath which spouted out a variety of tortuous streamlets, that are made to gurgle over artificial rocks, and to bathe the bodies of various sea-horses, tritons, and other marble monsters that are sprawling about in it.[71]

The very best time to visit the Trevi, most agree, is at night. It is then that the fountain, as Dickens put it, 'welling from a hundred jets, and rolling over mimic rocks, is silvery to the eye and ear'.[72] The Fontana di Trevi has a deserved reputation as a very romantic spot, and it has served as a backdrop for amatory interludes in a number of literary and cinematic fictions. Most of these do not have happy endings. An early example occurs in *Corinne ou L'Italie*, Madame de Staël's novel of 1807. Later in the nineteenth century Thomas Mann in *The Will to Happiness* (1896) has Paolo Hofmann and the narrator stroll through Rome on the eve of the former's departure for Germany where he is soon to be married. The night is tempestuous, and as Paolo raises a glass of the Trevi's water in a toast to his return, a flash of lightning knocks the glass to the ground and breaks it. It is not a good omen, and Paolo dies shortly after his wedding.

Lasting happiness escapes even the most glamorous figures of our own age who dare to dally at the fountain – Marcello Mastroianni and Anita Ekberg, stars of Fellini's *La dolce vita* (1960). The futility of their entanglement is symbolized by the fact that just as they are about to kiss – while standing in the fountain – the water is turned off and their ardour is lost.

The earlier habit of ensuring one's return to Rome by drinking from the Trevi's waters has in this century been replaced by the rite of throwing a coin over one's shoulder into the basin. So magical is the fountain's appeal that otherwise unsuperstitious and unsentimental individuals have been known to enrich the city coffers – or the pockets of enterprising urchins – by indulging in this practice on their last night in Rome. Those of a romantic nature and who have a love for the city may think twice, but seldom are they inclined to tempt fate by not doing so.

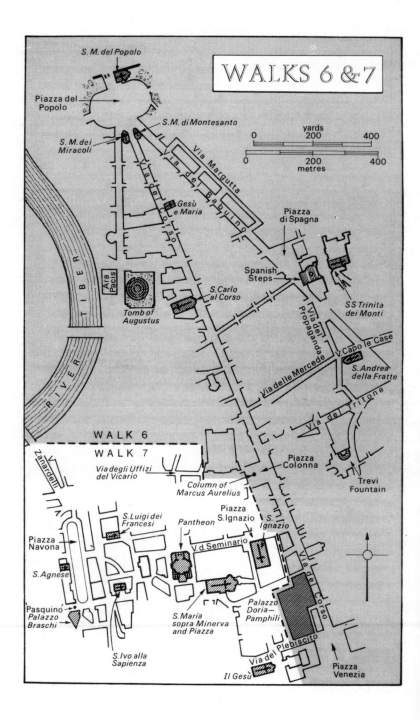

WALKS 6 & 7

S. M. del Popolo

Piazza del Popolo

S. M. di Montesanto

S. M. dei Miracoli

Via Margutta

Via del Babuino

Gesù e Maria

Piazza di Spagna

Via del Corso

Ara Pacis

Tomb of Augustus

S. Carlo al Corso

Spanish Steps

SS Trinita dei Monti

Via di Propaganda

Via delle Mercede

Capo le Case

S. Andrea della Fratte

Via del Tritone

RIVER TIBER

WALK 6

WALK 7

Zanardelli

Via degli Uffizi del Vicario

Piazza Colonna

Via del Tritone

Trevi Fountain

Column of Marcus Aurelius

S. Luigi dei Francesi

Pantheon

Piazza S. Ignazio

S. Ignazio

Piazza Navona

V. d. Seminario

S. Agnese

Pasquino Palazzo Braschi

S. Maria sopra Minerva and Piazza

Palazzo Doria–Pamphili

S. Ivo alla Sapienza

Via del Corso

Via del Plebiscito

Il Gesù

Piazza Venezia

yards
0   200   400

0   200   400
metres

7

SEVENTH WALK

*From the Piazza Venezia to the Pantheon and
the Piazza Navona*

THE CHURCH OF IL GESU

From the Piazza Venezia, it is but a mercifully short walk
down the narrow, fume-choked Via del Plebiscito to the once-
elegant Piazza del Gesù. The piazza takes its name from the
great church of Il Gesù, built in the late sixteenth century as the
Mother Church of the Jesuit Order. In keeping with the spirit
of the Counter-Reformation, the Gesù is spare and unpreten-
tious, at least by Italian standards. Yet for Protestants un-
accustomed to the display of any religious imagery, the church
made a powerful impression. The first English visitor to
record his observations was Grey Brydges, the fifth Lord
Chandos, who attended a service in 1620. In *Horae Subsecivae*
he noted that

> Wherein is inserted all possible inventions, to catch men's
> affections, and to ravish their understanding: at first, the
> gloriousness of their Altars, infinit number of images,
> priestly ornaments, and the divers actions [the Jesuits] use
> in that service; besides the most excellent and exquisite
> Musicke of the world, that surprizes our ears. So that
> whatsoever can be imagined, to expresse either Solem-
> nitie, or Devotion, is by them used.[1]

Non-Catholics by and large were deeply suspicious of what they viewed as the worldliness and sensuality of Catholic ritual. A few works in the Gesù that were added later in the Baroque period were found to be particularly offensive. Referring to Gaulli's ceiling painting of *The Triumph of the Holy Name*, and LeGros' transept sculpture of *Religion Triumphing over Heresy*, the Scottish Presbyterian minister Joseph Forsyth wrote in 1802–3:

> This church is horrible with the works of faith. Here you see a mob of poor allegorical wretches hurled down to hell by the lightning which issues from three letters of the alphabet: there, two ugly, enigmatical devils, which pass with the vulgar for Luther and his wife, blasted by a fine young woman, named Religion.[2]

For others, however, the experience was confusing if not truly oxymoronic. The Revd T. H. White found it 'a place of gloomy, of awful grandeur',[3] Ruskin thought the music 'exquisite in spite of all prejudice',[4] and Henry James concluded his description of a vesper service by commenting on 'the opulent-looking nun – possibly an abbess or prioress of noble lineage', who sat next to him. 'Can a holy woman of such a complexion', he asked, 'listen to a fine operatic barytone in a sumptuous temple and receive none but ascetic impressions? What a cross-fire of influences does Catholicism provide!'[5]

On the other hand, visitors with Catholic or more secular backgrounds found it easier to take the Gesù on its own terms. Père Teilhard de Chardin did not mince words when he noted in a letter of 1948 that 'despite its orgy of marbles and mouldings . . . one feels [in the Gesù] . . . the security of a faith that will not be sidetracked'.[6] A more effusive response occurs in the De Goncourt brothers' novel *Madame Gervaisais* (1869). The protagonist

> loved the vault over her head which resembled a golden arch, bedecked with ornaments, with coffers and arabesques, illuminated by windows where saints burst forth into the sunlight. She loved the blazing festivity of the

ceiling where, in Gaulli's glorious colours, the apotheosis of the Elect triumphs over vaporous clouds that seem like incense and which, garnished with flowers, overflows their borders. All poured forth, glimpses of sky and veritable clouds suspended from the vault where angels swirled with much thrashing of legs and beating of wings.[7]

In the twentieth century, as the subject matter of works of art became less important and stylistic expression became more of an issue, Italian Baroque painting began to find defenders among the general population. The American novelist Edith Wharton was among the first, and more recently, Barbara Grizzuti Harrison promoted *Roma barocca* with unabashed enthusiasm in *Italian Days* (1989). Ruminating upon the Gesù and the Baroque in general, she writes:

> If you do not love the agitated pleasure of the Baroque, you cannot love Rome. You do not have to love Roman ruins to love Rome, but you have to love the Baroque, otherwise you will think Rome is florid and vulgar and recoil from its extravagance.[8]

S. Maria sopra Minerva

From the Piazza del Gesù, it is not far to Rome's only Gothic church, S. Maria sopra Minerva. Northern visitors from any era would understand Sean O'Faolain's comment that while it is not a beautiful church, 'it is none the less an extraordinary relief to the eye to look again at the pointed arches, vaulted ceilings, dim clerestory, and broad aisles of the north'.[9] The Gothic style of S. Maria sopra Minerva could even rekindle old theological debates. In Zola's *Rome* (1896), the sceptical French cleric Pierre encounters a Roman monsignor while strolling through the church. The Italian wasted little time in coming right to the point as he

inveighed heavily against the Gothic style as rank heresy. The first Christian church, said the prelate, had been the basilica, which had sprung from the temple, and it was blasphemy to assert that the Gothic cathedral was the real Christian house of prayer, for Gothic embodied the hateful Anglo-Saxon spirit, the rebellious genius of Luther. At this a passionate reply rose to Pierre's lips, but he said nothing for fear that he might say too much.[10]

There is one monument of pre-eminent artistic importance in the Minerva, Michelangelo's marble statue *The Risen Christ*, placed just to the left of the high altar. Although modest in size and unprepossessing in character, this work has enjoyed immense popularity with tourists and the faithful alike.

Five popes and a bevy of cardinals are buried in S. Maria sopra Minerva, but one of the most moving funerals ever to take place there occurred only recently. It was that of Italy's most beloved modern actress, Anna Magnani, who died in 1975. Shortly before her death she had told a friend, 'in this country only the monuments survive', but at her funeral, according to William Murray, author of *Italy, the Fatal Gift*:

> when the service was over and her coffin was raised up to be carried out there was a spontaneous, startling burst of applause. It was as if the community were mourning for and applauding itself, because she had been, without willing it or realizing it, the living expression of its spirit. She, too, had at last become a monument.[11]

Grazing contentedly in front of the church is Bernini's whimsical sculpture of a small elephant carrying an obelisk on its back. This, in the words of Kate Simon,

> is one of the fancies of Rome, like peculiar fountains shaped of books or easels, of houses whose doors and windows are grotesque mouths and eyes, of lost, solitary Roman columns and dozens of etceteras. It is said that the elephant was chosen by Urban VIII to show that a solid healthy mind is needed to sustain wisdom and knowl- edge. Be that as it may, and one can think of better symbols for a solid mind than the patient plodding elephant, he is distinctly 'cute', a baroque cousin of a Walt Disney elephant . . .[12]

Several wall plaques in the Piazza della Minerva remind one of the notable people and events associated with the area. On the church façade itself, a cluster of marble tablets record the high-water marks from the worst inundations of the Tiber. The most damaging of these occurred in 1598 when the waters rose thirty-two feet and claimed several thousand lives. Across the square, plaques on the façade of the ever-fashionable Albergo della Minerva (the first hotel in Rome to offer central heating to its guests) commemorate the stays of Stendhal in 1834–6 and of Don José de San Martín, the liberator of Latin America, in 1845. George Eliot also stayed at the Minerva, but as she wrote so little about Rome, and her male companion was already married to someone else, the memory of her visit is not preserved. Another distinguished resident of the square whose name is not commemorated was Galileo. It was in 1633 in the Dominican convent to the left of the church that the brilliant Pisan stood before the Inquisitors and was made to retract his advocacy of the Copernican system.

THE PANTHEON

The inscription on the frieze of the portico – M·AGRIPPA·L·F·COS·TERTIUM·FECIT – is misleading. The present building was in fact not constructed by Marcus Agrippa in 27 BC but by Hadrian a century and a half later. The discrepancy in patronage and dating is explained by the fact that a temple of Agrippa originally did stand on the site, but it burned down and was replaced by Hadrian, who honoured his predecessor with the prominent inscription. Only in the late nineteenth century did archaeological investigation set the record straight. In Marguerite Yourcenar's fictional *Memoirs of Hadrian* (1951), the emperor confesses that

It mattered little to me to have my name recorded on this monument. . . . On the contrary, it pleased me that a text of more than a century ago should link this new edifice to the beginings of our empire. . . . Even in my innovations I liked to feel that I was above all a continuator.

'Hadrian' goes on the explain why he built the temple in the unusual shape of a domed rotunda:

> My intention had been that this sanctuary of All Gods should reproduce the likeness of the terrestrial globe and of the stellar sphere. . . . The cupola . . . revealed the sky through a great hole at the center, showing alternately dark and blue. This temple, both open and mysteriously enclosed, was conceived as a solar quadrant. The hours would make their round on that caissoned ceiling, so carefully polished by Greek artisans; the disk of daylight would rest suspended there like a shield of gold; rain would form its clear pool on the pavement below; prayers would rise like smoke toward that void where we place the gods.[13]

Stendhal claimed never to have met anyone who had been unmoved by the sight of the Pantheon which, in his words, 'has this great advantage: it requires only two moments to be penetrated by its beauty. You stop before the portico; you take a few steps, you see the church, and the whole thing is over'.[14] Indeed, few accounts of any sojourn in Rome fail to report their author's impressions of the Pantheon (Plates 15 and 16). Only in antiquity, surprisingly, is this most venerable and conspicuous of temples rarely mentioned. During the Middle Ages, on the other hand, it was frequently remarked upon, but always with a certain amount of suspicion. Despite its Christian consecration in the seventh century as S. Maria ad Martyres – a circumstance that aided in its preservation – there were those like the Venerable Bede who claimed it was inhabited by Satan and that it owed its existence to the sinister power of demons and not to the genius of an architect. The oculus in the cupola, for example, was explained as a hole broken through the roof by the devil in his desperate attempt to flee the building at the time of consecration by Boniface IV.[15]

It is said to have been Petrarch who changed people's

attitudes towards the Pantheon when in *De Remediis Utriusque Fortunae* he claimed that it was only the Virgin's intercession that saved the building from destruction.[16] Later Renaissance humanists freed the building from remaining superstition, and when Raphael chose to be buried there in 1520 – rather than in the Vatican – its fame as a paradigm of classical perfection was symbolically reconfirmed.

While the structure itself remained remarkably well preserved, the loss of its surface revetments and the squalor of its immediate surroundings were a cause of some concern. Hippolyte Taine in *Italy, Rome and Naples* (1868) found 'its begrimed surface, its fissures and mutilations, and the half-effaced inscription of its architrave, give it a maimed and invalid appearance'.[17] George Hillard, meanwhile, was not the first author of a popular guidebook to point out that

> The Pantheon stands in a narrow and dirty piazza, and is shouldered and elbowed by a mob of vulgar houses. There is no breathing-space around, which it might penetrate with the light of its own serene beauty. Its harmonious proportions can be seen only in front; and it has there the disadvantage of being approached from a point higher than that on which it stands. On one side is a market; and the space before the matchless portico is strewn with fish-bones, decayed vegetables, and offal.[18]

The market stalls around the Pantheon – and it was famous for its fishmongers and sellers of caged birds – have long disappeared, but the piazza today is no less colourful than it was in the past. Life in the square, according to a recent guidebook is 'worthy of Fellini. Half-naked beauties, pickpockets, street hawkers, introverts, extroverts, freaks and oddities of every ilk heap abuse on each other in an irresistible, spontaneous commedia dell'arte'.[19]

For good reason the Pantheon has also evoked more effusive praise than any other building in Rome. The grand simplicity of the portico was particularly alluring to those steeped in the Neo-Classical taste of the late eighteenth and early nineteenth centuries. Joseph Forsyth, a stern and fastidious architectural critic, even went so far in his *Remarks in Italy* (1802–3) as to

claim that 'the portal is more than faultless; it is *positively* the
most sublime result that was ever produced by such little
architecture'.[20]

The words simple and sublime appear over and over in early
descriptions. It was therefore with no great originality that
Byron used these very words to begin his stanza on the
Pantheon in *Childe Harold's Pilgrimage*:

> Simple, erect, severe, austere, sublime –
> Shrine of all saints and temple of all gods,
> From Jove to Jesus – spared and blest by time;
> Looking tranquillity, while falls or nods
> Arch, empire, each thing round thee, and man plods
> His way through thorns to ashes – glorious dome!
> Shalt thou not last? – Time's scythe and tyrants' rods
> Shiver upon thee – sanctuary and home
> Of art and piety – Pantheon! – pride of Rome![21]

While Byron's Romantic temperament could not resist the
temptation to see the building only in terms of human *vanitas*,
others viewed it in more positive terms, seeking to convey the
almost mystical aura of 'the simple sublime'. Henry James
certainly grappled with that notion in a letter he wrote to his
sister just one week after he arrived in Rome for the first time
in 1869:

> By far the most beautiful piece of ancientry in Rome is
> that simple and unutterable Pantheon to which I repeated
> my devotions yesterday afternoon. It makes you pro-
> foundly regret that you are not a pagan suckled in the
> creed outworn that produced it. It's the most conclusive
> example I have yet seen of the simple sublime. Imagine
> simply a vast cupola with its drum, set directly on the
> earth and fronted with a porch of columns and a triangu-
> lar summit: the interior lighted by a hole in the apex of the
> cupola and the circumference furnished with a series of
> altars. The effect is the very *delicacy* of grandeur – and
> more worshipful to my perception than the most mys-
> terious and aspiring Gothic. St Peter's, beside it, is ab-
> surdly vulgar.[22]

James at the age of twenty-six was not the first to experience the spiritual powers of the Pantheon. The young Goethe felt 'overwhelmed with admiration' for the monument during his first weeks in Rome in 1786 and 'wondered how can we, petty as we are and accustomed to pettiness, ever become equal to such noble perfection?'[23]

But it was undoubtedly the New England Protestant Nathaniel Hawthorne who allowed his imagination the freest play in ruminating upon the building. In a passage from his *French and Italian Note-Books* (1858) that he subsequently adapted for *The Marble Faun* (1860), Hawthorne stood inside the rotunda and contemplated the sunshine streaming through the oculus:

> The great slanting beam . . . was visible all the way down to the pavement, falling upon motes of dust or a thin smoke of incense imperceptible in the shadow. Insects were playing to and fro in the beam, high up towards the opening. There is a wonderful charm in the naturalness of all this; and one might fancy a swarm of cherubs coming down through the opening and sporting in the broad ray, to gladden the faith of worshippers on the pavement beneath; or angels bearing prayers upward, or bringing down responses to them, visible with dim brightness as they pass through the pathway of heaven's radiance, even the many hues of their wings discernible by a trusting eye; though, as they pass into the shadow, they vanish like the motes. So the sunbeam would represent those rays of divine intelligence which enable us to see wonders and to know that they are natural things.[24]

Of the several tombs of artists and Italian monarchs found in the Pantheon, that of Raphael (third *aedicule* on the left) has understandably attracted the most attention. The monument itself is modest, but it bears a graceful Latin epigram composed by his friend Cardinal Bembo. This was translated into English by Alexander Pope who, dropping the *Ille hic est Raphael*, reused it in an epitaph for the English painter Godfrey Kneller:

Living, great Nature feared he might outvie
Her works; and dying, fears herself may die.[25]

Naturally there have always been those who found the
Pantheon disappointing. Tobias Smollett was notoriously
censorious about everything he describes in *Travels through
Italy and France* (1766), so it is no surprise to hear that he
'visited [the Pantheon] several times, and each time it looked
more and more gloomy and sepulchral'.[26] Sightseers with the
ill fortune to enter in poor weather were most likely to remain
unenlightened by their visit. Florence Nightingale was plainly
unnerved by her experience in late November 1847:

> Last Sunday we had a rainy day – after church we went to
> the Pantheon – there was a great puddle under the [hole]
> and the lights from the altars and from the procession of
> the Host reflected in the dark puddle, for it was almost
> night, had such an effect, you cannot imagine. I thought
> of Charon ferrying over his souls by night, over the dark
> Styx.[27]

THE PIAZZA DI S. IGNAZIO AND THE CAMPO MARZIO

No fewer than eight streets lead out of the Piazza del
Pantheon, and for the unprepared, each can provide some
pleasant surprises. One of these, the Via del Seminario, leads
to what many consider to be Rome's most gracious square, the
Piazza di S. Ignazio. The principal features of this square are
the ponderous front of the seventeenth-century church of S.
Ignazio, and the more delicately worked façades of a cluster of
apartment blocks designed by Raguzzini a century later. The
contrast between the Baroque and the Rococo could not be
more strikingly exemplified.

Although travellers before the twentieth century seem not
to have paid much attention to the Piazza di S. Ignazio, it has
captivated a number of recent sightseers. Elizabeth Bowen in
A Time in Rome (1960), for instance, thought it 'Rome's most
perfect little outdoor drawing room'.[28]

To enter the church of S. Ignazio is to enter a different world. This is the second Jesuit church in Rome, built half a century after the Gesù. Like the earlier church, its architecture is fairly mundane but the decoration is spectacular. The great *trompe l'œil* ceiling fresco of *The Apotheosis of St Ignatius* was painted during the last decade of the seventeenth century, years after the completion of the church itself. Although its subject matter precluded its full appreciation by many visitors, its technical virtuosity and explosive style left nearly everyone spellbound. It was thus with some ambivalence that *Murray's Handbook* informed readers that 'its magnificence is not in the best taste, but it is interesting from its excessive ornament'.[29] Nathaniel Hawthorne, who would have found no mention of S. Ignazio in his friend George Hillard's guidebook, stumbled through on his own. In his *Note-Books* he reports finding

> the church . . . somewhat darkened . . . except the frescos . . . which were very brilliant, and done in so effective a style, that I could not satisfy myself that some of the figures did not actually protrude from the ceiling – in short, that they were not colored bas-reliefs, instead of frescos. No words can express the beautiful effect, in an upholstery point of view, of this kind of decoration.[30]

Both the Piazza di S. Ignazio and the Pantheon are in the *rione*, or quarter, known as Campo Marzio. In antiquity this was the Campus Martius or Field of Mars, but by the late Middle Ages the area had become densely populated and its character has changed very little since. Sean O'Faolain described this neighbourhood which he called 'the oldest living part of Rome' in *A Summer in Italy* (1949):

> Its so-called streets are often mere lanes, narrow, dark, grubby and odorous, sunless in summer, damp in winter, always busy and crowded, a terrible jumble of poverty and wealth, of palaces and garrets, of sophistication and simple virtue, of antiquity and modernism, so that all that most visitors, and I imagine most residents, too, know of it will be a few shopping streets, or their favourite churches which they dig out of the surrounding warrens, or a few favourite restaurants islanded in them.[31]

In the years that have passed since O'Faolain recorded his impressions, the streets have become no wider, brighter, or less congested, but they are less grubby than they used to be. Chic, well-designed shops have proliferated here, the most noticeable of them being *gelaterie* or ice-cream parlours. The good-humoured American food critic Calvin Trillin recently commented on this phenomenon in *Travels with Alice* (1989):

> Particularly around the Pantheon, there are streets in Rome where practically everyone seems to be carrying an ice-cream cone. In Rome there are serious disputes among connoisseurs about the relative merits of the slick Gelateria della Palma and the more traditional Giolitti. Alice was in the position of a chess fanatic who, after years of feeling a bit isolated in Newport Beach, suddenly finds himself in Leningrad.[32]

Notwithstanding the competition from smart newcomers, the venerable Giolitti establishment on the unappetizingly named Via degli Uffizi del Vicario remains in a class by itself. The definitive portrait of this *gelateria* is painted by Barbara Grizzuti Harrison in *Italian Days*:

> Giolitti looks as if it should be the scene of a *thé dansant*. Grandmothers and their small charges are there, and young Romans about whose beauty one can never cease exclaiming, and foreign cruisers and hustlers, and families. . . . You can eat inside – dismiss all notions of an American ice-cream parlor: chandeliers descend from pistachio-colored ceilings; walls are painted blueberry-blue, raspberry, and cream; tables are marble-topped and hold floral bouquets. You can eat outside, where you will become part of the *passeggiata* . . . the streets are narrow, Porsches and Alfa Romeos shriek; the Pantheon rises dark and everlastingly beautiful behind you.[33]

S. Luigi dei Francesi and S. Ivo alla Sapienza

There are literally dozens of churches in this part of Rome, but sightseers making their way towards Piazza Navona will not

want to miss seeing two in particular, S. Luigi dei Francesi and
S. Ivo alla Sapienza. S. Luigi, the French national church in
Rome, is not impressive from the outside and it traditionally
has received few encomiums in the literature of travel.
Stendhal, somewhat uncharacteristically for a Frenchman,
failed to list it among the twenty-two 'most remarkable'
churches in Rome,[34] and Nathaniel Hawthorne, ambling
through the dusky interior, thought it 'a most shamefully
dirty place of worship, the beautiful marble columns looking
dingy, for the want of loving and pious care'.[35] The attractions
of the place, apart perhaps from certain monuments erected to
illustrious Frenchmen, are chiefly found in the painted decoration of two chapels, the second on the right by Domenichino
and the fifth on the left by Caravaggio.

In years past, the Domenichino frescoes narrating scenes
from the life of St Cecilia were viewed with particular favour.
Their classical poise and idealized expressions had an almost
hypnotic effect on nineteenth-century viewers, but rarely are
these the qualities that move today's visitors, who will
probably prefer the dark and dramatic canvases of Caravaggio
in the Contarelli Chapel on the other side of the nave. Eleanor
Clark in *Rome and a Villa* (1952) was among the first non-art
historians to record her appreciation of these now-renowned
masterpieces depicting scenes from the life of St Matthew.
'Caravaggio', she writes,

> remains interesting even through the present excesses of
> rediscovery, with attendant publicizing of his luminism,
> homosexuality, propensity to murder, Trastevere
> models, flights and arrests and sorry death of malaria on
> the beach at Port' Ercole. There is a kind of somnam-
> bulism in all the paintings, round and round an infatua-
> tion with evil . . . [as well as] a powerful sensuality of
> remorse in nearly all of them, calling for more and more
> evil, which may fly in on angels' wings. He borrowed a
> pair of wings from a friend in Rome for a model, but his
> angels are never really held up by theirs; the one holding a
> palm branch toward Saint Matthew is under great gym-
> nastic strain to keep from falling off the edge of a cloud;

another there, over the altar, is a Roman dead-end kid
who has just broken through the wall Cocteau-fashion to
confuse the old saint.[36]

The second church in the neighbourhood that merits special
attention is S. Ivo alla Sapienza, located one block to the south.
Formerly the chapel of the University of Rome, S. Ivo is
Borromini's most unusual and fanciful creation. Early archi-
tectural critics of every nationality found the work of this
architect incomprehensibly bizarre, and sometimes offensive.
Colen Campbell, author of the neo-Palladian manifesto
Vitruvius Britannicus (1715) was genuinely irascible when he
asked his readers 'how wildly Extravagant are the Designs of
Borromini, who has endeavour'd to debauch Mankind with his
odd and chimerical Beauties, where the Parts are without
Proportion, Solids without their true Bearing, Heaps of
Materials without Strength, excessive Ornaments without
Grace, and the whole without Symmetry?'[37]
General travellers simply ignored the little church with the
conspicuous spiral lantern. There is no mention of it in
Murray's Handbook or Hillard's *Six Months in Italy* (1853), nor
for that matter in the widely read *New Picture of Rome* (1818) by
Mariano Vasi or in Augustus Hare's *Walks in Rome* (1871). The
few early sightseers who happened upon Borromini's work
often did not know what to make of it. Edward Wright noted
in his *Observations* (1730) that the architect 'was a little peculiar
in his fancy, but in the main a great master'.[38] Before the
twentieth century, only one American author deigned to
make any reference to S. Ivo, and that was Francis Marion
Crawford, himself a Catholic convert, who in *Ave Roma
Immortalis* (1898) breezily labelled it 'as bad a piece of Barocco
as is to be found in Rome'.[39]
Borromini's irksome personal traits did little to enhance his
early reputation. He dressed in a bizarre fashion, was quarrel-
some, unreliable, and irrationally jealous of the success of his
more gracious rival Bernini. In 1667, in a fit of despair, he
threw himself upon his sword and put an end to his troubles.
His star rose as the twentieth century slowly came to value
genius, imagination, and unfettered creativity. The literary

apogee of his fame probably occurred in the 1960s when in her novel *Birds of America*, Mary McCarthy used his work as a metaphor for what her young male protagonist was looking for in Rome. Fascinated by the 'dear, cracked' architect who was sneered at by rivals, had a strange sense of humour, and ended his life a suicide, the 19-year-old Peter Levi

> got attached to the dainty rhythms of concave and convex that seemed to be the master's 'language' and to the ribbony movement of plaster around windows that reminded him of his mother's boiled frostings as it swirled from her knife onto a birthday cake. . . .[40]

THE PIAZZA NAVONA

One block to the west of S. Ivo lies the Piazza Navona, one of Rome's most attractive squares (Plate 17). It is large but well-hidden, symmetrical yet informal, dramatic yet restful. Its long narrow shape follows that of Domitian's stadium on whose first-century foundations it was erected. Entering the airy piazza from any of the eight narrow streets that lead into it, one experiences, even after repeated visits, the sensation of unanticipated exhilaration. The sudden discovery or rediscovery of such majestic spaces is one of the great dividends of Rome's traditional lack of urban planning.

The American poet Henry Wadsworth Longfellow lived in the piazza during his first visit to Rome in 1828–9. In *Outre-Mer* (1833–5) he describes the view from the apartment of the family with which he was staying:

> Our windows look out upon the square, which circumstance is a source of infinite enjoyment to me. Directly in front, with its fantastic belfries and swelling dome, rises the church of St Agnes; and sitting by the open window, I note the busy scene below, enjoy the cool air of morning and evening, and even feel the freshness of the fountain, as its waters leap in mimic cascades down the side of the rock.[41]

The fountain to which Longfellow refers – one of three in
the square – is Bernini's Fountain of the Four Rivers. Although the association with Bernini was enough to prompt
Murray's Handbook to caution sightseers that 'the figures and
the design of the whole fountain are almost below criticism',[42]
the sheer exuberance of the work seduced almost everyone
who came under its spell. Even the cynical Tobias Smollett
had to admit in his *Travels through France and Italy* (1766)
that he found the fountain 'perhaps the most magnificent in
Europe. . . notwithstanding [the fact that] the piazza is almost
as dirty as West Smithfield, where the cattle are sold in
London'.[43]

'The busy scene' that Longfellow noted beneath his window in the Piazza Navona centred on the outdoor markets
which for centuries had been held there. In 1830, Samuel F. B.
Morse, the inventor and painter, commented in his *Letters and
Journals* that 'the scene here is very amusing; the variety of
wares exposed, and the confusion of noises and tongues, and
now and then a jackass swelling the chorus with his most
exquisite tones'.[44]

Among the items for sale were fish, fruit, vegetables,
clothing, farm equipment, tools, and some lesser *objets d'art*
and antiquities. In 1858 Nathaniel Hawthorne described in his
Note-Books how 'women and men sit with these things for
sale, or carry them about in trays, or on boards on their heads,
crying them with shrill and hard voices. There is a shabby
crowd and much babble'. Like Smollett, Hawthorne also
found the square 'dingy in its general aspect, and very dirty',
but admitted that 'there is more life in it than one sees
elsewhere in Rome'.[45]

In the twentieth century, the produce market was relocated
in the nearby Campo dei Fiori while the dry goods and
(mostly bogus) antiquities have gone to Porta Portese. The
festive aspect of Piazza Navona has, if anything, increased as a
result. It is now a sort of urban park, thronged at any hour of
the day or night with tourists, pavement artists, bicyclists, and
a miscellany of Roman 'types'. The lines of Rome's renowned
vernacular poet of the nineteenth century, Giuseppe
Gioacchino Belli, have never been truer than they are today:

> It's not a square, it's an open field,
> a stage, a fair, a merry time.[46]

The façade of the church of S. Agnese casts its shadow over the centre of the square as proudly as the *scenae frons* of an ancient theatre. Built in the mid-seventeenth century for Innocent X Pamphili, S. Agnese was the creation of four architects, including Borromini and Bernini. Its self-confident, swaggering presence ensured the usual debates in later centuries between those who accepted and those who abhorred the rhetorical promotions of the Baroque papacy. Visitors from Catholic countries like France found it '*admirable*', '*jolie*' and '*très agréable*', while those from other backgrounds frequently pretended it did not exist.

A work of art with a very different flavour is found just outside the south end of the Piazza Navona. This is the Pasquino, the most famous of Rome's 'talking statues'. Its legend is recounted by H. V. Morton:

> At the back of the Palazzo Braschi is the battered fragment of a marble group which once represented Menelaus supporting Patroclus, and has been known for centuries as Pasquino. During the Renaissance, witty and sometimes libelous puns and comments would be found attached to this statue, and were answered by the statue of Marforio, who reclines so plumply on the Capitol. Some popes resented these pasquinades – so-called from a tailor named Pasquino who was believed to be the originator – and rewards were offered to those who had composed them. The bait was rarely taken, but on one occasion a guileless punster went to claim the reward, but was unable to carry it away, for both his hands were cut off. Journalism was a dangerous occupation in Renaissance Rome.[47]

According to Rodolfo Lanciani, author of *New Tales of Old Rome* (1901), the first critical pasquinades appeared in the sixteenth century and were 'mostly the work of inexperienced and silly boys' directed at their university professors.[48] Only later did they become an outlet for anti-papal sentiments such

as the notorious one directed toward Urban VIII Barberini
chiding him for having cannabalized ancient monuments:

> Quod non fecerunt barbari
> fecerunt Barberini.

The tradition continues in the twentieth century. During
the Fascist era the addendum 'Et quod non fecerunt Barberini,
fecit Mussolini' appeared one morning,[49] while even today
some Romans continue to find the hapless statue a convenient
place to air their grievances, either in spray paint or in the
traditional medium of the attached paper memorandum.

Of the several *ristoranti* in the neighbourhood around the
Piazza Navona, Passetto, just to the north of the square on the
Via Zanardelli, can rightly claim the most celebrities among
its former patrons. Those who have inspected the guest book
have found the names of countless film stars and political
figures, but the name of one modern literary giant, William
Faulkner, is absent. Yet in 1954, four years after he won the
Nobel Prize for Literature, Faulkner dined at Passetto while in
Rome for the casting of his screenplay *Land of the Pharaohs*. His
friends Humphrey Bogart and Lauren Bacall were also in
Rome at the time and, according to his biographer, it was in
this restaurant that Bacall asked the alcohol-prone author,

> 'Bill, why do you drink?' Liking the slim, green-eyed
> girl, he answered. 'When I have one martini', he said, 'I
> feel bigger, wiser, taller. When I have a second, I feel
> superlative. When I have more, there's no holding me.'[50]

Faulkner's reaction to Rome was not very different from
that of most tourists on their first visit. 'I like this city,' he
wrote at the time to a young friend, 'it is full of the sound of
water, fountains everywhere, amazing and beautiful – big
things full of marble figures – gods and animals, naked girls
wrestling with horses and swans with tons of water cascading
over them'. To a press correspondent whom he met at a party,
the creator of the fictional Yoknapatawpha County admitted,
'I've fallen in love with Rome, I want to see much more of
it'.[51] One need not be from Oxford, Mississippi to understand
why he felt just as he did.

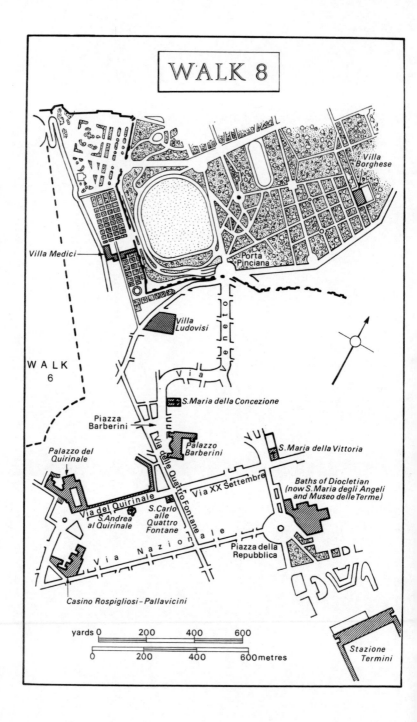

8

EIGHTH WALK

From the Stazione Termini to the Borghese
and Pincian Gardens

THE BATHS OF DIOCLETIAN

Within sight of the Stazione Termini, the newest building in
old Rome, are several remnants of Roman antiquity. The
Servian Wall meanders along one side of the station, but
directly across the field of idle orange buses in the Piazza del
Cinquecento lies a more substantial ancient structure, the
1,500-year-old Baths of Diocletian. The sensation of seeing
this for the first time as one exits from the train station is neatly
evoked in Bernard Malamud's *Pictures of Fidelman* (1969).
The American art student Arthur Fidelman has just arrived
from Naples

> and at the moment, as he stood in front of the . . . station,
> after twenty minutes still absorbed in his first sight of the
> Eternal City, he was conscious of a certain exaltation that
> devolved on him after he had discovered directly across
> the many-vehicled piazza stood the remains of the Baths
> of Diocletian. Fidelman remembered having read that
> Michelangelo had helped in converting the baths into a
> church and convent, the latter ultimately changed into the
> museum that presently was there. 'Imagine,' he mut-
> tered. 'Imagine all that history.'[1]

The Baths of Diocletian were the largest of Rome's public
spas, covering an area of 32 acres and accommodating some

3,000 patrons. It has since been converted, as Fidelman noted, into a church, S. Maria degli Angeli, and a museum, the Museo Nazionale Romano or Museo delle Terme. This museum houses one of the world's finest collections of ancient art. In *Rambles with Anatole France*, the novelist's travelling companion Georges Bölöni (Sándor Kémeri) informs the reader that:

> For weeks we had spent the greater part of the day in the Museo delle Terme. This museum was one of France's favourites. We arrived before it was open and left when everybody had gone. The guards knew us and called our attention to the closing hour when they could not stay any longer. On such occasions France was always much surprised. 'Time flies fast among things of the past', he complained.[2]

France was fortunate to have seen so much when he visited in 1910. In recent years, most of the rooms have without explanation been closed to the public. Nonetheless, one of the most attractive features of this gloomy and exasperating museum, which Elizabeth Bowen suggests is best 'enjoyed on a sleepy, wet afternoon',[3] is its central cloister. The charm of this cloister 'with its warm yellow walls and its travertine colonnades' was captured earlier this century by Olave Potter in *The Colour of Rome* (1909):

> Even in December it is full of flowers – canea and chrysanthemum, rose and iris, heliotrope and purple veronica. Broken statues and columns peep from among the greenery; here the marble bust of a dead Roman is crowned by a spray of tiny red roses which have not realized in this sheltered pleasaunce that winter has come; there some broken amphorae are half hidden in a clump of yuccas. In the heart of the garden where the four paths meet is a lichen-covered fountain almost smothered in waterplants, which never tires of singing to a dying cypress, the only one of all the five planted by the hand of Michelangelo himself, which still stretches its tired old limbs in the sunshine.[4]

The largest chambers of Diocletian's baths are taken up by the sixteenth-century church. It is doubtful that anyone has left a clearer impression of this structure than Nathaniel Hawthorne who in his *Note-Books* of 1858 wrote:

> The exterior of this church has no pretensions to beauty or majesty, or indeed, to architectural merit of any kind, or to any architecture whatever; for it looks like a confused pile of ruined brickwork, with a façade resembling half the inner curve of a large oven. No one would imagine that there was a church under that enormous heap of ancient rubbish. But the door admits you into a circular vestibule, once an apartment of Diocletian's Baths, but now a portion of the nave of the church, and surrounded with monumental busts; and thence you pass into what was the central hall; now with little change, except of detail and ornament, transformed into the body of the church. This space is so lofty, broad, and airy, that the soul forthwith swells out and magnifies itself, for the sake of filling it. It was Michel Angelo who contrived this miracle; and I feel even more grateful to him for rescuing such a noble interior from destruction, than if he had originally built it himself.[5]

The modern Piazza della Repubblica (formerly Piazza dell'Esedra) was built on the foundations of the curved *exedrae* of Diocletian's Baths. The pair of quadrantal *palazzi* that define this circular square date from 1888 and have been likened to a chastened version of the Paris Opera and other works of questionable French taste. The piazza is alive with activity at all hours of the day and night, but it is not the gracious manners of other Roman squares that lure people here. It is rather the fast pace of life, the blur and squeal of speeding taxis, the swiftness with which a gypsy troop can encircle a bewildered tourist, and the meretricious glamour of its central fountain that give the piazza its special personality.

The Via Nazionale will probably always be the 'commercial riot' and 'hell of neon' that Eleanor Clark described in *Rome and a Villa*, but for many, this broad modern avenue that runs from the Piazza della Repubblica to the Piazza Venezia remains the 'real' Rome. In his fictional travelogue *Roman Pictures* (1923), Percy Lubbock adopts an unnamed café on the street as the locus of discovery for his protagonist, Deering. When there, Deering 'entered a company which belonged – he insisted on it – to the *real* Rome, the city unsuspected of our gaping countrymen. His secret was to "live the life of the place", he said; and let there be no mistake, the life of the place is to be found among the shops and tramways of the business quarter, nowhere else'.[6]

When Scott and Zelda Fitzgerald stayed in Rome in the winter of 1924–5, the hotel they chose was the Albergo Quirinale at Via Nazionale, 7. As they were making their way back to the hotel late one evening, Fitzgerald provoked the encounter that years later he described as 'just about the rottenest thing that ever happen in my life'.[7] He got into a drunken brawl with, of all people, a plainclothes policeman. In a travel sketch, 'The High Cost of Maccaroni' (1924–5) and again in *Tender is the Night* (1934), Fitzgerald recounted the unhappy tale. In the sketch, the author confesses that 'what happened had been provided for about fifteen years previously when I took four boxing lessons from Tommy Gibbons'.[8] Just what occurred next is unclear. In 'The High Cost of Maccaroni', the scene ends with the author finally realizing the identity of the man he has knocked to the ground; in *Tender is the Night*, the protagonist Dick Diver 'was dragged through the bloody haze, choking and sobbing, over vague irregular surfaces into some small place where he was dropped upon a stone floor. The men went out, a door clanged, he was alone'.[9]

BERNINI'S ECSTASY OF ST TERESA

No visit to the area round the Piazza della Repubblica would be complete without a detour up the Via Orlando to see Bernini's Cornaro Chapel in S. Maria della Vittoria. 'If one is going to put one's love for the Baroque to the test, the place to go is Santa Maria della Vittoria', observed Barbara Grizzuti Harrison.[10] This small church was once a spare Counter-

Reformation structure, but later embellishments have left it, in the words of Stendhal, looking 'like a boudoir'.[11] Its fame is now almost entirely due to the presence of Bernini's *Ecstasy of St Teresa*, a work that reproduces in stone a vision experienced by the sixteenth-century mystic Teresa of Avila. In her autobiography, Teresa speaks of a very beautiful angel appearing at her side:

> In his hands I saw a great golden spear, and at the iron tip there appeared to be a point of fire. This he plunged into my heart several times so that it penetrated to my entrails. When he pulled it out, I felt that he took them with it, and left me utterly consumed by the great love of God. The pain was so severe that it made me utter several moans. The sweetness caused by this intense pain is so extreme that one cannot possibly wish it to cease, nor is one's soul then content with anything but God. This is not a physical, but a spiritual pain, though the body has some share in it – even a considerable share. So gentle is this wooing which takes place between God and the soul that if anyone thinks I am lying, I pray God in His goodness, to grant him some experience of it.[12]

Bernini himself was an extremely devout Catholic, and there is no sensible reason to doubt that the *Ecstasy of St Teresa* was the product of his sincere effort to give concrete expression to the mysteries of the faith. Yet for many viewers, it was impossible to see Teresa's ecstatic transport in anything more than secular terms. 'I feel within myself, if I may so say, a kind of mental blush', confessed one French cleric of the eighteenth century.[13] 'Certainly the most unfit ornament to place in a Christian church that can be imagined', exclaimed an Englishman of the nineteenth century.[14] The sharpest comments were voiced by the French. Madame Vigée LeBrun found Teresa's expression so 'scandalous [that it] cannot be described',[15] while the President De Brosses simply noted 'if this is Divine Love, I know all about it'.[16]

Post-Revolutionary French visitors were inclined to see the work in a more sympathetic light. Stendhal, in his *Roman Journal* acknowledged the matchless technical perfection of the

work when he asked 'has the Greek chisel produced anything
to equal the head of St Teresa?', while at the same time
addressing the question of the sculpture's expressive content.
Quoting the monk who guided him through the church,
Stendhal added 'it is a great shame that these statues can easily
convey the idea of a profane love'.[17]

To the less judgemental eyes of the twentieth century, the
Ecstasy of St Teresa has become merely one of the great
masterpieces in the history of art. In *Rome and a Villa*, Eleanor
Clark sounded the neutral tone of the modern viewer when
she wrote:

> time was when the piece was considered in dreadful taste
> and there is certainly some amusement in one's liking it
> now, but it is hard not to, when its candor is so engaging,
> it rapture so true to the writings of the mystics, the talent
> so great and all Rome around to cushion the blow. The
> smile of the angel as he poises his golden arrow is one of
> the best smiles in sculpture.[18]

BORROMINI'S S. CARLO AND BERNINI'S S. ANDREA

A short distance down the Via XX Settembre are two churches
that were designed from the ground up by Borromini and
Bernini respectively. Four corner fountains mark the intersection at the Via delle Quattro Fontane. These fountains are
not the most beautiful in Rome and few would probably
disagree with William Dean Howells's assessment that

> No fountain can be quite ugly, but some fountains can be
> quite stupid, like, for instance, those which give its pretty
> name to the Street of the Four Fountains and which
> consist of two extremely plain Virtues and two very dull
> old Rivers, diagonally dozing at each other over their
> urns in niches of its four converging edifices.[19]

Borromini's church of S. Carlo alle Quattro Fontane, or
S. Carlino as it is affectionately called, rises from one corner of
the intersection. In *Roman Mornings* (1956), James Lees-Milne

correctly observed that 'the front of San Carlino has, like much Baroque architecture of an advanced sort, aroused extreme censure and extreme eulogy. It seems as though this particular style must invite the most unbalanced judgements from eclectic and otherwise level-headed critics'.[20]

Even among seventeenth-century Romans, opinion was sharply divided over the merits of this kind of architecture. The patrons of S. Carlo boasted that 'nothing similar with regard to artistic merit, fantasy, excellence, and singularity can be found anywhere in the world', while Filippo Titi's widely read guidebook labelled the work 'bizarre' and G. P. Bellori pronounced Borromini 'a complete ignoramus, the corrupter of architecture, the shame of our century'.[21] The critical fortunes of S. Carlino have continued to fluctuate depending on one's attitude towards tradition and innovation, creative regulation and expressive freedom. Our own age, now so weary of modernist reduction, is by and large attracted by S. Carlo's 'kaleidoscope of whirling line and ornament', as Edith Wharton described it nearly a century ago.[22]

The enthusiasm of the later twentieth century for Baroque music has prompted some viewers to recognize fugue-like cadences in Borromini's design. 'The flow of rhythms, the alternations of concave and convex immediately introduced by the façade, the brightening of a concave space by loose arabesques of stone around oval windows, and the deep portal that balances, in its turn, a convexity of steps' are what make the building 'sing' according to Kate Simon, who concludes her remarks on the church by saying 'if ever there was architecture that suited the definition "frozen music", it is Borromini's.'[23]

Just down the street from S. Carlino is Bernini's contemporary church of S. Andrea al Quirinale. Borromini viewed Bernini as his chief rival, and a comparison between the two small buildings reveals the extent to which they viewed their practices differently. S. Andrea, although built of more lavish coloured marbles, is a calmer, more taciturn building, more 'correct' in classical Vitruvian terms. For those naturally suspicious of the Baroque, it was easy to leave this relatively unassuming little church off their itinerary. Catholic visitors, on the other hand, often found it irresistible. Eighteenth-century Frenchmen seem to have been particularly responsive. The President De Brosses called it 'a miniature masterpiece' and 'one of the three finest works in the city', while the Abbé Richard pronounced it 'le bijou de Rome'.[24]

The most lavish praise for S. Andrea, however, comes from an unexpected source. Undeterred by the omission of the church in popular guidebooks, Nathaniel Hawthorne ventured inside with his wife Sophia one winter evening in 1858. In his *Note-Books* he wrote, 'I have not seen, nor expect to see, anything else so entirely and satisfactorily finished as this small oval church; and I only wish I could pack it in a large box, and send it home'.[25]

THE QUIRINAL HILL

Directly opposite S. Andrea is the Palazzo del Quirinale, a papal palace of the late Renaissance now the residence of the president of Italy. The Quirinal Hill on which it stands is, according to Frances Elliot, 'a respectable and visible eminence, conspicuous from all quarters of the city', while the palace itself 'crowns the hill like a diadem, descending through whole streets in its interminable length. It impresses the imagination from the very simplicity of its architecture, so essentially different from the florid magnificence prevailing at the Vatican'.[26]

Indeed so simple is the exterior of the palace itself that it has been virtually eclipsed in most accounts by the monument that stands in the piazza before its main portal. There, an Egyptian obelisk, colossal ancient sculptures of the Dioscuri, and a great Roman basin have been conjoined to make a fanciful fountain.

The Dioscuri Castor and Pollux were once believed to be the work of Phidias and Praxiteles. Singled out in the medieval pilgrims' guide *Miribilia Urbis Romae*, and praised by Petrarch for their 'ingenium et ars', these over-sized horsemen have rarely gone unnoticed.[27] Percy Shelley arrived in Rome in the winter of 1818, just a few months after the marble basin was added to the existing ensemble. In a letter to Thomas Love

Peacock of 1819, Shelley first described the Trevi and Four
Rivers' fountains, and then added:

> The fountain on the Quirinal, or rather the group formed
> by the statues, obelisk, and the fountain, is, however, the
> most admirable of all . . . a vast basin of prophyry, in the
> midst of which rises a column of the purest water . . .
> collects into itself all the overhanging colours of the sky,
> and breaks them into a thousand prismatic hues and
> graduated shadows – they fall together with its dashing
> water-drops into the outer basin. . . . On each side, on an
> elevated pedestal, stand the statues of Castor and Pollux,
> each in the act of taming his horse. . . . These figures
> combine an irresistible energy with the sublime and
> perfect loveliness supposed to have belonged to their
> divine nature.[28]

One of the most celebrated paintings in Rome, Guido
Reni's fresco of *Aurora*, is located in the Casino Rospigliosi-
Pallavicini, just down the hill on the Via 24 Maggio. 'It
requires a great effort of imagination and intellect for a
present-day viewer to recreate for himself even partially the
effect – emotional and aesthetic – that works by Reni wrought
on his contemporaries', one art historian recently observed.[29]
Those in the past who sought ideal or transcendental beauty
were usually enthralled by the grace of the *Aurora*. Because the
painting did not have a religious subject, it never gave offence
in the way of so many other Baroque works and Jonathan
Richardson spoke for many when, in his 1722 *Account of the
Statues and Pictures in Italy*, he found the picture 'a Gay
Subject. . . . Tis Beautiful, Gracious, and . . . the Heads
Exquisite!'[30] With slight variations, the same sentiments were
expressed by viewers of every nationality right through the
nineteenth century.

Naturally the work was widely reproduced. Nine engravings of it were made before 1900, and on a typical day in
February 1858, Nathaniel Hawthorne reported that 'three or
four [painters] were copying it . . . [while] two other attempted copies [were] leaning against the wall'.[31] With so
much prior exposure, few early visitors were able to view the

work free from roseate preconceptions. Those whose previous acquaintance with the work was in the comfort of their
own drawing room were often surprised to discover that the
Aurora was actually painted on a ceiling. 'Would it were not!'
exclaimed Anna Jameson in her widely read *Diary of an
Ennuyée* (1826), 'for I looked at it till my neck ached, and my
brain turned giddy and sick'.[32] It later became fashionable to
comment on the inadequacy of either the reproduction or the
original, since the two were so frequently compared with one
another.

   But tastes eventually changed and Reni's star plummetted as
Ruskin's notion of 'sincerity' and veristic impressionism came
into favour in the late nineteenth century. By the 1950s
Bernard Berenson would write 'our grandfathers were thrilled
by Guido Reni's ecstatic visages, whose silly emptiness now
rouses our laughter'.[33] Indeed, while the 1985 edition of the
Blue Guide to Rome continues to make the claim that the
Aurora is 'a work remarkable in Rome for its classical restraint
and colouring', the 1989 edition dispenses with even that faint
praise, saying only that 'it was greatly admired by travellers to
Rome in the nineteenth century'.[34] Nowadays the *Aurora* can
only be seen on the first day of every month, for two hours in
the morning, and two in the afternoon. It does not attract large
crowds and to be among the few that seek it out is to be
reminded of the fickleness of taste in every period.

THE PALAZZO BARBERINI

One searches in vain at the intersection of the Quattro Fontane
for any sign of the house in which John Milton is said to have
resided during his brief sojourn in the autumn of 1638. Not
only is the exact building in which he stayed unknown but, as
Laurence Hutton in *Literary Landmarks of Rome* (1897) notes:

   unfortunately he left no record of his impressions here, or
   of what he did or saw. He is perhaps the only Man of
   Letters who ever visited the Eternal City without telling,
   in prose, to the world what he thought about it; and his

pictures of Rome written in *Paradise Regained* might have
been the work of a man who had never seen Rome at all.[35]

As one turns down the Via delle Quattro Fontane towards
the Piazza Barberini, the rakish façade of the Palazzo Barberini
is soon on one's right. The family palace of Pope Urban VIII
(1623–44), this handsome structure is attributable in varying
shares to Bernini, Borromini, and Carlo Maderno, but its
literary fame is based more on the collections it houses and the
personalities who frequented it in later periods.

William Wetmore Story, the American author and sculptor,
was its most distinguished resident, and he lived in the *palazzo*
for most of the second half of the nineteenth century. Story
played host in those years to virtually every visitor to Rome
with an interest in literature or the arts. In 1903, Henry James
published *William Wetmore Story and his Friends*, a two-volume
biography recounting the life and times of this now mostly
forgotten figure. Among its most charming recollections is
that of a children's party the Storys gave in 1854. Hans
Christian Andersen began by reading aloud from *The Ugly
Duckling* and Robert Browning followed with the *Pied Piper*,
which in turn 'led to the formation of a grand march through
the spacious Barberini apartment, with Story doing his best on
a flute in default of bagpipes'.[36] But James's book was also, he
admits, partly the tale of the 'possession of Europe in the
American consciousness', a piece of cultural baggage that
Story carried about 'as the Mohammedan pilgrim carries his
carpet for prayer', and partly the evocation of the Palazzo
Barberini as the very symbol of 'the grand style . . . the old
social appearances, old manners, figures, features, the delightful, dreadful old conception of conduct, of life'.[37] By the latter
part of his life, after the political and social transformation
brought about by the Risorgimento, Story had become as
much of an anachronism as the patrician palace in which he
chose to live.

In another context and an altogether different medium, the
Palazzo Barberini played a comparable role in William Wyler's
1953 film *Roman Holiday*. Audrey Hepburn is improbably cast
as a head of state who, in the course of a brief visit to Rome

conducts a clandestine relationship with Gregory Peck, an American journalist. The Barberini palace serves as the embassy in which she stays, but its 'grand style' is now interpreted as being grimly stultifying and symbolic of the formal restraints imposed on a figurehead in what American audiences would have viewed as an anachronistically stratified society.

The collections of the Palazzo Barberini (now the Galleria Nazionale d'Arte Antica) contain many works of artistic merit, but two paintings in particular captured the imagination of earlier viewers. The first was the so-called portrait of Beatrice Cenci, long-believed to be the work of Guido Reni. Now moved across town to another branch of the same museum, it was aptly described not long ago by Stuart Curran, a literary critic:

> The portrait that is not by Guido Reni of a girl who is not Beatrice Cenci, which legend has it was rendered in prison shortly before her execution for parricide, today hangs modestly in the Palazzo Corsini among the cast-offs of Rome's more august museums. Its ascription disproved by modern scholars, its soft tones too decadent for modern taste, the soulful portrait . . . has been effectively retired from the tourist circuit. A century ago it held a place of honor in the grand gallery of the Palazzo Barberini, and the grand tour sidled by in dutiful homage. Beatrice Cenci was one of the most famous attractions of Rome; reproduced ubiquitously, the portrait was hardly less compelling to visitors than the Bernini fountains or the Sistine frescoes. Dickens hung it reverently among his *Pictures from Italy*; Hawthorne, praising it as 'the saddest picture ever painted or conceived', made it central to the seventh chapter of *The Marble Faun*; and Melville appeared haunted by 'that sweetest, most touching, but most awful of all feminine heads'.[38]

Stendhal and Shelley were the most ambitious of those who retold the sixteenth-century tale of a monstrous father whose unsolved murder led to the torture and execution of his wife, son, and daughter. Shelley's five-act drama *The Cenci* (1819),

said by Swinburne to be the greatest blank verse tragedy since
Shakespeare, is a romantic tribute to a girl he found to be the
very symbol of the human spirit in revolt against all that is
unjust or oppressive. Scrutinizing the 'Reni' portrait, Shelley
concluded in his preface that 'in the whole mien there is a
simplicity and dignity which united with her exquisite
loveliness and deep sorrow are inexpressibly pathetic'.[39]

The second painting in the Barberini palace that mesmerized yesterday's museum-goers was likewise a portrait of
a young woman, and this carried an equally dubious attribu-
tion to Raphael. *La Fornarina* was reportedly Raphael's mistress, but as no tragic legends were attached to their
relationship, viewers were free to see her for just what she
was, a bare-bosomed *sensualista* whose dark eyes make no
effort to avert one's own. Prudish individuals like George
Hillard naturally felt compelled to moralize on what they saw.
In *Six Months in Italy* (1853) he noted:

> Some writer has remarked, that a man in choosing his
> wife should ask himself what are her resources for a rainy
> day in the country. Judging from her countenance, the
> Fornarina would seem to be very indifferently supplied
> with such capacities and accomplishments; in short, an
> artist's model, a sensual toy, whose power over an intel-
> lectual man, if she had any, would be yielded to with
> something like self-contempt.[40]

But there was no denying the picture's immense popularity.
In the very year that Hillard's book was simultaneously published in Boston and London, a rambunctious young American named Theodore Witmer published *Wild Oats, Sown
Abroad* in Philadelphia. In the footsteps of countless (male)
Grand Tourists of the past, Witmer stood in front of the work
and found the girl

> a vain, passionate-looking creature, but deuced attractive
> withal. She has the real Italian intensity of gaze which
> challenges and yet retreats – which woos and yet com-
> mands. There is no dallying about that face; she will
> brook no denial – you must either proceed to extremities,
> or not commence at all; no Platonic warfare there.[41]

The Piazza Barberini and the Via Veneto

The Piazza Barberini is not one of Rome's prettiest or most charming squares, but its literary history is second only to that of the Piazza di Spagna. Among the many authors who resided in the square were Louisa May Alcott, Hans Christian Andersen, Margaret Fuller, and Nathaniel Hawthorne, while James Fenimore Cooper and Henry Wadsworth Longfellow stayed on the contiguous Via S. Nicola da Tolentino and Nikolai Gogol and Percy Shelley, like Franz Liszt and G. B. Piranesi, lived on the Via Sistina. A portion of one major literary work, Friedrich Nietzsche's *Also Spracht Zarathustra* (1883–5) was perhaps even inspired by the ambience of the piazza. In his autobiography *Ecce Homo* (1888), Nietzsche informs us that 'in a chamber high above the Piazza from which one obtained a general view of Rome, and could hear the fountains plashing far below, the loneliest of all songs was composed – "The Night-Song"'.[42]

The fountain to which Nietzsche alludes is Bernini's Fountain of the Triton. Exceptionally for a work by him, this modest sculpture has been almost universally praised. Indeed it would seem hard to dislike a work that Andersen described in 1840–1 as 'a massive stone Triton, blowing with full cheeks into a conch-shell, so that the water-jet spurts up high into the sunshine and plays out like a prism with all the colours of the rainbow'.[43]

Robert Browning, among others, was particularly struck by the appearance of the fountain in the off-season. In his epic poem *The Ring and the Book* (1868–9), he portrays it in the chill of winter:

> O' the Barberini by the Capuchins;
> Where the Old Triton, at his fountain-sport,
> Bernini's creature plated to the paps,
> Puffs up steel sleet which breaks to diamond dust,
> A spray of sparkles snorted from his conch,
> High over the caritellas, out o' the way
> O' the motley merchandizing multitude.[44]

A very different kind of experience awaits one in the Capuchin church of S. Maria della Concezione, just a few steps up the Via Veneto. Enthusiasts of Guido Reni have always delighted in his elegant portrayal of *St Michael Slaying the Devil* in an interior chapel, but the most remarkable aspect of this Capuchin church is the cemetery in its crypt, described in a recent popular guidebook as 'Rome's most ghoulish chamber of horrors'.[45]

To be taken at the age of six to visit this place is not a pleasant prospect, but that is just what happened to the narrator in Hans Christian Andersen's novel *The Improvisatore* (1833). Led by his mother's confessor, the lad later recalls that:

We descended, and now I saw round me skulls upon skulls, so placed one upon another that they formed walls, and therewith several chapels. In these were regular niches, in which were seated perfect skeletons of the most distinguished of the monks, enveloped in their brown cowls, and with a breviary or a withered bunch of flowers in their hands. Altars, chandeliers, and ornaments were made of shoulder-bones and vertebrae, with bas-reliefs of human joints, horrible and tasteless as the whole idea.

I clung fast to the monk, who whispered a prayer, and then said to me –

'Here also I shall some time sleep; wilt thou thus visit me?'[46]

In *The Marble Faun* (1860), Nathaniel Hawthorne devotes an entire chapter to the crypt, but leaves the reader in no doubt as to what he thinks of it himself:

There is no possibility of describing how ugly and grotesque is the effect, combined with a certain artistic merit, nor how much perverted ingenuity has been shown in this queer way, nor what a multitude of dead monks, through how many hundred years must have contributed their bony framework to build up these great arches of mortality.[47]

The Via Veneto, the most opulent of Rome's boulevards, was opened only in 1886 as a thoroughfare running through a newly developed residential quarter. The posh hotels, restaurants, and nightclubs of the area have always attracted the rich and famous, but the real Golden Age occurred in the early 1960s after Federico Fellini made it the setting for much of *La dolce vita* (1960). In a 1962 essay entitled 'Via Veneto: Dolce Vita', Fellini discussed the part he and his film played in shaping the street's glamorous new identity:

> I know that since *La dolce vita* my name has been insistently linked with it and with the more or less smart nightlife that goes on there, with the lovely women and talented men who see the small hours in at the café tables . . .
>
> The truth is that, in response to *La dolce vita*, Via Veneto has transformed itself and has made a violent effort to come up to the image I gave it in the film. Photographers have multiplied on every corner, muckraking and gossip have become the order of the day, and starlets looking for publicity have started appearing there in nightdresses or riding into cafés on horseback.[48]

But much of the glamour has worn off in recent years, and an accurate portrait of the Via Veneto in the 1980s is painted by Paul Hofmann in *Rome, the Sweet Tempestuous Life* (1982). In the chapter entitled 'Dolce Vita, Good-Bye', Hofmann wrote:

> The street that Fellini glamorized has become tawdry, lined with travel bureaus, airline offices, a hamburger eatery, stores selling overpriced shoes and apparel, a double procession of neon signs, and café terraces with South Seas decor. The boulevard is populated with tourists, cabdrivers, high-class streetwalkers, touts for nightclubs, news vendors, pimps, mafiosi, and plainclothes policemen. Romans stay away from it if they can, especially after dark.
>
> Yet Fellini's version of the Via Veneto remains in people's minds. . . . No single film has done so much as *La dolce vita* for fixing the image of a city, even on the

mental screens of persons who have seen neither the movie nor Rome.[49]

The Via Veneto and its expensive modern environs were built on the grounds of the Villa Ludovisi, a *vigna* which itself occupied the site of the ancient villas of Sallust and Luculus. Henry James strolled through the Ludovisi park in 1873 and thought there was 'nothing so blissfully *right* in Rome, nothing more consummately consecrated to style'.[50] The main villa and a small part of the gardens survived the urban development of the 1880s and can, with special permission, still be seen today. The highlight of the tour is no longer its superb but now dispersed collection of antique sculpture, but the spectacular ceiling fresco of *Aurora* by Guercino. Painted seven years after the *Aurora* in the Casino Rospigliosi, this lively and illusionistic Baroque work has always, and rightly, been compared with Reni's more refined and classical composition. Stendhal captured the visual experience of Guercino's dramatic masterpiece in *A Roman Journal*.

This morning we revisited the Villa Ludovisi; we are more than ever charmed by Guercino's frescoes; it is a sudden passion, which in the case of one of our lady friends amounts to exaltation. It is somewhat like love at first sight. An instant reveals to you what your heart had needed for a long time without recognizing it. She was very partial to the delicacy of Guido's women, and suddenly she worships Guercino who is quite the opposite!

There is a whole system of painting to be discussed here. Is it better to be stingy of light, like Guercino, Rembrandt, Leonardo da Vinci, Correggio, or to be lavish with it like Guido?[51]

THE BORGHESE AND PINCIAN GARDENS

The glittery ambience of the Via Veneto ends abruptly at the Porta Pinciana, the fortified gateway that leads almost magically into the serene world of the Borghese Gardens. Now a

public park, the Borghese Villa and Gardens were laid out by
Cardinal Scipione Borghese, nephew of Paul V, in the early
years of the seventeenth century. They have been a popular
tourist attraction ever since and many a written account of a
trip to Rome recalls the pleasure its author took in strolling
through the enchanted setting. In *The Voyage of Italy* (1670),
Richard Lassels gives a list of the attractions:

> here you have store of Walkes, both open and close, fish
> ponds, vast cages for birds, thickets of trees, store of
> fountaines, a park of deere, a world of fruit trees, statues
> of all sizes, banqueting places, grottos, wetting sports,
> and a stately palace adorned with so many rare statues and
> pictures.[52]

For many tourists, the Gardens' appeal lay in the respite
they offered from the exhausting rounds of visits to museums
and monuments. Rainer Maria Rilke obviously felt that way
when he reminisced later in his life about his earliest days in
Rome. 'To us', he recalled in a letter to a friend, 'the Borghese
Gardens were a familiar place of refuge . . . and we had need of
a retreat, as the museums especially, with their many
wretched statues, made us desolate'.[53]

The American critic Edmund Wilson put a finer point to
this theme when in *Europe without Baedeker* (1947) he observed
that:

> Here one always finds an atmosphere of gaiety, of leaf-
> age, of light bright color . . . and enchanting with a
> freedom and felicity that are characteristic only of Rome –
> all a little not precisely tinselly, not precisely flimsy, but
> slightly both tempting and teasing the foreigner by a
> careless disregard of plan, a cheerful indifference to pur-
> pose, that, nevertheless, acquire a certain insolence from
> blooming among the monuments of so much solid civic
> building, so much noble and luxurious beauty. With all
> this behind them, these immense rambling grounds
> can afford to lack foundation, be perishable – like
> D'Annunzio's *Elegie Romane* and Respighi's *Fontane di
> Roma*.[54]

Other discourses on the Borghese Gardens invite comparisons with the gardens of England and France or play on its reputation as a trysting spot for romantically inclined couples of every imaginable type. In Gore Vidal's early novel *The Judgement of Paris* (1952), Phillip Warren arranges to meet Regina Durham in the Gardens, 'for both were a little shy and he hesitated about inviting her up to his [hotel] room: he was not yet free of that American fear of desk clerks which has rendered the great game so depressing in his own country'.[55]

If Phillip and Regina's rendezvous was of an unremarkably common sort, what surely must be the most unusual romance to ever blossom in the park occurred during a festival held there in 1779. In his *Memoirs*, the painter Thomas Jones speaks of another English artist, John James Ruby.

> It was at these festive sports that poor *Rouby* lost his heart to a little Roman gipsey, who every Afternoon mounted one of the Chairs of the horizontal Wheel – Rouby constantly took his Station at a Spot where he could completely command a full view of her various attitudes in the Act of throwing her javelin, & every time his Dulcinea came round, cried out in Extacy – O che bella, quanto bella, quanto graziosa!!! a short time afterward with the Consent & Approbation of his Patron Mr Hackaert, he turn'd Roman Catholic and married her – and it was talked of in Rome as a match equaly prudent on the One hand as it was accomodating on the Other.[56]

The Villa Borghese itself was modelled after villas of ancient Rome, and Cardinal Borghese used it to house his extensive collection of classical sculpture. Centuries later, as a public museum, it continues to do so. In *A Letter from Italy* (1701) Joseph Addison described the timeless ambience:

> In solemn silence a majestic band
> Heroes & Gods & Roman consuls stand
> Stern Tyrants whom their cruelities renown
> And Emperors in parian marble frown.
> While the bright dames to whom they humbly sued
> Still shew the charms that their proud hearts subdued.[57]

The original collection also contained 'modern' works by
Bernini, augmented in later years by sculpture and paintings
culled from other members of the Borghese family. Since the
early nineteenth century, the most eye-catching sculpture in
the villa has been Antonio Canova's 1805 portrait of Pauline
Borghese, the sister of Napoleon, reclining nude on an Empire
couch in the pose of Venus Victrix. That this figure is both
coolly Neo-Classical in style but, less ideally, the portrait of a
living person, virtually guaranteed ambivalent appraisals
through the ages. The reputation of Pauline herself did
nothing to suppress the murmurs of lurid gossip. In a much
repeated anecdote, one prudish lady is supposed to have said
reproachfully to Pauline, 'But you must surely feel uncomfortable, having to pose in the nude?' To which Pauline
replied, with an angelic smile, 'Not at all, Canova's studio is
adequately heated'.[58]

Twentieth-century viewers of Canova's sculpture surely
see it differently from those in the past. In *A Traveller in Rome*
(1957), H. V. Morton encounters a young Italian at a luncheon
party who 'argued that modern women have an infinitely
higher standard of beauty than women born before the age of
cinema and cheap cosmetics, and drew a sad picture of Pauline
passing unnoticed today among the crowds on the Lido'.[59]

To the west of the Borghese Gardens lie the gardens of the
Pincio and the Villa Medici. The latter has been the home of
the French Academy in Rome since 1803 and has housed
legions of Prix de Rome winners from Ingres to Debussy.
Although its grounds are no longer open to the public, they
are little changed from the time Henry James described them
so beautifully in 'From a Roman Note-Book' (1873). This, he
wrote, is

> perhaps the most enchanting place in Rome. The part of
> the garden called the Boschetto has an incredible, imposs-
> ible charm; an upper terrace, behind locked gates,
> covered with a little dusky forest of evergreen oaks. Such
> a dim light of a fabled, haunted place, such a soft suffusion
> of tender grey-green tones, such a company of gnarled
> and twisted little miniature trunks – dwarfs playing with

each other at being giants – and such a shower of golden
sparkles drifting in from the vivid west![60]

The Pincian Gardens, laid out by Giuseppe Valadier in
1809–14, offer the perfect picture-postcard view of the city
stretching out to the 'vivid west'. A century ago, Pius IX,
accompanied by his cardinals, enjoyed his *passeggiata* here
every afternoon in a carriage drawn by white mules, and
countless painters and photographers have rendered the perspective under every atmospheric condition and at every time
of day. But among literary impressions of the spot, there is
none more picturesque than that evoked by Emile Zola in
Rome. After first describing the varying cloud formations
that can be seen at dusk, sometimes 'sanguineous . . . sometimes a rosy mist . . . sometimes a triumphal cortège of gold
and purple cloud chariots', Zola describes one evening in
particular when

> the sublime spectacle presented itself to Pierre with a
> calm, blinding, desperate grandeur. At first, just above
> the dome of St Peter's, the sun, descending in a spotless,
> deeply limpid sky, proved yet so resplendent that one's
> eyes could not face its brightness. And in this resplen-
> dency the dome seemed to be incandescent, you would
> have said a dome of liquid silver. . . . Then, as the sun
> was by degrees inclined, it lost some of its blaze, and one
> could look; and soon afterwards sinking with majestic
> slowness it disappeared behind the dome, which showed
> forth darkly blue, while the orb, now entirely hidden, set
> an aureola around it, a glory like a crown of flaming rays.

Zola's description continues for several more lines until
'finally . . . the glow of the heavens departed, and nothing
remained but the vague, fading roundness of the dome of St
Peter's amidst the all-invading night'.[61]

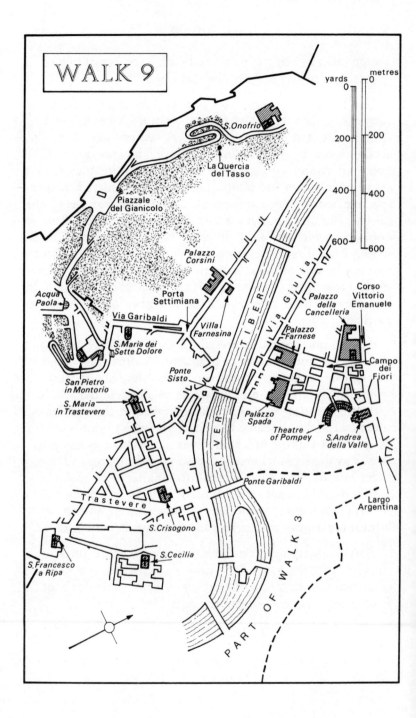

WALK 9

yards   metres
0   0

200   200

400   400

600   600

S. Onofrio

La Quercia
del Tasso

Piazzale
del Gianicolo

Palazzo
Corsini

Acqua
Paola

Porta
Settimiana

TIBER

Via Giulia

Palazzo
della
Cancelleria

Corso
Vittorio
Emanuele

Via Garibaldi

Villa
Farnesina

Palazzo
Farnese

S. Maria dei
Sette Dolore

Campo
dei
Fiori

San Pietro
in Montorio

Ponte
Sisto

S. Maria
in Trastevere

RIVER

Palazzo
Spada

Theatre
of Pompey

S. Andrea
della Valle

Ponte Garibaldi

Trastevere

Largo
Argentina

S. Crisogono

PART OF WALK 3

S. Francesco
a Ripa

S. Cecilia

9

NINTH WALK

From the Largo Argentina through Trastevere to the Janiculum Hill

THE CORSO VITTORIO EMANUELE

From the Largo Argentina, the most direct route to Trastevere is to walk or ride a bus down the charmless and commercial Via Arenula and cross the river on the modern Ponte Garibaldi. However, a more interesting and adventurous route can be taken by walking westwards a short distance along the Corso Vittorio Emanuele before turning off to explore an older quarter of the city and crossing the Tiber at Ponte Sisto.

The Corso Vittorio, like the Via Nazionale, was built in the 1870s as a main artery to channel the increased flow of traffic in the new capital city. Both streets have been decried ever since for introducing the ills of modern urban life to what many still consider an amiable small town atmosphere. The chief complaint naturally has been the traffic, with its relentless din echoing in the canyons of the tall buildings that tightly skirt the roadway. By 1930 there were already about 30,000 motor vehicles in the city and Mussolini himself became concerned about the noise they produced. His solution for dampening the sound was, paradoxically, to increase the number of cars. In a speech of 1932 the Duce asserted that with more vehicles in the streets 'all must channel themselves one after the other, and then there will no longer be any motive for annoying the public with useless honking'.[1]

Mussolini clearly misjudged the Italian character. A more astute appraisal was offered two years later by an Englishman, Philip Gibbs, who wrote in his *European Journey* (1934):

> Rome is the noisiest capital in Europe. The Italians love noise. It seems to give them an exhilaration of spirit. It is their way of expression, vitality, dynamic purpose, and the joy of life. The motorcar has given them an easy means of indulging in this form of self-expression, and they make full use of it. Their motor horns have a strident and ear-piercing timbre not possessed by any other make of horn in any other country.[2]

The Corso Vittorio is not an ugly street, but its narrow pavements are not inviting to pedestrians in search of the perfect *passeggiata*. In *Italy Builds* (1955), George Kidder Smith was only being realistic when he suggested that

> This handsome avenue in Rome realizes its optimum impression at a speed of from twenty to thirty miles per hour. Its sinuous pulsating quality, highlighted by tri-angles of trees and glimpses of fine buildings, at this speed reaches its apogée, while to stroll down it afoot is guaranteed to produce ennui.[3]

The large church on the left is S. Andrea della Valle, built by the Theatine Order early in the Baroque period to rival the Jesuits' nearby Gesù and the Oratorians' Chiesa Nuova farther down the street. Like other Counter-Reformation churches, S. Andrea has an oversize façade that loudly proclaims the spiritual riches to be found within. In the minds of some non-believers, however, sumptuous structures like this were as renowned for providing sanctuary to criminals as they were for inducing Christian piety. 'Most of the churches in Italy are refuges for rogues', the English anecdotist Joseph Spence wrote to his mother in 1732. In front of one he visited were 'eight or ten idle fellows lying on the grass, some of which we soon learned were robbers, but the greater part murderers'.[4] In Puccini's opera *Tosca* (1900), Angelotti's crime was only

political, but having escaped from prison he made straight for
S. Andrea della Valle where the first act of the tragic tale is set.
This indeed is the only church in which an Italian opera is set,
and for some that gives S. Andrea an aura as least as scintillat-
ing as that conferred by Domenichino's frescoes depicting
scenes from the life of St Andrew on the tribune vault and
pendentives. 'There are days when it seems to me that painting
can go no further', was the way that Stendhal remembered
these works in his *Roman Journal* (1828).[5]

THE THEATRE OF POMPEY AND THE CAMPO DEI FIORI

The Theatre of Pompey once stood just behind and to the right
of S. Andrea della Valle, but only the outline of its vast
auditorium remains. A model of conspicuous consumption in
its time, the theatre's inaugural celebrations lasted five days
and included, among other things, the slaughter of five hundred lions and eighteen elephants. Some years later, in AD 66,
Nero had the entire structure – which held 40,000 people –
covered with gold to impress King Tiridates of Armenia on
the one day he came to see it. But the most dramatic per-
formance held in this once-magnificent and now forgotten
theatre complex occurred on 15 March 44 BC. It was on that
day that Julius Caesar was murdered in an attached senate
chamber. After muttering the lines now known to every
schoolchild, 'Et tu, Brute?', the legendary Roman, according
to Shakespeare

> . . . Then burst his mighty heart,
> And, in his mantle muffling up his face,
> Even at the base of Pompey's statue,
> Which all the while ran blood, great Caesar fell.[6]

Connoisseurs of public murder need only stroll to the
nearby Campo dei Fiori to witness another infamous execution site. There a lofty statue of the brooding Giordano Bruno
reminds visitors of the approximate spot where the 'impeni-
tent, tenacious, and obstinate' church reformer and specu-
lative thinker was burned for heresy in February 1600. The

statue was only erected, of course, after papal rule came to an end in Rome and the square was transformed into a public market-place in 1869. The accounts of early travellers who witnessed capital punishment as public entertainment are not hard to find. Lord Byron's reaction to a triple execution he attended in 1817 was fairly typical. In a letter to his friend and publisher John Murray, the poet admits that:

> The first [beheading] turned me quite hot and thirsty, and made me shake so that I could hardly hold the opera-glass (I was close, but determined to see, as one should see everything, once, with attention); the second and third (which shows how dreadfully soon things grow indifferent), I am ashamed to say, had no effect on me as a horror, though I would have saved them if I could.[7]

The name Campo dei Fiori means 'Field of Flowers', and every day but Sunday this once grim piazza functions as an outdoor produce market. With the incongruously sombre figure of Giordano Bruno gazing down upon it, the square is alive with colour and movement. In *The Colour of Rome* (1909), Olave Potter remarks:

> A gayer scene is not imaginable. The sunlight filters between a forest of enormous white umbrellas on to the brilliant fruits and flowers piled up in their shade; and glitters on the silver fish still lying in the round tubs in which they were brought to the market. . . . The women are as gay as their own wares, with their full swinging skirts bunched up on their hips, and their velvet stays, and brilliant flowered kerchiefs. There are all sorts and conditions of attire – here you see an old woman with a face as wrinkled as a walnut, wearing blue stays over a pink bodice, and a bright scarlet cloth on her head; there a girl, as beautiful as a Madonna, with a *tovaglietta* [headcloth] on her glossy hair, and red stays over a St Anna green bodice.[8]

Foreign visitors have often been surprised by the kind of food offered for sale in Italian markets. In Rome in the 1660s,

the English naturalist John Ray frequented the market-place
and was astonished to find for sale

> such birds as in England no man touches, *viz*. kites,
> buzzards, spar-hawks, kestrels, jayes, magpies, and
> woodpeckers. Nothing more commonly sold and eaten
> here in Italy, than coots and stares. They spare not the
> least and most innocent birds, which we account scarce
> worth the dressing, much less powder and shot, v.g.
> robin red-breasts, finches of all kinds, titmice, wagtails,
> wrens etc.[9]

Browsing round other food shops, Ray was even more
puzzled by another staple of the Roman diet that he had not
seen before:

> Paste made into strings like pack-thread or thongs of
> whit-leather (which if greater they call maccaroni, if
> lesser vermecelli) they cut in pieces and put in their pots
> . . . these boil'd and oil'd with a little cheese scraped upon
> them they eat as we do buttered wheat or rice. The
> making of these is a trade and mystery; and in every great
> town you shall see several shops of them.[10]

THREE RENAISSANCE PALACES

The immediate environs of Campo dei Fiori abound with
stately Renaissance *palazzi*. In 'Italy Revisited' (1877), Henry
James pondered the genre in the most general terms:

> We laugh at Italian 'palaces', at their peeling paint, their
> nudity, their dreariness; but they have the great palatial
> quality – elevation and extent. They make of smaller
> things the apparent abode of pigmies; they round their
> great arches and interspace their huge windows with a
> proud indifference to the cost of materials. . . . If the
> Italians at bottom despise the rest of mankind and regard
> them as barbarians, disinherited of the tradition of form,
> the idea proceeds largely, no doubt, from our living in
> comparative mole-hills. They alone were really to build
> their civilisation.[11]

The grandest of the nearby *palazzi* is the Cancelleria, located just to the north of the Campo. Georgina Masson, in her *Companion Guide to Rome* (1965), praises its 'delicately wrought façade [which] in the golden light of a fine Roman afternoon resembles some ancient casket of mellowed ivory, hoarding as a treasure the most beautiful courtyard in Rome'. Masson also relates the oft-told tale of how the palace came to be built:

> The heraldic stone roses above the windows of the *piano nobile* indicate that the palace was built for Raffaele Riario, nephew of Sixtus IV (1471–84). If ever there was a monument to nepotism surely it is this. The famous 60,000 scudi which went to its building were won in a night's gambling from another papal nephew, Franceschetto Cibo, whose uncle was to become Pope Innocent VIII (1484–92). Whatever the sober-sides of fifteenth-century Rome may have thought of the matter, we are bound to admit that no one who has broken the bank at Monte Carlo has ever left the rest of the world so much richer in beauty.[12]

Over the centuries the Cancelleria has also achieved a dubious notoriety for its role in housing the apostolic tribunal charged with the dissolution and annulment of marriages. William Murray, in a chapter devoted to the subject in his book *Italy: The Fatal Gift* (1982) notes that:

> The court sits in an enormous, appropriately gloomy medieval *palazzo* called the Cancelleria, which, like apparently every other building owned by the Vatican in Old Rome, seems to be unequipped with electricity, for it never shows a light burning. Inside the Cancelleria, the Rota judges weigh the merits of the petitions . . . which have already been scrutinized and passed on by one of the Church's eighteen lower regional courts. . . . The process historically has been glacially slow (a matter of years), costly (as high as twenty thousand dollars), and never less than humiliating to the petitioning parties, even when the proceedings, as often happens, dip refreshingly into areas of low comedy and farce.[13]

The Palazzo Farnese is located one block to the south in a broad square of the same name. Cardinal Alessandro Farnese originally commissioned a more modest building, but after being elected to the papacy in 1534, he enlarged the structure to its present blockbuster proportions. Hippolyte Taine described this imposing residence in *Italy, Rome and Naples* (1868):

> Alone in the middle of a dark square, rises the enormous palace, lofty and massive, like a fortress capable of giving and receiving the heaviest ordinance. It belongs to the grand era; its architects, San Gallo, Michael Angelo and Vignolles [sic] . . . have stamped upon it the veritable Renaissance character, that of virile energy. It is indeed akin to the torsoes of Michael Angelo; you feel in it the inspiration of the great pagan epoch, the age of tragic passions and of unimpaired energies that foreign dominion and the catholic restoration were about to weaken and degrade.[14]

A few years after Taine made his comments, the palace was turned over to the French government for their embassy. French tourists may thereafter have felt differently about the building, but even their responses are rarely affectionate. In Zola's *Rome* (1896), Pierre stands and ruminates before the structure:

> Ah! that colossal, sumptuous, deadly dwelling, with its vast court whose porticus is so dark and damp, its giant staircase with low steps, its endless corridors, its immense galleries and halls. All was sovereign pomp blended with death. An icy, penetrating chill fell from the walls.[15]

Opera fans may recall that the second act of *Tosca* is set in Scarpia's apartment in the Palazzo Farnese, an appropriate setting for the tragedy that ensues. But even Zola had to admit that the palace did have its attractions. In the same paragraph that begins so lugubriously, he goes on to add:

> The only part of the building which was at all lively and pleasant was the first storey, overlooking the Tiber,

which the ambassador himself occupied. From the gallery there, containing the famous frescoes of Annibale Carracci, one can see the Janiculum, the Corsini gardens, and the Acqua Paola above San Pietro in Montorio.

For those enthralled with Bolognese classicism, the Carracci Gallery (now closed to the public) is the very *urtext* of the genre in Rome. Early connoisseurs like the eighteenth-century portrait painter and critic Jonathan Richardson proclaimed that the gallery possessed

> a Copious, and Rich, a Solid, and Judicious way of Thinking, Strong, and Just Expressions, a Colouring between the Gravity of Rafaelle, and the Gaiety of Guido, and inclining to that of Correggio . . . the nobile Attitudes, and Contours of the Antique, and the Roman Schools somewhat reduc'd towards Common Nature, but very Great, and Open. . . . In a Word all that . . . can be Wish'd for in Painting is here to be found.[16]

Scholarly types like Richardson were not the only ones to be moved by the sight of the frescoes with their frisky depictions of Ovidian love scenes. Florence Nightingale and her companions gazed up at the ceiling in 1847 'and dislocated our spines at the résumé of all Mythology, but I think, in the midst of that roaring, gushing, tide of physical enjoyment, the glimpses of higher life in the melancholy of the faces . . . is very touching'.[17]

Another major attraction of the palace was the Hellenistic sculpture known as the Farnese Hercules. This was described by Goethe in 1787, the year the original was transported to Naples and a copy put in its place, as 'one of the most perfect works of antiquity'.[18] John Moore, the Scottish physician and author of *A View of Society and Manners in Italy* (1781) wrote of the effect the gigantic statue had on some viewers of his day:

> I am told that the women in particular find something unsatisfactory, and even odious, in this figure; which, however majestic, is deficient in the charms most agreeable to them. . . . A lady whom I accompanied to the Farnese palace, turned away from it in disgust. I could not

imagine what had shocked her. She told me, *after recollec-tion*, that she could not bear the stern severity of his countenance, his large brawny limbs, and the club with which he was armed; which gave him more the ap-pearance of one of those giants that, according to the old romances, carried away virgins and shut them up in gloomy castles, than the gallant Hercules, the lover of Omphale. Finally, the lady declared, she was convinced this state could not be a just representation of Hercules; for it was not in the nature of things that a man so formed could ever have been a reliever of distressed damsels.[19]

A third patrician palace of the sixteenth century, the Palazzo Spada, lies one block to the south. To Georgina Masson, 'After the sober magnificence of Palazzo Farnese, the exuber-ant stucco decorations of Palazzo Spada strike an unexpectedly frivolous note . . . and it is difficult to believe that less than fifty years separate the beginnings of the two palaces.'[20] Since its recent restoration, the palace can no longer be faulted for its 'decayed and impoverished aspect' or the 'dirt, discomfort, and delapidation' that put off nineteenth-century viewers like Nathaniel Hawthorne or Anna Jameson.[21]

The collections of the Palazzo Spada contain one work that particularly fascinated early visitors. This was not the in-genious and charming *trompe l'œil* perspective corridor that Borromini built off a second courtyard in the seventeenth century, but the colossal statue of Pompey that was widely if mistakenly believed to be the very one at whose feet Plutarch tells us that Caesar was murdered. Lord Byron wrote stir-ringly of this work in *Childe Harold's Pilgrimage*, and in his *Memoirs* (1830), Charles C. F. Greville went so far as to proclaim that:

It is impossible for the coldest imagination to look at this without interest, for it calls up a host of recollections and associations, standing before you unchanged from the hour when Caesar folded his robe round him and 'con-sented to death' at its base. Those who cannot feel this had better not come to Rome.[22]

Those who do come to the Palazzo Spada to see the statue will be disappointed to discover that Pompey is now hidden away in the offices of a government agency and can only be viewed with special permission.

Via Giulia runs behind the Farnese and Spada palaces. 'Half a mile long, it has a preternaturally calm look, as though it were its own picture in a book of engravings', is how Elizabeth Bowen described it in *A Time in Rome* (1960).[23] This elegant street was planned by Pope Julius II as a thoroughfare to the Vatican, and its essential Renaissance character has remained intact.

TRASTEVERE

The narrow, slightly ramshackle Ponte Sisto is an ancient bridge reconstructed in the fifteenth century by Sixtus IV. It still takes pedestrians and cyclists across the river to Trastevere, the most exotic of Rome's *rioni* or districts. Early visitors like Fynes Moryson attributed the special character of Trastevere to a distinctive climate. His *Itinerary* of 1617 informs readers that 'because the aire is unwholesome, as the winde is that blowes heere from the South, it is onely inhabited by Artisans and poore people'.[24]

The poverty and picturesqueness of the place have provided sightseers with the inspiration for countless literary sketches. One of the warmest is found in Henry James's early novel *Roderick Hudson* (1875). The protagonist Rowland Mallet takes 'a long afternoon ramble' through the area because

He was particularly fond of this part of Rome, though he could hardly have expressed the charm he found in it. As you pass away from the dusky swarming purlieus of the Ghetto, you emerge into a region of empty, soundless, grass-grown lanes and alleys, where the shabby houses seem mouldering away in disuse and yet your footstep brings figures of startling Roman type to the doorways. There are few monuments here, but no part of Rome seemed more historic, in the sense of being weighted with a ponderous past, blighted with the melancholy of things that had had their day. When the yellow afternoon sun-shine slept on the sallow battered walls and lengthened the shadows in the grassy courtyards of small closed churches, the place acquired a strange fascination.[25]

A less romantic image is portrayed in Zola's *Rome* where the naturalism is as harsh as can be found anywhere in the long novel. Drawn by 'his compassion for all who suffered', Pierre also goes for 'a long ramble' in Trastevere. He finds that

the whole district teemed with ragged, grimy denizens, children half-naked and devoured by vermin, bare-headed, gesticulating and shouting women, whose skirts were stiff with grease, old men who remained motionless on benches amidst swarms of hungry flies.[26]

Another common stereotype of the local populace is evoked by Augustus Hare in *Walks in Rome* (1871):

They pride themselves upon being born 'Trasteverini', profess to be the direct descendents of the ancient Romans, seldom intermarry with their neighbours, and speak a dialect peculiarly their own. It is said that in their dispositions also they differ from the other Romans in that they are a far more hasty, passionate, and revengeful, as they are a stronger and more vigorous race. The proportion of murders . . . is larger in this than in any other part of the city.[27]

Since few foreigners could converse in the dialect, ex-changes were naturally limited. However, one amusing encounter is reported in H. V. Morton's *A Traveller in Rome* (1957). The author and an Italian friend are leaving a café when they meet a local resident whom he dubs 'the spitfire':

She was a bold, sturdy young girl who kept pace with us, and said to her friend, in a voice intended for us:

'Pah, these foreigners! They come to Rome and look at palaces, but why don't they come and look at the filthy hole I have to live in!'

'Quickly, tell her we'd like to see it!' I whispered.

Rather reluctantly, afraid of cutting a *brutta figura* I suppose, my friend overtook her and did as I suggested. Finding herself addressed courteously in Italian, she was deflated. Her eyes travelled in contempt from our feet to our eyes, then uttering a Trasteverine insult, which even my friend could not understand, she looked for a moment as though she were about to fly at us. Instead, she shrugged her shoulders and walked haughtily away; and I pitied the man who ever tried to argue with her or get the better of her.[28]

Trastevere's proudest sons are the two satirical poets Giuseppe Gioachino Belli (d. 1863) and Carlo Alberto Salustri, known as Trilussa (d. 1950). Both have been accorded the honour of commemorative monuments in piazzas named after them: Trilussa's opposite the Ponte Sisto, and Belli's opposite Ponte Garibaldi. Belli has been called Rome's 'one and only great poet' and 'the Chaucer-cum-Phil May of Trastevere'.[29] He wrote more than a thousand sonnets in the local dialect, and

There was nothing in Roman life that wasn't caught by his mordant eye and pen: the abuses of the clergy, quarrels of market women, the pouter-pigeon strut of a lady *per bene*, the zesty comments of her maids, bitter howls about the human condition, lyrics to the freshness of a Roman morning. He sits now in his comfortable paunch and top hat, reciting to his loved, pitied, and hated neighbors.[30]

A few lines from his poem 'Er Lavore' gives a sketch of a lazy Trasteverino:

> Don't wanna work, I don't, so what the Hell?
> I'm not cut out for it, and work's a bore.
> Don't wanna work, I don't, need I say more?
> Or can I save my breath and take a spell?[31]

Near the Piazza Trilussa in the former Carmelite monastery of S. Egidio is one of Rome's most unconventional museums, the Museo del Folklore e dei Poeti Romaneschi. On the floor above the galleries of topographical paintings and *tableaux vivants*, there is a recreation of Trilussa's study filled with memorabilia of the poet's life and work.

FOUR CHURCHES

The most venerable church in Trastevere is the fourth-century basilica of S. Maria in Trastevere. Its solemn grandeur has rarely failed to impress those who enter it, but it has left many at a loss for words, and even unnerved a few sensitive souls. 'I call this a terrible church. It quite frightened me, it looked altogether so stern', wrote Frances Elliot in her *Diary of an Idle Woman in Italy* (1871).[32]

Sharp-eyed individuals sometimes took delight in the church's lesser details. In her *Notes in England and Italy* (1869), Sophia Hawthorne observed that

> One of the chapels was prepared for Domenichino to paint in fresco; and in one corner of an arch he commenced with a little cherub, and then he fell ill and died. No other hand has carried on the work. The little cherub remains alone. . . . There was something inexpressibly affecting in these void spaces, watched over by the cherub.[33]

By contrast, the piazza that stands before S. Maria in Trastevere is festive and, at any hour of day or night, alive with activity. Two colourful (if overpriced) alfresco restaurants compete with two outdoor cafés and an illustrious fountain for the attention of large numbers of people of every age, nationality, and economic circumstance. The highlight of the local calendar is the 'Festa de Noantri', a spirited outdoor festival held in July. Towards the end of Fellini's *Roma* (1972), there is a segment filmed in the piazza as the festival is in full swing. Artists and intellectuals are shown dining at Sabatini where the film crew comes upon the American author Gore Vidal. Asked why he chooses to live in Rome, he replies sardonically that 'Rome is the city of illusion', and 'as good a place as any to wait for the end of the world'.

S. Crisogono borders the Largo Sonnino a few blocks down
the Via della Lungaretta. A Romanesque structure with Baroque embellishment, this is described by Barbara Grizzuti
Harrison as a 'happy church'. In *Italian Days* (1989), she tells of
a visit she paid to it with her Italian friend Lala:

> Lala would walk on her hands on this floor if she could;
> she has a special love for the Fratelli Cosmati, the medi-
> eval family of marble cutters who scavenged ruins for
> pretty marbles – especially rare red and green porphyry –
> and cut them into circles, squares, and cubes with which
> to make infinitely varied hand-set geometric patterns.
> Lala scampers about San Crisogono like a child, amused
> even by the *spingere* candles – candles with electric flames
> activated by buttons (tsk-tsk the tourists say). I link arms
> with her, confident that her unconventional piety, if not
> her interior-decorator sensibilities, will not be offended
> before a statue of the Madonna locked behind plate glass,
> festooned with jewels: a simple string of coral beads such
> as one might find in any souvenir shop; a nineteenth-
> century brooch of seed pearls and diamonds; many gold
> rings, a gold cross; a tarnished silver watch and watch fob
> girdling Mary's waist.
>
> When people say that Catholics in Rome are not 'really'
> Catholic, I wonder what they think these manifestations
> of thanks and supplication to the Virgin mean.[34]

The most popular church in Trastevere has traditionally
been S. Cecilia, immured in a great Benedictine convent on
the other side of the Viale Trastevere. The relentless cacoph-
ony and miasmic fumes of that modern thoroughfare make
the fragrant silence of the cloistered church seem all the
sweeter by comparison. The church's special appeal derives
from its dedication to St Cecilia, a fourth-century martyr who
later, somewhat inexplicably, became the patron saint of
musicians. Stefano Maderno's marble statue of the recumbent
saint encased beneath the main altar had a very special appeal
for viewers in the past whose tastes ran to the expression of
ideal beauty. In his *Classical Tour through Italy* (1813), the

(Catholic) Reverend John Chetwode Eustace was moved to write that

> The posture and drapery are natural as well as graceful, and the whole form wrought with such exquisite art, that we seem to behold the martyred virgin, not locked in the slumbers of death, but in the repose of innocence, awaiting the call of morning.[35]

Henry James attended a vesper service in S. Cecilia in 1869 and duly reported in a letter to his mother that

> The music and singing on this occasion draws great crowds and is most divinely beautiful. Much of it was immensely florid and profane in tone – as far at least as I could judge; but in spite of the crowded and fetid church and the revolt provoked in my mind by the spectacular catholicism . . . I truly enjoyed the performance.[36]

The young American Charles Eliot Norton had a very different experience when he witnessed a young woman taking her vows in the church one morning in 1856:

> Any one who desires to retain his imagination of what this solemn and affecting scene might be should not go to witness the ceremony. I did not know this, and therefore went to the church to see it. . . . There was not one word of earnest exhortation, of sincere joy, or of religious counsel. The friends of the girl were utterly unmoved through the whole; she herself sat with little expression of feeling; and the foreign spectators seemed to care only that the sermon should be finished quickly. . . .
>
> In spite of all the want of feeling in the forms that had been gone through with, it was impossible not to have a profound sense of the melancholy of this ceremony. Whether the nun who has now to begin her convent life had before been happy or unhappy, it was equally sad to see her, a girl, thus renounce the world, and confine herself within limits so narrow that neither the affections nor the intellect could escape being stunted and crushed by them.[37]

The literary reputation of the nearby S. Francesco a Ripa was established in 1837 when Stendhal used its name for the title of a short story. The protagonist of this story is chased into S. Francesco by a band of assassins, but the author unfortunately fails to say anything more about this much-rebuilt church whose most remarkable feature is a late work by Bernini. In *Italy, Rome and Naples*, Hippolyte Taine pointed to S. Francesco as a striking example of the contrasts between a Roman church and its surroundings. 'On leaving San Francesco a Ripa', he wrote, 'you stop your nose, so strong is the odour of codfish; the yellow Tiber rolls along, between remnants of piles near large mournful edifices and before silent lugubrious streets'.[38]

The last word on church-going in Trastevere must go to Kate Simon. In *Rome: Places and Pleasures* (1972) she recommends that

> Trastevere is not a place to leave on a religious note in spite of its many and splendid churches. Walk back along the Via di S. Francesco a Ripa, have a pizza at Ivo's, or a *porchetta* sandwich on the viale and a gelato on the great S. Maria square, while you watch the bambini watching the hippies, and be comforted when the rest of the city pours out to the beaches on Sundays, leaving the streets tongue-less and bloodless, to know that Trastevere stays at home, arms folded, guarding its shambles, drinking its wine, rumbling its big-voiced greetings and arguments.[39]

TWO PALACES

In his *Roman Journal*, Stendhal claimed that there are only twelve 'Outstanding palaces in Rome [that] are well worth going out of one's way to visit'.[40] Two of these, the Villa Farnesina and the Palazzo Corsini, are in Trastevere, facing one another on the Via della Lungara, just past the Porta Settimiana.

The Palazzo Corsini is the massive structure on the left. Its interminable façade was built during an eighteenth-century restructuring of a more modest Renaissance *palazzo*. Over the years some notable individuals have resided there: Michelangelo, Queen Christina of Sweden, and Madame Letizia, the mother of Napoleon. Most sightseers have been drawn by the Corsini family collection which since 1883 has been part of the Galleria Nazionale d'Arte Antica. There are paintings here for every taste. According to Charlotte Eaton:

> A certain quantity of Landscapes, a great many Holy Families, a few Crucifixions, two or three Pietàs, a reasonable proportion of St Jerome's, a mixture of other Saints and Martyrdoms, and a large assortment of Madonnas and Magdalens, make up the principal part of all the collections in Rome; which are generally composed of quite as many bad as good paintings, like this at the Corsini Palace.
>
> How much more pleasure there would be in seeing them, if the good were placed apart for your inspection, and you were not sickened and disgusted with the quantity of rubbish you must sift, to find those really worth looking at![41]

Unfortunately not everyone would agree with Mrs Eaton's ranking of the good and bad. She, for instance, found Guercino's *Ecce Homo* 'full of such deep and powerful expression, so elevated in its conception, and so faultless in its execution, that it awakens our highest admiration, and leaves an indelible impression on the mind'.[42] However, the American painter Rembrandt Peale studied the painting just a few years later and responded rather differently. In his *Notes on Italy* (1831) he acknowledged that 'it is exquisitely finished and natural in the colouring', but nonetheless considered it 'a most ignoble, disgusting, and unfortunate exhibition of the Saviour'.[43]

When Gustave Flaubert visited the gallery in 1851, the painting that most aroused him was Murillo's *Madonna*. The Frenchman, who was then at work on *Madame Bovary*, devoted 49 lines in his *Notes de Voyages* to an affectionately detailed description of the picture that is more painstaking than any lavished on Emma Bovary herself.[44] Yet Mrs Eaton, whose tastes were more rarified, wrote of this, 'there is nothing elevated or ideal in it. Let us fancy a mother and baby in the lower walks of life, and it will have no fault'.[45]

Across the street at the Villa Farnesina there are even more notable works of art to be seen. George Eliot, in Rome in 1860, recalls them in her *Life and Letters*:

> It is here that Raphael painted the 'Triumph of Galatea', and here this wonderful fresco is still bright upon the wall. In the same room is a colossal head, drawn by Michael Angelo with a bit of charcoal, by way of *carte-de-visite*, one day that he called on Daniele di Volterra, who was painting detestably in this room, and happened to be absent. In the entrance-hall, preceding the Galatea room, are the frescoes by Raphael representing the story of Cupid and Psyche; but we did not linger long to look at them, as they disappointed us.[46]

Raphael's *Galatea* received the most praise of any work in the Farnesina, and accounts of it are monotonously laudatory of its ideal beauty. One of the few early critics not overcome by its reputation was the classical purist, J. J. Winckelmann. In his influential *History of Ancient Art* (1763), the great German scholar took Raphael to task:

> the conception of the head of his Galatea is common; women of greater beauty are to be found everywhere. Moreover, the figure is so disposed, that the breast, the most beautiful part of the naked female form, is completely covered by one arm, and the knee which is on view is much too cartilaginous for a person of youthful age, to say nothing of a divine nymph . . .[47]

THE JANICULUM

To ascend from Trastevere to the Janiculum Hill is to enter a world that is greener, quieter, and more salubrious than the one below. From Porta Settimiana, the most direct route is up Via Garibaldi, past Borromini's practically unknown church of S. Maria dei Sette Dolori, and bearing to the left, to S. Pietro in Montorio. John Ruskin followed such a path in December 1840

and had a delicious walk up a sunny hill, with masses of
shattered wall covered with vegetation above, rising with
lines of broad buttresses to several ranges of massy buildings; convent and cypress and cedar, everything imaginable in the way of material, without a grain of rigidity.
The city lying below, exquisitely clear; the sky without a
cloud and several pieces of glowing snow on the moun-
tain background. The Coliseum coming in nobly as a
square mass; the pyramid equally well; the stones of the
burial ground gleaming under the shadow of the walls; a
piece of the Tiber to the south flashing back the sun.[48]

It was in S. Pietro in Montorio that Raphael's *Transfiguration*
mesmerized legions of art-lovers before it was transferred to
the Vatican in 1809. Since then, the primary attraction has
been Bramante's Tempietto. Reportedly built on the very spot
where St Peter was crucified, this small commemorative
structure, according to *Murray's Handbook*, 'has been universally admired as a *bijou* of architecture and is in every respect
one of the most elegant works of modern times'.[49]
   On first viewing this paragon of High Renaissance design
and proportion, one is usually struck by its diminutive size.
Gregorovius called it 'an elegant trifle'; Eleanor Clark
'toyish'.[50] In *Roman Mornings* (1956), James Lees-Milne explains why the little building enjoys such a large reputation:

> Small the Tempietto undoubtedly is, but as a work of art
> and as an archetype it is of immense stature, of far-
> reaching influence. Size, I need hardly say, is absolutely
> no criterion in assessing the merits of its architecture.
> Scale on the other hand is everything. Helvellyn in rela-
> tion to the neighboring peaks of the miniature Cumbrian
> range is every bit as majestic and awe-inspiring as Monte
> Rosa surrounded by its fellow Alpine giants. So too every
> part of the Tempietto is perfectly related to the whole
> structure. It has all the dignity and solemnity of St Peter's
> and is far more beautiful. It is as beautiful in its economy
> of line and form as any building of the ancient Romans
> known to us.[51]

Just behind S. Pietro in Montorio is the early Baroque fountain known as the Acqua Paola. In *The Fountains of Rome* (1966), H. V. Morton wrote:

> Mounted high upon the Janiculum, with the whole of Rome beneath it, this fountain stands magnificently situated amid the last surviving tranquillity of the nineteenth century. It is off the tourist run so that the thousands who linger around the Trevi are unaware of its existence, while many who follow the antiquarian route laid down in the eighteenth century generally lack the time to go there. I think it is one of the most rewarding sights in Rome.[52]

One early tourist who did take the time to visit the Acqua Paola was Henry Wadsworth Longfellow. In *Outre-Mer* (1835) the American poet noted that:

> as often as once a week we pass the day there, amid the odor of its flowers, the rushing sound of its waters, and the enchantments of poetry and music. How pleasantly the sultry hours steal by! Cool comes the summer wind from the Tiber's mouth at Ostia. Above us is a sky without a cloud; beneath us the magnificent panorama of Rome and the Campagna, bounded by the Abruzzi and the sea. Glorious scene! one glance at thee would move the dullest soul, – one glance can melt the painter and the poet into tears.[53]

The view from the Janiculum has captivated poets since the city was founded. Livy, Martial, Ovid, and Pliny sang its praises before the first tourist sallied up the hill. Although many since have tried, it would be difficult to improve upon the lines written by Martial nearly two thousand years ago:

> From here you can see the seven lordly hills,
> and measure the whole of Rome –
> The Alban Hills, too, and those of Tusculum,
> and every cool retreat outside the city walls,[54]

Indeed the view from this spot is so legendary that Zola's French abbé in *Rome* comes here straight from the station after having spent two days on the train. In Zola's time, the Janiculum underwent a vast improvement: in the 1880s the lovely Passeggiata del Gianicolo was begun, and at its highest point, the Piazzale del Gianicolo, a large equestrian statue of Garibaldi was erected. Nowadays, among the entertainments offered in the surrounding park are pony rides, a merry-go-round, and an open-air Punch and Judy show.

From the puppet show, a short amble down the Passeggiata del Gianicolo brings one to the celebrated literary landmark known as La Quercia del Tasso or Tasso's Oak. The twisted, blackened, iron-corsetted trunk of this long-dead tree is a relic of the Renaissance poet's last days in Rome. Tasso is said to have planted it himself when he was living in the nearby monastery of S. Onofrio. This tree, along with the monk's cell in which he died and his simple tomb inside the tiny church have become shrines for many a literary pilgrimage. Goethe, Chateaubriand, Longfellow, Henry James, and John Cheever were just a few of those who came to what Herman Melville called the 'quaint, damp, and doleful' S. Onofrio to pay their respects to the epic poet.[55] For many authors, and especially for romantics like Byron and Shelley, Tasso's appeal partly lay in the kind of life he led. Melancholic, passionate, and deeply distrustful of others, his seven-year imprisonment at the behest of a dissatisfied patron made him the very archetype of the alienated artist who, punished by society for his differences, continued to create works of enduring nobility and fame.

One of the most moving tributes to Tasso and to the serene beauty of S. Onofrio is that of Chateaubriand, first published in his *Mémoires d'outre-tombe* (1848–50), and later transcribed on a marble plaque on the side wall of the church:

If I have the good fortune to end my days here, I have arranged to have a retreat at Sant'Onofrio adjoining the room where Tasso died. . . . In one of the most beautiful spots on earth, among the orange-trees and the holly oaks, with all Rome under my eyes every morning, as I sit down to work, between the deathbed and the tomb of the poet, I shall invoke the genius of glory and misfortune.[56]

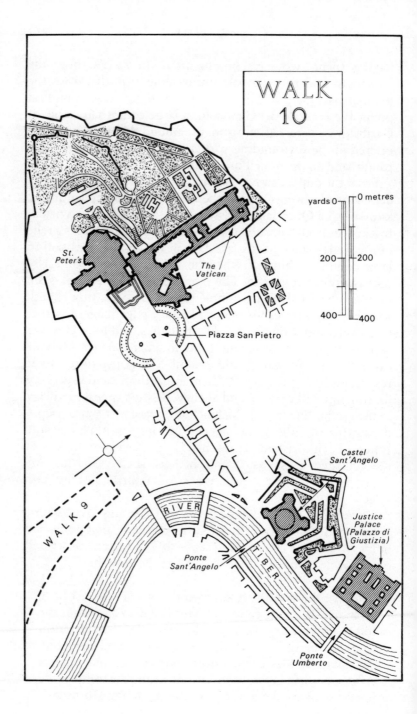

WALK 10

St. Peter's

The Vatican

Piazza San Pietro

yards 0   0 metres

200   200

400   400

WALK 9

RIVER

TIBER

Ponte Sant'Angelo

Castel Sant'Angelo

Justice Palace (Palazzo di Giustizia)

Ponte Umberto

10

TENTH WALK

From the Tiber past the Castel Sant' Angelo to the Vatican

THE TIBER

One could see all of old Rome, apart from excursions to
Trastevere or the Vatican, without realizing that this is a city
built on a river. Visitors from London or Paris are especially
struck by the physical separation of the Tiber from the life of
the city, but in fact, this has not always been the case. Before
the massive marble embankments were built to control flood-
ing in the late nineteenth century, the river did play a somewhat more prominent and conspicuous role in everyday life.

Corot's view (Plate 18) from the 1830s shows the Tiber
before the embankments. His was a particularly popular
viewpoint for artists to take, for in the foreground it captures a
moment in the lives of some ordinary boatmen while St
Peter's, the Castel Sant' Angelo, and the Ponte Sant' Angelo
stand resolutely in the background. George Stillman Hillard
sought out this very vista and went on to report in *Six Months
in Italy* (1853):

> A thousand times had I seen it in engravings, and it was
> with a peculiar feeling – half recognition and half surprise
> – that I beheld the real group in the smokeless air of a
> Roman December. The combination is so happy and
> picturesque that they appear to have arranged themselves
> for the especial benefit of artists, and to be good-

naturedly standing, like models, to be sketched. They make a picture inevitable.[1]

Corot's muddy river view also reveals why some commentators were unenchanted by the Tiber of old. Puzzled by ancient encomiums like Virgil's reference in the *Aeneid* to 'the Tiber of the blue waters, the river most dear to heaven',[2] a seventeenth-century tourist like Richard Lassels could only wonder 'to finde it such a small river, which poets with their hyperbolical inke had made swell into a river of the first rate'.[3] A sampling of later comments demonstrates the contempt with which the legendary river was often held:

'A scurvy draught' (David Garrick, 1763)[4]
'An inconsiderable stream' (Tobias Smollett, 1765)[5]
'A ditch, yellow as saffron' (Herman Melville, 1857)[6]
'After a heavy rain, it looks like pease-soup' (Nathaniel Hawthorne, 1858)[7]
'Don't flow, just oozes along' (Will Rogers, 1926)[8]
'A menacing serpent, with no more life than the Dead Sea' (Federico Fellini, 1972)[9]

Among the Tiber's impressive bibliography, one title stands out in its defence. In 1871 Strother A. Smith published a book entitled *The Tiber and its Tributaries*. In this the author went so far as

to form an opinion as to the time within which it might be drunk, I filled a large flagon with it at a time when it was greatly discoloured by a sudden flood. At the end of five hours I found that it had deposited its yellow mud, but still retained a slightly milky hue. . . . [Five days later] it had become as clear as crystal, and in no way distinguishable from the water of the Acqua Vergine.

I drank a portion, used another portion for making tea, and found it excellent. A trial of it with soap shewed it to be of a medium degree of hardness. . . . A bottle of it well corked was left at Rome during the summer, to see whether it would undergo fermentation owing to the presence of organic material, and develop any unpleasant taste or smell. On my return, after an interval of four months, the water was found to be perfectly sweet to the taste, and free from any disagreeable odour.[10]

THE PONTE SANT'ANGELO AND CASTEL SANT'ANGELO

The bridge known as the Ponte Sant'Angelo dates to the time of Hadrian, but it was Bernini and his circle that added the ten angels during a major restoration in the seventeenth century. While a handful of visitors like Hippolyte Taine were 'put out of humour' by these angelic figures that 'express a tender, coquettish air, and wriggle about in Greek or Roman drapery as in an eighteenth-century petticoat',[11] most of those who ambled across the bridge came away with a more positive impression. After John Ruskin crossed on New Year's Day 1841 while 'scarlet Turner clouds' passed overhead and the papal standard waved 'broad in the sun', he noted in his diary 'The best thing I have seen in Rome yet'.[12] That same year, Frances Trollope made her way on foot from Piazza di Spagna to the Vatican and found the walking

> wretched, there being no pavement, or only a few yards here and there, and carriages, waggons, carts, barrows, horses, asses, dogs, men, women, and children, all seeming well disposed to run at and over you without ceremony. My first reward for encountering all this was passing the statued bridge of St Angelo, with the castle directly before my eyes at the end of it. I would at that moment have willingly agreed to receive sundry hard knocks rather than have been enclosed in any vehicle more encumbering than a triumphal car.[13]

The Castel Sant'Angelo looms large as one crosses the bridge from the *centro*. According to *The Travels of the Learned Father Montfaucon* (1702), during the Middle Ages this mighty structure was considered one of the Seven Wonders of the World, ranking third behind the city of Thebes and the walls of Babylon (but coming just ahead of the pyramids).[14]

The building began its history as the mausoleum of the Emperor Hadrian and became a fortress and bridgehead defence with the construction of the Aurelian Wall in 270–5. Late in the sixth century, when Rome was being decimated by pestilence, the Archangel Michael, guardian of the sick, reportedly appeared in the sky over it. His sheathing of his sword was a sign the plague would soon end and, in gratitude, a chapel dedicated to St Michael was built above the mausoleum and the entire fortress renamed the Castel Sant' Angelo. From the twelfth century until the Unification in 1870, it remained the principal fortress of the popes.

No other building in the world has had so varied and tragic a history. Among the notable individuals who ended their days there were Beatrice Cenci, who was executed at the far end of Ponte Sant' Angelo, and Puccini's Tosca, who threw herself off the parapet. A glimpse of a prisoner's life in the sixteenth century is preserved in Benvenuto Cellini's *Autobiography* (1558–62). A vain and arrogant sculptor and goldsmith, Cellini was imprisoned for having spoken contemptuously of the artistic taste of his patron, Paul III:

> I was taken into a gloomy dungeon below the level of a garden, which swam with water, and was full of big spiders and many venomous worms. They flung me a wretched mattress of coarse hemp, gave me no supper, and locked four doors upon me . . .
>
> For one hour and a half each day I got a little glimmering of light, which penetated that unhappy cavern through a very narrow aperture. Only for so short a space of time could I read; the rest of the day and night I abode in darkness, enduring my lot, nor ever without meditations upon God and on our human frailty.[15]

Although he was greatly impressed with the man-powered lift that Leo X had installed, and the 'glorious little bathroom' of Clement VII, H. V. Morton nevertheless felt that

> it is one of the most frightening buildings in the world. One does not need to be psychic, or even unduly sensitive or fanciful, to feel that agony and suffering still cling to the dark corridors. Mounting the stone steps in the dim light, it would not surprise one to hear a fearful scream, or

opening a door to come upon some scene of murder or torture. There are beautiful rooms in which a man might sit listening to music, while a few yards off are dungeons; in at least one of the gayest rooms a trapdoor opens on an oubliette. Compared with S. Angelo, the Tower of London is almost a happy place.[16]

The historical blend of past excesses and modern tourism is the subject of Richard Hugo's poem 'Castel Sant' Angelo' in his collection *Good Luck in Cracked Italian* (1969). The middle stanzas read:

Banquets lasted days, meat roasted black
to gnaw on after girls and endless wine.
When gluttony and love had turned them mean, they brought
the sadist and the virgins in.
Where they dropped the bores in the canal
is grated, and a horny guard points out
the best of the pornography above.

Popes came puffing down that wall to hide
where cruelty and orgy used to blend
before they locked the drawbridge down,
burned invitations, charged admission,
found if everyone came in that no one
had a knife or thought, or was interesting.
They fired guards and opened dungeons
so touring girls from Iowa can peek.[17]

THE APPROACH TO ST PETER'S

To the right of the Castel Sant' Angelo is the Palazzo di Giustizia, a Risorgimento structure that has been called 'the most licentious, depraved, orgiastic building ever conceived'.[18] Not surprisingly, few tourists linger before it when St Peter's and the Vatican beckon from the opposite direction. The route from here to the basilica takes one down the Via della Conciliazione, a stark yet curiously pompous avenue built between 1936 and 1950 in place of the warren of medieval streets of the old *borgo*. Walking along this wide boulevard with its double row of imitation obelisks, 'the most revered church in Christendom can now be approached like a pavilion at a world's fair', observed Eleanor Clark.[19] Quite apart from 'its shops with their souvenirs poignant and execrable in equal part' Barbara Grizzuti Harrison underlines the real failure of the new street: 'it robs the pilgrim of surprise'.[20]

Nevertheless, to enter St Peter's square (Plate 19) is an overpowering experience. On his first day in Rome in 1845, Charles Dickens, though in 'a very indifferent humour' the night before, was instantly taken with what he saw. In *Pictures from Italy* he wrote, 'The beauty of the Piazza . . . with its clusters of exquisite columns, and its gushing fountains – so fresh, so broad, and free, and beautiful – nothing can exaggerate'.[21] George Eliot had the 'sense of having entered some millennial new Jerusalem, where all small and shabby things were unknown'.[22] Even the curmudgeonly Smollett had to admit that he found the piazza 'altogether sublime'.[23]

Comparisons with the forms of nature was a popular theme in many nineteenth-century accounts. In Zola's *Rome* (1896), for instance, the author evokes metaphors of nature on each of the three occasions his protagonist enters the square. On a visit early in the morning, Pierre 'never realized the enormity of those four curving rows of columns, forming a forest of gigantic stone trunks among which nobody ever promenades. In fact, the spot is a grandiose and dreary desert, and one asks oneself the why and wherefore of such a majestic porticus'.[24] In subsequent visits at night, he 'fancied that he was losing himself in a murky sea', thought 'the forests of pillars showed up their trunks in fantastic fashion', and between the 'thickets of stone' found the 'jets of the fountains . . . rising like thin phantoms'.[25]

Lesser literary talents occasionally stumbled under the weight of their own conceits. Where George Eliot at least had the good sense not to extend her vision of the 'millennial new Jerusalem', Florence Nightingale was out of her depth when in a letter home she likened the moonlit piazza to a vision in Revelations. One of the fountains, she wrote 'was the life of the spirit – the retiring contemplative life, the Angel of peace, and love, while the other was the Angel of joy and glory'.[26]

St Peter's

There is scarcely an account of any Roman sojourn that does not contain the impressions of a visit to St Peter's. Those who remained silent about virtually everything else often found their voices inside the great basilica. The sole record of Fyodor Dostoevsky's thoughts during his 1863 stay are that the church 'sent a shiver down the spine'.[27] Such is the sheer grandeur and majesty of the structure that many sceptical souls, otherwise repulsed by run-of-the-mill Counter-Reformation architecture, simply melted before it. Thus Goethe wrote in 1786, 'since we were determined to enjoy its magnitude and splendour, we did not, this time, allow our over-fastidious taste to put us off and abstained from carping criticism. We enjoyed everything that was enjoyable'.[28]

Catholics were not alone in their rapturous transport before the shrine of Peter. 'One cannot help worshipping the religion that produces such things', admitted Stendhal in *A Roman Journal*.[29] The young Boswell even felt refreshed by his plunge into Catholicism's deepest waters. His journal for April 1765 notes that he 'prayed fervent to the unchangeable Father of all to drive away melancholy and keep clouds of Presbyterian Sundays from rendering mind gloomy'.[30]

Truly negative reactions are surprisingly rare, and even then frequently tempered by some positive afterthought. Thus George Stillman Hillard, who was among the most disapproving critics of Catholic iconography, found that St Peter's 'is so vast and it contains so much', that it is 'among buildings what Shakespeare is among poets: both are characerized by universality'.[31] Hillard may also have been inclined favourably toward St Peter's because it provided him with a physical comfort that he often found lacking in Roman interiors:

In winter, we leave behind the dampness and the cold, and pass into a dry atmosphere of vernal softness, which refreshes the frame and soothes the spirit. In summer, we escape from the fiery heat and dazzling sunshine, and breathe, with a sense of luxury, the cool airs which are

stored up in those capacious caverns. . . . When we
dream of the climate of heaven, we make it warmth
without heat, and coolness without cold, like that of St
Peter's.[32]

Hector Berlioz was another who found the environment to
his liking. In his *Autobiography* (1831) he notes that 'during the
fierce summer heat I used to spend whole days there, comfortably established in a confessional, with Byron as my
companion'.[33] Some years later, in his essay 'A Roman
Holiday' (1873), Henry James spoke frankly of how St Peter's
could serve as a sanctuary from the vexations of modern life:

When you are weary of the swarming democracy of your
fellow-tourists, of the unremunerative aspects of human
nature on Corso and Pincio, of the oppressively frequent
combination of coronets on carriage panels and stupid
faces in carriages, of addled brains and lacquered boots, of
ruin and dirt and decay, of priests and beggars and takers
of advantage, of the myriad tokens of a halting civilis-
ation, the image of the great temple depresses the balance
of your doubts, seems to rise above even the highest tide
of vulgarity and make you still believe in the heroic will
and the heroic act. It's a relief, in other words to feel that
there's nothing but a cab-fare between your pessimism
and one of the greatest of human achievements.[34]

On the other hand, some resident foreigners went to St
Peter's not to flee humanity but to seek social contact. Panini's
engraving of 1766 (Plate 20) depicts a handful of religious
pilgrims outnumbered by a splendid assortment of ladies and
gentlemen apparently engaged in some higher level of secular
discourse. Indeed, in James's own Roman novels, *Roderick
Hudson* (1875), *Daisy Miller* (1878), and *The Portrait of a Lady*
(1881), there are scenes of social encounter that might as well
take place in a salon as in a church. In *Daisy Miller*, for instance,
Winterbourne's aunt sets up a campstool and receives visitors
not far from the seated statue of St Peter himself.[35]

In his avowedly secular guidebook *Rome* (1926), the author-
composer Gabriel Fauré even complains that

These spectators in the galleries with their opera glasses in their hands, these people strolling round or rushing to get a better view, those women fanning themselves, talking, greeting one another as if in the foyer of the Opera, those boys perched on the pillars, those Suisses in striped costumes, all are a little disconcerting.[36]

Browning's poem 'Christmas Eve' (1850) captures the spirit of the art-filled and crowded basilica during a holiday mass:

> And I view inside, and all there, all,
> As the swarming hollow of a hive,
> The whole Basilica alive!
> Men in the chancel, body and nave,
> Men on the pillars' architrave,
> Men on the statues, men on the tombs
> With popes and kings in their porphyry wombs,
> All famishing in expectation
> Of the main-altar's consummation.[37]

One of the more amusing topoi in many recollections of St Peter's concerns its size. A particular preoccupation of Anglo-Saxon authors, this inevitably led to fruitless comparisons with St Paul's, London, the Capitol in Washington and, more improbably, Niagara Falls. In *The Innocents Abroad* (1875), Mark Twain exemplifies this obsession with precise measurement.

> Of course we have been to the monster Church of St Peter frequently. I knew its dimensions. I knew it was a pro-digious structure. I knew it was just about the length of the Capitol at Washington – say seven hundred and thirty feet. I knew it was three hundred and sixty-four feet wide, and consequently wider than the Capi-tol. . . . Thus I had one gauge. I wished to come as near forming a correct idea of how it was going to look as possible; I had a curiosity to see how much I could err. I erred considerably. St Peter's did not look nearly so large as the Capitol, and certainly not a twentieth part as beautiful, from the outside.[38]

Other ruminations upon its scale stress the subjective element rather more. In *The Portrait of a Lady*, Henry James

scripted the following conversation between Isabel Archer
and the self-centered Gilbert Osmond:

> 'What's your opinion of St Peter's?' Mr Osmond asked
> of Isabel.
> 'It's very large and very bright', said the girl.
> 'It's too large; it makes one feel like an atom.'
> 'Is not that the right way to feel – in a church?' Isabel
> asked, with a faint but interested smile.
> 'I suppose it's the right way to feel everywhere, when
> one *is* nobody. But I like it in a church as little as anywhere
> else.'[39]

Even Byron had an opinion on the matter. In *Childe Harold*
(1818) he posits the relationship between church and beholder
as a dynamic one:

> . . . even so this
> Outshining and o'erwhelming edifice
> Fools our fond gaze, and greatest of the great,
> Defies at first our Nature's littleness,
> Till, growing with its growth, we thus dilate
> Our spirits to the size of that they contemplate.[40]

Despite its enormous popularity in our own age,
Michelangelo's *Pietà*, in the first chapel on the right, did not
engender widespread praise in the past. Tobias Smollett was
'not at all pleased' by the work and criticized the dead Christ
for being 'emaciated, as if he had died of a consumption', and
the whole thing 'indelicate, not to say indecent, in the attitude
and design of a man's body, stark naked, lying upon the knees
of a woman'.[41] Readers of *Murray's Handbook* would later find
amid 42 lines of pedantic documentation, the solitary responsive phrase 'some portions of it are extremely beautiful'.[42]

Across the wide nave, a monument that has been of particular interest to English visitors is visible in the side aisle –
Canova's archly Neo-Classical tomb of the last Stuarts. It is
sensitively described by James Lees-Milne:

> Of the utmost simplicity, it takes the form of a Greek
> funerary *stele*. A bust in relief of each of the three crown-

less kings appears above an inscription. Alas, that the
head of Bonny Prince Charlie resembles a prosperous
butcher's with double chin! On either side of the closed
door of the tomb, symbolizing the exit of the old and
unfortunate dynasty, stand a pair of mourning angels.
These partly draped figures, with wings folded, heads
bowed, and arms leaning upon extinguished torches,
revive the very spirit of ancient Hellas. . . . The beauty
of the mourners is undeniable. But it is a classical and
impersonal beauty. I find it difficult to understand Roger
Peyrfitte's insinuation that what the guide books describe
as 'l'indicibile soavità della morbida patina' of the marble
thighs of these sexless ephebes is caused by the libidinous
fingers of passers-by.[43]

There is a moving passage in Lockhart's *Memoirs of Sir
Walter Scott* that records Scott's visit to this tomb in 1832, the
last year of his own life:

> Soon after his arrival I took Sir Walter to St Peter's . . .
> that he might see the tomb of the last of the Stuarts. I took
> him to one of the side doors, in order to shorten the
> walk. . . . We contrived to tie a glove round the point of
> his stick, to prevent his slipping in some degree; but to
> conduct him was really a service of danger and alarm,
> owing to his infirmity and total want of caution.[44]

Some decades later, the Yorkshire poet and man of letters
Richard Monckton Milnes was inspired by this passage
to write 'Sir Walter Scott at the Tomb of the Stuarts in St
Peters':

> A few more moments and that labouring brow
> Cold as those royal busts and calm will lie;
> And, as on them his thoughts are resting now,
> His marbled form will meet the attentive eye.
>
> Thus, face to face, the dying and the dead,
> Bound in one solemn ever-living bond
> Communed; and I was sad that ancient head
> Ever should pass those holy walls beyond.[45]

Maderno's nave, it should be realized, is but an early
Baroque afterthought attached to the perfectly centralized
church of Bramante and Michelangelo. Its Renaissance symmetry forever ruined, the area around the crossing then became a gallery for Baroque art of the most energetic and
persuasive variety. Bernini contributed the bronze baldachin,
the design of the niches and sculptures in the four piers that
face it, the *Cathedra Petri*, the altar of the Cappella del SS.
Sacramento, and the tombs of Urban VIII and Alexander VII.
A feast for those able to appreciate the rhetoric of the *Ecclesia
Triumphans*, the crossing was anathema to others whose religious and cultural backgrounds were of a more introverted
nature. Thus a French Catholic like François Raguenet could
write in *Les Monuments de Rome* (1700) that the 'beauty of the
cathedra is so dazzling that the whole world owes its author a
tribute',[46] whereas a New England puritan like George Stillman Hillard indignantly declared that

> The huge, uncouth structure, reared over the high altar
> awakens, both from its ugliness and inappropriateness, a
> double effusion of iconoclastic zeal. It is a baldachino, or
> canopy, of bronze, ninety-three feet high, and resting on
> four twisted columns of the same material; the whole
> elaborately ornamented and richly gilded. It is difficult to
> imagine on what ground, or for what purpose, this costly
> fabric was placed here. It has neither beauty nor grandeur;
> and resembles nothing so much as a colossal four-post
> bedstead without the curtains.[47]

For centuries, the crowning glory of many a visit to St
Peter's has been an ascent to the top of Michelangelo's stately
dome. In a short essay entitled 'Mea Culpa, a Travel Note',
John Updike relates what it was like to make this excursion in
the early 1960s:

> In recent times a Stigler-Otis elevator, manufactured in
> Milan, has been installed, whereby . . . one may ascend
> to the roof. Here, on an uneven terrain of tarred pebbles,
> rusty octagonal huts house those bits of sunlight and blue
> mosaic which, seen from within the nave, seem like

glimpses of the Empyrean. A little low shack with a Coca-Cola sign sells souvenir trinkets and sweetens the air with popular recordings of 'Mamma Mia' and 'Ave Maria'.[48]

From the roof to the dome itself, one proceeds on foot along 'a seemingly endless spiral of stone steps', leading to a second flight with sharply sloping walls, which in turn culminates in a third that 'only a Titan or a monkey could have climbed comfortably'. Then one steps out into the loggia atop the majestic cupola. Updike goes on to comment that

This island in the sky already supported a tame little population – several phlegmatic guards, one ancient nun, two pairs of lovers, a family whose father carried a baby in his arms, and a nudging, snickering quartet of Roman youths. All seemed at home on this height. Only I, leaning desperately back from the precipitous parabola of metal that fell away on all sides, seemed to feel the impossibility of our position. Some birds wheeled far below my feet. The view was a map and a postcard mixed, and in the Vatican gardens designs had been executed in shrubbery apparently for our benefit; my retinas received these sights mechanically. My mind was too obsessed by fear to see.[49]

Had Updike chosen to test the real limits of terror, he might have attempted the feat accomplished a century and a half earlier by the English naturalist Charles Waterton. 'As our nerves were in excellent trim', Waterton relates in his *Autobiography* (1838), he and an old school friend

mounted to the top of St Peter's, ascended the cross, and then climbed thirteen feet higher, where we reached the point of the conductor, and left our gloves on it. After this, we visited the castle of St Angelo, and contrived to get on to the head of the guardian angel, where we stood on one leg.[50]

Those more affected by churchly ceremony and ritual have customarily sought a papal audience. Oscar Wilde, who described himself as 'not a Catholic: I am simply a violent Papist',[51] attended several public audiences while in Rome in the spring of 1900. In a letter to his friend Robert Ross, he wrote:

> How did I get the ticket? By a miracle, of course. I thought it was hopeless, and made no effort to any kind. On Saturday afternoon at five o'clock Harold and I went to have tea at the Hôtel de l'Europe. Suddenly, as I was buttering toast, a man, or what seemed to be one, dressed like a hotel porter, entered and asked me would I like to see the Pope on Easter Day. I bowed my head humbly and said '*Non sum dignus*' or words to that effect. He at once produced a ticket!
>
> When I tell you that his countenance was of super-natural ugliness, and that the price of the ticket was thirty pieces of silver, I need say no more.

Wilde attended the audience with Leo XIII and found the 90-year-old pontiff

> wonderful as he was carried past me on his throne, not of flesh and blood, but a white soul robed in white . . .
>
> I have seen nothing like the extraordinary grace of his gesture, as he rose, from moment to moment, to bless – possibly the pilgrims, but certainly me.[52]

Years later, on what would be his last visit to the Eternal City, Thomas Mann had just as memorable an experience. Himself nearly eighty, he wrote a letter home stressing the symbolic aspect of his private audience with Pius XII:

> The unbeliever and heir of Protestant culture, without the slightest spiritual inhibition, bent his knee before Pius XII and kissed the ring of the Fisherman, since it was no man nor politician before whom I knelt, but a white idol, which, surrounded by the most formal spiritual and courtly ceremonial, meekly and a little sadly represented two thousand years of Western history.[53]

The Vatican Museums

Chateaubriand may have exaggerated when in his *Mémoires* (1848–50) he claimed that the Vatican Museums contained eleven thousand rooms,[54] but there is no reason to disagree with Mrs Jameson who, 'lost in wonder and enchantment', noted in her *Diary* (1862) that

> gallery beyond gallery, hall within hall, temple within temple, new splendours opening at every step; of all the creations of luxurious art, the Museum of the Vatican may alone defy any description to do it justice, or any fancy to conceive the unimaginable variety of its treasures.[55]

Even a laconic Dylan Thomas, indisposed to 'vast exhausting tours of inexhaustible galleries and churches' had to admit in a 1947 letter to his parents that 'dizzily moving down marble miles' he was greatly impressed with the Vatican's 'huge cool galleries that seem the size of public squares and corridors like the terraces of gods'.[56]

Of all the works of art on view, only a handful have consistently provoked comment. Surprisingly perhaps, the Sistine frescoes of Michelangelo did less to titillate early viewers than some antiquities and the paintings of Raphael. The most admired works – the *Apollo Belvedere* and the *Laocoön* – are still found in the Belvedere courtyard of the Museo Pio-Clementino. The *Apollo* was for centuries the crown prince of the entire Vatican collection. A Hadrianic copy of a bronze original by Leochares, this sublime marble had an appeal that verged on the transcendental, particularly among those acquainted with Winckelmann's famous panegyric in his *History of Ancient Art* (1764):

> Before this miracle of art I forget the entire universe and my soul takes on a nobility befitting its dignity. From admiration I pass to ecstasy; I feel my breast dilate and expand as if at the height of prophetic frenzy; I am transported to Delos and to the groves of Lycia, places

that Apollo honoured with his presence; the statue takes
on life, as did the beautiful creation of Pygmalion.[57]

While many have tried, no one has ever written more
stirringly or soulfully of the work. Even Goethe, who greatly
admired 'that inexhaustible topic of artistic conversation', fled
from the challenge.[58] It fell in fact to the first American in
Rome, the Pennsylvania artist Benjamin West, to offer a
markedly different interpretation from the one that would
remain standard throughout the nineteenth century. According to a contemporary biographer, the young Quaker was
escorted through the Vatican in 1760 by a group of 'the
principal Roman nobility and strangers of distinction', and

> it was agreed that the Apollo should be first submitted to
> his view, because it was the most perfect work among all
> the ornaments of Rome, and, consequently, the best
> calculated to produce that effect which the company were
> anxious to witness. . . . [When he saw it] the Artist felt
> himself surprised with a sudden recollection altogether
> different from the gratification which he had expected;
> and without being aware of the force of what he said,
> exclaimed, 'My God, how like it is to a young Mohawk
> warrior!'[59]

The dramatic *Laocoön* group occupies the niche just to the
right of the *Apollo*. Lavishly praised by Pliny as 'of all paintings and sculptures, the most worthy of admiration',[60] this,
like the *Apollo* was rediscovered and installed in the Vatican by
Julius II. In the eighteenth and nineteenth centuries, learned
essays by Lessing, Herder, Schiller, Goethe and Shelley de-
bated the nature of Laocoön's emotion, while artists from
Rubens to the Romantics paraphrased it whenever expressive
pathos was required in works of their own.

Lord Byron was naturally drawn to it. Among ancient
sculptures, only the *Laocoön* and the 'manly' *Gladiator* in the
Capitoline Museum appear in *Childe Harold's Pilgrimage*. In
Canto IV, he implores:

> Or, turning to the Vatican, go see
> Laocoön's torture dignifying pain –

A father's love and mortal's agony
With an immortal's patience blending: – Vain
The struggle; vain, against the coiling strain
And gripe, and deepening of the dragon's grasp,
The old man's clench; the long envenomèd chain
Rivets the living links, – the enormous asp
Enforces pang on pang, and stiffles gasp on gasp.[61]

The epic struggle between man and beast was too rich for some people's blood, however. The young Boswell felt his 'nerves contracted by it',[62] Florence Nightingale wrote 'I cannot bear the Laocoön',[63] and Henry James, in his various essays and novels, ignored it altogether. Charles Dickens likewise fails to mention it in *Pictures from Italy*, but in *A Christmas Carol*, there is a comic description of Scrooge struggling with his stockings 'and making a perfect Laocoön of himself'.[64]

A third sculpture in the Museo Pio-Clementino, the so-called *Belvedere Torso* also enjoyed an exalted reputation. While aesthetes like Sir Joshua Reynolds likened this sadly mutilated sculpture to the highest efforts of poetry, others responded to such mythically brave, well-developed males in a less ethereal fashion. Thus the legend ensued, embellished in a variety of fanciful ways, that one day Michelangelo himself was surprised by a cardinal while kneeling suppliantly before it.[65]

This muscular work is now in a gallery designated the Sala delle Muse. In one of the most charming of his Roman poems, Thomas Hardy used this chamber as the setting for a delightful fantasy. His six-stanza poem begins:

I sat in the Muses' Hall at the mid of the day,
And it seemed to grow still, and the people to pass away,
And the chiselled shapes to combine in a haze of sun,
Till beside a Carrara column there gleamed forth one.

She looked not this nor that of those beings divine,
But each and the whole – an essence of all the Nine;
With tentative foot she neared to my halting-place,
A pensive smile on her sweet, small, marvellous face.[66]

Sated with all the ancient statuary, Oscar Wilde sought his
solace in the quietude of the Vatican Gardens. In one of several
letters to Robert Ross from the spring of 1900, he mentions
that

> Today, on coming out of the Vatican Gallery, Greek gods
> and the Roman middle-classes in my brain, all marble to
> make the contrast worse, I found that the Vatican
> Gardens were open to the Bohemian and the Portuguese
> pilgrims. I at once spoke both languages fluently, ex-
> plained that my English dress was a form of penance, and
> entered that waste, desolate park, with its faded Louis XIV
> gardens, its sombre avenues, its sad woodland. The
> peacocks screamed, and I understood why tragedy dogged
> the gilt feet of each pontiff. But I wandered in exquisite
> melancholy for an hour. One Philippo, a student, whom I
> culled in the Borgia room, was with me: not for many
> years has Love walked in the Pope's pleasaunce.[67]

The Pinacoteca, or picture gallery, houses what was long
considered to be the most perfect painting in Rome. This is
Raphael's large *Transfiguration*, moved here in the early nineteenth century from S. Pietro in Montorio. In his *Lives* (1550),
Giorgio Vasari proclaimed:

> In this work the master has, of a truth, produced figures
> and heads of such extraordinary beauty, so new, so
> varied, and at all points so admirable that, among the
> many works executed by his hand, this by the common
> consent of all artists, is declared to be the most worthily
> renowned, the most excellent, the most divine.[68]

Centuries would pass before anyone challenged the picture's singular perfection. Late in the nineteenth century,
Murray's Handbook still informed its loyal readers that this was
'the last and greatest oil picture of the immortal master, and
justly considered as the first oil painting in the world'.[69]
Although he refrained from saying so in print, Henry James
was among the earliest to question the canon. In an 1869 letter
to his sister, he wrote:

Without going into metaphysics, it is easy to say that the
great works of Rafael are vitiated by their affected classicism – their elegance and coldness. I sat staring stupidly at
the *Transfiguration* and actually *surprised* at its thinness –
asking myself whether *this* was the pretended greatest of
pictures.[70]

Nowadays, one might say that maybe James was right. Like
its perennial runner-up in popularity at the Pinacoteca,
Domenchino's *Last Communion of St Jerome*, the *Transfiguration* is less likely to enrapture viewers of our era than Raphael's
own earlier work in the nearby apartments or *stanze*. The three
stanze di Raffaello were painted before the *Transfiguration*
was commissioned in 1517, and thus are more typical of what
art historians now call the 'High' Renaissance.

In *Rome and a Villa* (1952) Eleanor Clark gives an accurate
sketch of what the modern sightseer can expect to see in these
rooms:

In the Vatican, tourists of every nation with their
Babeling guides are being squeezed through the Stanze. It
is an awful rush, to get your money's worth in paint,
philosophy, allegory and general information; you
should be able to recognize every ancient philosopher in
the School of Athens (*and* the famous self-portrait) and
every poet in Parnassus (and know why Apollo is looking
up in that idiotic way instead of so much more hand-
somely down as he was in the original sketch) and which
pope and what pupil and the difference between Prudence
and Wisdom. Furthermore the crowds are terrible, you
are lucky if you can see anything or get close enough to
your own guide to catch one word out of ten of his
broken Swedish or whatever he is being paid to talk.

The second room, the *Stanza della Segnatura*, is the most
pleasing to today's tastes, but as Clark goes on to point out:

this is the real nut to crack; if there were only the four or
rather three main walls, but the lunettes! the ceiling! –
almost all Raphael too, the room he did first, before he
was all worn out and having to run a factory to fill his

orders: Original Sin, the Judgement of Solomon, Temporal and Spiritual Justice, Apollo and Marsyas . . . a sibyl showing the Virgin to Augustus, sounds strange but it makes a link, like the Borgo or the School of Athens – you have really got the whole Renaissance right there in a nutshell if you could get it open . . .[71]

THE SISTINE CHAPEL

Echoing James's private remarks of a century earlier, Kate Simon deflates Raphael's reputation even further in *Rome: Places and Pleasures* (1972). 'Raphael', she writes, 'is not everyone's painter; the sheer versatility and enameled perfection put some people off'.[72] To judge from the sale of gift-shop reproductions and the size of the crowds, Michelangelo's recently restored frescoes in the Sistine Chapel are now unquestionably the most popular attraction in the Vatican.

This was not the case in the past when *grazia* counted for more than *gravitas*. As recently as a century ago, Guy de Maupassant could write that 'the Last Judgement looks like the canvas of a fair, painted for a wrestling booth by an ignorant coal heaver'.[73] Evidently he did not agree with Hippolyte Taine who explained to readers of *Italy, Rome and Naples* (1868) about Michelangelo's true virtues:

> Superhuman personages as miserable as ourselves, forms of gods rigid with earthly passion, an Olympus of jarring human tragedies, such is the sentiment of the ceiling of the Sistine Chapel. What injustice to compare with his works the 'Sibyls' and the 'Isaiah' of Raphael! They are vigorous and beautiful, I admit, and I do not dispute that they testify to an equally profound art; but the first glance suffices to show that they have not the same soul: they do not issue like these from an impetuous, irresistible will; they have never experienced like these the same thrill and tension of a nervous being, concentrated and launching itself forth at the risk of ruin. There are souls whose impressions flash out like lightning, and whose actions

are thunderbolts. Such are the personages of Michael Angelo.[74]

While the average early tourist may have been disaffected by displays of such passion and impetuosity, those creative artists who were themselves passionate and impetuous often discovered in Michelangelo a wellspring of energy and inspiration. For true Romantics, tired of the endless discussions over 'correctness' of design, these were powerful forms that could be associated with Nature and God. Indeed, the Sistine frescoes were the only paintings in Rome that moved a number of creative individuals. Otherwise unyielding, Samuel Taylor Coleridge 'lost himself in veneration' in the chapel in 1808;[75] Géricault 'trembled and lost all self-confidence' in 1816;[76] and Piotr Tchaikovsky, in his only known comment on Rome's art, felt 'for the first time in my life, maybe, a real artist's enthusiasm for painting'.[77]

In *Italian Days* (1989), Barbara Grizzuti Harrison informs us why we are fortunate to be able to visit the Vatican in the late twentieth century:

> During the Counter-Reformation the *Last Judgement* came under attack for its 'filth' and for its supposed lack of orthodoxy – the naked figures of the damned, lumpish, heavy as sin itself. Lovers of Raphael, whose works are sweet, could not abide the *Last Judgement*. We are fortunate to live now, at this remove. We can love them, Raphael and Michelangelo, both.[78]

STENDHAL'S SYNDROME AND SOME FINAL IMPRESSIONS

The museum-goer who at this point feels fatigued and a little glassy-eyed may take solace in knowing he or she is in good company. In 1857, Herman Melville noted in his *Journal*, 'staid in Vatican till closed. Fagged out completely, and sat long time by the obelisk, recovering from the stunning effect of a first visit to the Vatican'.[79] A few decades later, Anton Chekhov wrote from Rome to a friend in Moscow, 'sauntering around the Vatican, I wilted from exhaustion, and when I

got home, my legs left as if they were made out of cotton'.[80]
Melville and Chekhov's condition nowadays would be diag-
nosed as 'Stendhal's Syndrome', a malady identified in 1979
by Dr Graziella Magherini, chief of Psychiatry at a Florentine
hospital. The name derives from several passages in Stendhal's
Journal where, for example, he warns, 'if the foreigner who
enters St Peter's attempts to see everything, he will develop a
furious headache, and presently satiety and pain will render
him incapable of any pleasure'.[81]

Notwithstanding the numbing fatigue of so much sightsee-
ing, today's tourist may still feel upon leaving the Vatican as
Ralph Waldo Emerson did on the eve of his departure from
Rome in 1833. In his *Journal* he noted, 'I love St Peter's church.
It grieves me to think that after a few days I shall see it no
more'.[82]

The experience of a Roman sojourn can also be enduring. If
memory is our second life, memories of Rome can haunt one
forever. The reflections of those for whom a stay in Rome held
lasting significance may add resonance to feelings of our own.

Maria and I have just come back from a week in Rome,
where we had been lent a flat to do some sightseeing.
What a place! It inspires one at once with a kind of passion
to know it utterly and inside out. We came back through
Florence and the spectacle of that second-rate provincial
town with its repulsive Gothic architecture and its acres
of Christmas card primitives made me almost sick. The
only points about Florence are the country outside it, the
Michelangelo tombs, Brunelleschi's dome and a few rare
pictures. The rest is simply dung when compared with
Rome.

Aldous Huxley, *Letter* (1921)[83]

I do not much wish to see Florence or any other place on
our way home. I should like to keep my vision of Rome as
a purely distinct and undivided recollection of my life, a
jewel for which no setting is wanted, for which no setting
is sufficiently valuable. Rome, alone, isolated, lifted up,
like a queen whom no meaner thing is permitted to
approach, an island in the sea, is how I should like to keep

her, and to go home as we came out, without any other aim or object to divide our attention.

Florence Nightingale, *Letter*, (1848)[84]

Do you remember Rome, dear Lou? How is it in your memory? In mine sometimes there will be only its waters, those clear, exquisite, animated waters that live in its squares; its steps, built on the pattern of falling water, so strangely thrusting stair out of stair like wave out of wave; its gardens' festiveness and the splendour of great terraces; its nights that last so long, still and filled to overflowing with great constellations.

Rainer Maria Rilke, *Letter*, (1903)[85]

When we have left Rome in such a state as this, we are astonished by the discovery, by and by, that our heart-strings have mysteriously attached themselves to the Eternal City, and are drawing us thitherward again, as if it were more familiar, more intimately our home, than even the spot where we were born.

Nathaniel Hawthorne, *The Marble Faun* (1860)[86]

NOTES

PREFACE

1. Petrarch, *Rerum familiarum*, VI, 2, p. 293.
2. Gibbon, *The Decline and Fall*, III, p. 2439.
3. Pine-Coffin,. *Bibliography*; other standard bibliographies include Andrieux, *Le français à Rome*, Schudt, *Italienreisen*, and Tresoldi, *Viaggiatori tedeschi*.

INTRODUCTION

1. Howell, *Instructions*, p. 14.
2. Goethe, *Italian Journey*, p. 116.
3. Ibsen, *Correspondence*, p. 78.
4. *The Correspondence of Erasmus*, p. 94.
5. Turgenev, *Letters*, p. 139.
6. Gibbon, *Autobiography*, p. 85.
7. Miola, *Shakespeare's Rome*, p. 238.
8. Ferguson, 'The Afflatus', p. 29.
9. Chekhov, *Letters*, p. 192.
10. Butor, *A Change*, pp. 517–18.
11. Mewshaw, *Playing Away*, p. xvi.
12. Byron, *Don Juan*, IV, 63, in *The Complete Poetical Works*, V, p. 29.
13. Jonas, *Thomas Mann*, pp. 24–5: 31–41.
14. Nashe, *The Unfortunate Traveller*, p. 96.
15. Eustace, *A Classical Tour*, I, p. 67.
16. Cradock, *Literary Memoirs*, p. 67.
17. James, *Roderick Hudson*, p. 27.
18. Sterne, *A Sentimental Journey*, p. 79.
19. Rogers, *Keats, Shelley*, p. 27.
20. Chitty, *That Singular Fellow*, p. 184.
21. Matthews, *Diary*, I, p. 2.
22. Chateaubriand, *Memoirs*, p. 356.
23. Stevens, 'To an Old Philosopher', in *Poems*, p. 161.
24. Macaulay, *Pleasure*, p. 40.

25. Greene, 'Resurrecting Rome', pp. 48–9.
26. Dyer, 'The Ruins', p. 2.
27. Goldstein, *Ruins and Empire*, chapter 6.
28. Byron, *Childe Harold*, IV, 78, in *The Complete Poetical Works*, II, p. 150.
29. Goldstein, *Ruins and Empire*, p. 208.
30. Lee, *The Spirit*, p. 111.
31. Howell, *Epistolae*, quoted in Bates, *Touring*, p. 303.
32. Pomfret quoted in Black, *The British*, pp. 40–1.
33. Walpole quoted in Pine-Coffin, *Bibliography*, p. 12; Smollett, *Travels*, p. 196.
34. Craven quoted in Fitzgibbon, *A Taste*, p. 110.
35. Fussell, *Abroad*, p. 40.
36. Ibid. pp. 39, 41.
37. Osborne, *Advice*, p. 80.
38. Sherlock, *New Letters*, p. 43.
39. Bates, *Touring*, p. 327.
40. Montaigne, *Journal*, II, p. 74.
41. Bates, *Touring*, p. 242.
42. Eustace, *A Classical Tour*, I, p. 48.
43. Gardiner, *Sights*, pp. 168–72.
44. Mewshaw, *Playing Away*, p. 90.
45. Hildebert quoted in Ross, 'A Study', p. 305.
46. Pine-Coffin, *Bibliography*, p. 55.
47. James, *Roderick Hudson*, pp. 237–8.
48. Lowell, *Fireside Travels*, p. 197.
49. Sala, *Rome*, p. 430.
50. Story, *Roba*, I, pp. 6–7.
51. Harrison, *Italian Days*, p. 259.
52. Dickens, *Pictures*, p. 498.
53. *United States Catholic Magazine*, VI (1847) pp. 401–2.
54. Canepa in *English Miscellany*, pp. 107–46.
55. Shelley, *Letters*, in *The Complete Works*, X, p. 12.
56. Wharton, *Italian Backgrounds*, p. 181.
57. Huxley, *Along the Road*, p. 43.
58. Petrarch, *Rerum familiarium*, II, 14, p. 113.
59. Luther in *Selections*, p. 429.
60. Garrick, *Letters*, I, p. 396.
61. M. Shelley, *Letters*, I, p. 89.
62. Gogol, *Letters*, pp. 74–5.
63. James, *Letters*, p. 610.
64. James, *Daisy Miller*, p. 178.
65. Fitzgerald, *Correspondence*, p. 99.
66. Woolf, *Letters*, III, p. 365.

1. First Walk

1. Horace, Epistle XVII, p. 361; Juvenal, *Thirteen Satires*, p. 20.
2. Simon, *Rome*, p. 426.
3. Clark, *Rome*, (1952 ed.) p. 33.
4. Meeks, *Italian Architecture*, pp. 346–7.
5. Dudley, *Urbs Roma*, p. 57.
6. Goethe, *Italian Journey*, p. 496.
7. Evelyn, *Diary*, p. 226.
8. De Sade, *Voyage*, p. 210.
9. Forsyth, *Remarks*, p. 206.
10. James, *Italian Hours*, p. 141.
11. James, *Letters*, p. 176.
12. Eliot, *Life and Letters*, p. 340.
13. Morton, *A Traveller*, p. 47.
14. Hazlitt, *Notes*, p. 239.
15. Morton, *A Traveller*, p. 261.
16. Evelyn, *Diary*, II, p. 235. Evelyn saw the work in the Villa Ludovisi before it was transferred to the Capitoline.
17. Trollope, *A Visit*, p. 324.
18. Byron, *Childe Harold*, IV, 140, in *The Complete Poetical Works*, II, p. 171.
19. Emerson, *Journals*, pp. 98–9.
20. *Nightingale in Rome*, pp. 93–4.
21. M. Shelley, *Letters*, I, p. 88.
22. Hawthorne, *Note-Books*, pp. 172–3.
23. White, *Fragments*, p. 78.
24. Hillard, *Six Months*, p. 183.
25. Mortoft, *His Book*, p. 64.
26. De Staël, *Corinne*, p. 18.
27. Jameson, *Diary*, p. 136.
28. Spear, *Domenichino*, I, p. 111.
29. Ruskin, *Letters*, no. 136.
30. Thackeray, *Letters*, p. 340.
31. Symonds quoted in Spear, *Domenichino*, I, p. 119.
32. Jameson, *Diary*, p. 137; Eliot, *Life and Letters*, p. 348.
33. Hawthorne, *Note-Books*, pp. 110–11.
34. Dickens, *Pictures*, pp. 495–6.
35. Berenson, *The Passionate Sightseer*, p. 26.
36. Potter, *The Colour*, pp. 70–1.
37. Bowen, *A Time*, p. 46.
38. O'Faolain, *A Summer*, p. 145–7.
39. Kostof, *The Third Rome*, p. 60.
40. Clark, *Rome* (1982 ed.), p. 109.
41. Ammianus Marcellinus XVI, 10, 15–16, quoted in Pollitt, *The Art of Rome*, p. 170.
42. Cassiodorus, *Variae* VII, 6, 1, quoted in Pollitt, ibid. p. 170.

NOTES

43. Wordsworth, 'The Pillar', in *The Poetical Works*, pp. 646–7.

2. SECOND WALK

1. Joyce, *Letters*, p. 165.
2. Fauré, *Rome*, p. 68.
3. Gibbon, *Autobiography*, p. 84.
4. Hillard, *Six Months*, pp. 186–7.
5. Howells, *Italian Journeys*, p. 151.
6. Shelley, *Letters*, in *The Complete Works*, X, p. 14.
7. Vidal, *The Judgement*, p. 46.
8. Harrison, *Italian Days*, p. 221.
9. Cooper, *Gleanings*, p. 200.
10. De Brosses, *Viaggio*, p. 447.
11. Potter, *The Colour*, p. 28.
12. MacMillan, *Roman Mosaics*, p. 168.
13. Harrison, *Italian Days*, p. 222.
14. Zola, *Rome*, I, pp. 228–9.
15. Shelley, 'Notes', in *The Complete Works*, VI, p. 309.
16. Stendhal, *A Roman Journal*, p. 146.
17. Peale, *Notes*, p. 103.
18. Andersen, *A Visit*, p. 136.
19. Lear quoted in Chitty, *That Singular Fellow*, p. 40.
20. Eaton, *Rome*, I, p. 142.
21. Hardy, 'Rome: On the Palatine', in *Complete Poems*, pp. 102–3.
22. *Boswell on the Grand Tour*, p. 62.
23. Plautus, *Curculio*, 470–83, in Pollitt, *The Art of Rome*, pp. 48–9.
24. Vedder, *Digressions*, p. 452.
25. Seneca, *Moral Epistles* VII, 3–5 in Lewis and Reinhold, *Roman Civilization* II, p. 230.
26. *Nightingale in Rome*, p. 144.
27. De Staël, *Corinne*, p. 65.
28. Martial, *Liber de Spectaculis* XV, in Quennell, *The Colosseum*, p. 139.
29. De Sade, *Voyage*, p. 366.
30. Moore, *A View*, p. 417.
31. Head, *Rome*, II, p. 194.
32. Beckford, *Dreams*, Letter XXII, in Hawcroft, *Travels*, p. 44.
33. Dyer, *The Ruins*, pp. 8–9.
34. Goethe, *Italian Journey*, p. 125.
35. Cole, *Notes at Naples* in Quennell, *The Colosseum*, p. 145.
36. James, *Italian Hours*, p. 144.
37. Andersen, *A Visit*, p. 142.
38. Byron, *Manfred* II, IV, in *The Complete Poetical Works* IV, pp. 97–8.
39. Poe, *Collected Works*, p. 228.
40. Chateaubriand, *Recollections*, p. 26.

41. Stendhal, *A Roman Journal*, p. 14.
42. Zola, *Rome*, I, p. 230.
43. Dickens, *Pictures*, p. 475.
44. Hillard, *Six Months*, p. 193.
45. Twain, *The Innocents Abroad*, p. 198.
46. James, *Italian Hours*, pp. 144–5.
47. Goethe, *Italian Journey*, pp. 156–7.
48. Byron, *Childe Harold*, IV, 144, in *The Complete Poetical Works*, II, pp. 172–3.
49. Elliot, *Diary*, II, p. 20.
50. Hawthorne, *The Marble Faun*, I, p. 184.
51. Twain, *The Innocents Abroad*, p. 205.
52. Byron, *Childe Harold*, IV, 144, in *The Complete Poetical Works*, II, p. 172.
53. Joyce, *Letters*, II, p. 146.
54. Vance, 'The Colosseum', p. 136.
55. James, *Daisy Miller*, (1879 ed. only) in Vance, *America's Rome*, I. p. 62.
56. Lassels, *Voyage*, II, p. 122.
57. Chrysoloras quoted in Baxendall, *Giotto*, p. 81.
58. Moore, *A View*, I, p. 439.
59. Stendhal, *A Roman Journal*, p. 148.
60. Suetonius, *The Lives*, in Keaveney, *Views*, p. 103.
61. Bowen, *A Time*, p. 178.
62. Ibid. p. 180.

3. THIRD WALK

1. Mewshaw, *Playing Away*, p. 57.
2. Clark, *Rome*, p 109.
3. Kostof, *The Third Rome*, p. 22.
4. Gunther, 'S.P.Q.R.', p. 142.
5. Brint quoted in Mewshaw, *Playing Away*, p. 89.
6. Morton, *The Fountains*, pp. 99–100.
7. Eaton, *Rome*, II, p. 117.
8. Ibid. p. 118.
9. Evelyn, *Diary*, II, p. 294.
10. Simond, *A Tour*, p. 257.
11. Jameson, *Diary*, p. 157.
12. De Tuddo, *Rome*, p. 73.
13. Eaton, *Rome*, I, p. 284.
14. Story, *Roba*, I, p. 5.
15. James, *Transatlantic*, p. 129.
16. Harrison, *Italian Days*, pp. 273–4.
17. Hare, *Walks*, p. 210.
18. Vedder, *Digressions*, p. 340.
19. Meeks, *Italian Architecture*, p. 72.

20. White, *Fragments*, pp. 66–7.
21. Potter, *The Colour*, p. 190.
22. Head, *Rome*, II, p. 146.
23. Nashe, *The Unfortunate Traveller*, p. 76.
24. Kostof, *The Third Rome*, p. 14.
25. Hazlitt, *Notes*, p. 235.
26. Hawthorne, *Note-Books*, pp. 128–9.
27. Hillard, *Six Months*, p. 205.
28. James, *Letters*, pp. 175–6.
29. Elliot, *Diary*, p. 147.
30. Potter, *The Colour*, p. 109.
31. Berenson, *The Passionate Sightseer*, p. 21.
32. Morton, *A Traveller*, p. 212.
33. Naval, *A Roma*, p. 197.
34. Fitzgibbon, *A Taste*, p. 12.
35. Lassels, *Voyage*, II, p. 82.
36. Morton, *A Traveller*, p. 213.
37. Gardiner, *Sights*, p. 263.
38. Ovid, *Ars Amatoria*, I, 33–9, in Keaveney, *Views*, p. 97.
39. Hutton, *Rome*, p. 270.
40. Bowen, *A Time*, p. 177.
41. Clark, *Rome*, p. 22.
42. Meeks, *Italian Architecture*, p. 64.
43. Stendhal, *A Roman Journal*, p 51.
44. Ibid. p. xvii.
45. Elliot, *Diary*, p. 144.

4. Fourth Walk

1. Montaigne, *Journal*, II, pp. 131–2.
2. Evelyn, *Diary*, II, pp. 306–7.
3. Howells, *Roman Holidays*, p. 141.
4. James, *Italian Hours*, p. 199.
5. Liszt, *Letters*, p. 162.
6. De Staël, *Corinne*, p. 80.
7. Rogers, *Italy*, p. 161.
8. James, *Italian Hours*, p. 194.
9. Shelley, *Adonais*, in *The Complete Works*, II, p. 387.
10. Morton, *A Traveller*, p. 245.
11. *The Protestant Cemetery in Rome*, p. 9.
12. Shakespeare, *Henry VIII*, IV, II, 45–6, in *The Complete Works*, p. 1535.
13. Severn, *Letters*, quoted in Cacciatore, *A Room*, p. 56.
14. Hillard, *Six Months*, p. 271.
15. Shelley, *Adonais*, in *The Complete Works*, II, p. 403.
16. *The Protestant Cemetery*, p. 17.

4244   NOTES

17. Eliot, *Life*, p. 349; Ruskin, *Diaries*, p. 117; James, *Italian Hours*, p. 194.
18. Ellmann, *Wilde*, p. 74.
19. Wilde, *Poems*, p. 130.
20. James, *Daisy Miller*, p. 201.
21. Gardiner, *Sights*, pp. 289–90.
22. Clark, *Rome*, (1982 ed. only), p. 329.
23. Morton, *A Traveller*, p. 248.
24. Gibbon, *The Decline and Fall*, I, p. 234.
25. Bowen, *A Time*, pp. 32–3.
26. James, *Italian Hours*, pp. 161–2.
27. Addison, *Remarks*, p. 116.
28. Melville, *Journal*, p. 209.
29. Hawthorne, *The Marble Faun*, II, p. 474.
30. Dickens, *Pictures*, pp. 476–7.
31. Bowen, *A Time*, p. 35.
32. Eaton, *Rome*, II, p. 365.
33. Byron, *Childe Harold*, IV, 103, in *The Complete Poetical Works*, II, p. 158.
34. Cooper, *Gleanings*, p. 206.
35. Dupaty, *Travels*, pp. 149–50.
36. *Murray's Handbook*, (1871 ed.) p. 70.
37. Byron, *Childe Harold*, IV, 102, in *The Complete Poetical Works*, II, p. 158.
38. Ibsen, *Correspondence*, p. 82.
39. Trollope, *A Visit*, p. 193.
40. Dickens, *Pictures*, p. 472.
41. Arms, *Italian Vignettes*, p. 90.
42. Pliny, *Natural History*, XXXVI, in Pollitt, *The Art of Rome*, p. 137.
43. James, *Italian Hours*, pp. 146–47.
44. Adams, *Letters*, p. 144.
45. Chateaubriand, *Recollections*, p. 20.
46. James, *Italian Hours*, p. 168.
47. Ruskin, *Modern Painters*, I, II, II, II, p. 153.
48. Hillard, *Six Months*, p. 318.
49. Respighi, *The Pines of Rome*, cover notes.
50. Woolf, *Letters* p. 367.
51. *De Locis*, in Krautheimer, *Rome: Profile*, p. 83.
52. Capgrave, *Ye Solace*, in Gaston, 'English Travellers', p. 145.
53. Munday, *The English*, in Gaston, ibid. p. 146.
54. Dickens, *Pictures*, p. 504.
55. Goethe, *Italian Journey*, p. 461.
56. Dickens, *Pictures*, p. 502.
57. Miller, *Letters*, III, pp. 51–6, in Gaston, 'English Travellers', p. 154.
58. Castiglione, *The Book*, (1900 ed.), in Gaston, ibid. p. 148.
59. De Blainville, *Travels*, II, pp. 541–5, in Gaston, ibid. p. 153.
60. Andersen, *The Improvisatore*, p. 11.

5. FIFTH WALK

1. Wilbur, 'For the New Railway Station', in Williams, ed., *A Roman Collection*, p. 68.
2. O'Faolain, *A Summer*, p. 124.
3. Darretta, *Vittorio de Sica*, pp. 69–73.
4. Bagot, *My Italian Year*, p. 152.
5. Berlioz, *Autobiography*, p. 193.
6. Cooper, *Gleanings*, pp. 186–7.
7. Hawthorne, *Note-Books*, p. 152.
8. Simon, *Rome*, p. 319.
9. Stendhal, *A Roman Journal*, p. 195; Hawthorne, *Note-Books*, p. 65; Eliot, *Life and Letters*, p. 344; Berenson, *The Passionate Sightseer*, p. 21.
10. James, *Italian Hours*, p. 148.
11. Potter, *The Colour*, p. 102.
12. Howells, *Roman Holidays*, pp. 139–40.
13. Simon, *Rome*, p. 335.
14. De Brosses, *Viaggio*, p. 507.
15. Simon, *Rome*, p. 335.
16. Stendhal, *A Roman Journal*, p. 254.
17. Trollope, *A Visit*, p. 372.
18. Head, *Rome*, II, p. 322.
19. James, *Italian Hours*, p. 147.
20. Jameson, *Diary*, I, p. 183–4.
21. Dante, *The Divine Comedy, Paradiso*, XXXI, pp. 183–4.
22. Morgan, *Italy*, in Keaveney, *Views*, p. 160.
23. Morton, *A Traveller*, p. 187.
24. Head, *Rome*, II, p. 249; Hawthorne, *Note-Books*, p. 73.
25. Batcheller, *Glimpses*, p. 106.
26. Clark, *Rome*, p. 45.
27. Longfellow, *Outre-Mer*, pp. 247–8.
28. Taine, *Italy*, p. 263.
29. Morgan, *Italy*, in Keaveney, *Views*, p. 160.
30. Hillard, *Six Months*, p. 211.
31. Gardiner, *Sights*, pp. 167–8.
32. Evill, *A Winter Journey*, pp. 119–20.
33. Panciroli and Posterla, *Roma Sacra*, p. 63.
34. Gardiner, *Sights*, p. 104.
35. James, *Italian Hours*, p. 214.
36. Lanciani, *Wandering*, p. 208.
37. Eaton, *Rome*, I, p. 444.
38. Stendhal, *A Roman Journal*, p. 199.
39. De Sade, *Voyage*, p. 289.
40. Dickens, *Pictures*, p. 500.
41. *Nightingale in Rome*, p. 120.
42. Elliot, *Pictures*, pp. 39–40.

43. Zola, *Rome*, I, p. 231.
44. Taine, *Italy*, p. 136.
45. James, *Letters*, pp. 163–4.
46. Shelley, *Prometheus*, in *The Complete Works*, II, p. 172.
47. Melville, *Journal*, pp. 192–3.
48. Berenson, *The Passionate Sightseer*, pp. 33–4.

6. Sixth Walk

1. Stendhal, *A Roman Journal*, p. 77.
2. Zola, *Rome*, I, p. 206.
3. Montaigne, *Journal*, II, p. 106.
4. Evelyn, *Diary*, II, pp. 381–2.
5. Goethe, *Italian Journey*, pp. 445–69.
6. Dickens, *Pictures*, p. 484.
7. Ibid. p. 482.
8. Crawford, *Ave Roma*, pp. 184–5.
9. Waddington, *Italian Letters*, pp. 244–5, quoted in Vance, *America's Rome*, II, p. 279.
10. Hawthorne, *Note-Books*, p. 121.
11. Donaldson, *Cheever*, p. 153.
12. Ruskin, *Diaries*, p. 119.
13. Melville, *Journal*, p. 208.
14. Taine, *Italy*, p. 227.
15. Wilde, *The Letters*, p. 823.
16. Marcus Aurelius, *The Communings*, X, 10, p. 227.
17. Potter, *The Colour*, p. 197.
18. Harrison, *Italian Days*, p. 227.
19. Adams, *Letters*, p. 150.
20. Chekhov, *Letters*, p. 192.
21. Juvenal, *Thirteen Satires*, III, p. 17.
22. Hutton, *Literary Landmarks*, p. 50.
23. Morton, *A Traveller*, p. 304.
24. Augustus, *Monumentum*, II, 12, in Pollitt, *The Art of Rome*, p. 118.
25. Morton, *A Traveller*, pp. 305–6.
26. Pepper, *See Rome*, pp. 26–30.
27. Lewis, *Babbitt*, pp. 97, 196.
28. Schorer, *Sinclair Lewis*, p. 577.
29. Smollett, *Travels*, p. 239.
30. Elliott, *Pictures*, pp. 9–10.
31. Howells, *Roman Holidays*, pp. 175–6.
32. Ruskin, *Diaries*, p. 120.
33. Simon, *Rome*, p. 38.
34. O'Faolain, *A Summer*, p. 140.
35. Simon, *Rome*, p. 36.

36. Montaigne, *Journal*, II, pp. 89–90.
37. Matthews, *Diary*, p. 267.
38. Dickens, *Pictures*, p. 506.
39. Harrison, *Italian Days*, p. 298.
40. Dixon, 'Handel's Music', pp. 29–30.
41. Moretti, *Artists*, p. 2.
42. Adams, *Letters*, p. 156.
43. Lubbock, *Roman Pictures*, pp. 237–8.
44. Moretti, *Artists*, p. 2.
45. Jones, *Memoirs*, p. 54.
46. Chitty, *That Singular Person*, p. 41.
47. Canova, *I quaderni, passim*.
48. Angeli, *Le cronache*, p. 13.
49. Mendelssohn, *Letters*, pp. 77–8.
50. Wilson, *Europe*, p. 246.
51. Fitzgibbon, *A Taste*, p. 5.
52. Keats, *Selected Poems*, pp. 299–300.
53. Cacciatore, *A Room*, p. 10.
54. Rogers, *Keats*, pp. 17–18.
55. MacMillan, *Roman Mosaics*, p. 13.
56. Inturrisi quoted in Harrison, *Italian Days*, p. 304.
57. Story, *Roba*, I, p. 40.
58. Wharton, *A Backward Glance*, p. 29.
59. Andersen, *A Visit*, p. 106.
60. Simon, *Rome*, p. 103.
61. Coleridge, *Note-Books*, II, n. 2759.
62. Spence, *Observations* [1732], II, n. 1368. p. 503.
63. Zeyer, *Jan Maria Plojhar*, in Parpagliolo, *Italia*, V, p. 373.
64. Potter, *The Colour*, p. 201.
65. Norton, *Notes*, p. 39.
66. Sitwell, *Baroque*, p. 98.
67. Clark, *Rome*, p. 264.
68. Hutton, *Literary Landmarks*, p. 44.
69. Ruskin, *Diaries*, p. 126.
70. Wilde, *Letters*, p. 826.
71. Eaton, *Rome*, II, p. 29.
72. Dickens, *Pictures*, p. 518.

7. Seventh Walk

1. Brydges, *Horae*, quoted in Haskell, *Patrons*, p. 63.
2. Forsyth, *Remarks*, p. 184.
3. White, *Fragments*, p. 62.
4. Ruskin, *Diaries*, p. 131.
5. James, *Italian Hours*, p. 201.

6. Teilhard de Chardin, *Letters*, p. 300.
7. De Goncourt, *Madame Gervaisais*, p. 162.
8. Harrison, *Italian Days*, p. 320.
9. O'Faolain, *A Summer*, p. 138.
10. Zola, *Rome*, II, p. 123.
11. Murray, *Italy*, p. 176.
12. Simon, *Rome*, pp. 167–8.
13. Yourcenar, *Memoirs*, pp. 167–8.
14. Stendhal, *Roman Journal*, p. 111.
15. Buddenseig, 'Criticism', pp. 259–60, and 'Classical Influence', p. 336.
16. Buddenseig, 'Criticism', p. 261.
17. Taine, *Italy*, p. 133.
18. Hillard, *Six Months*, p. 199.
19. Gault Millau guide quoted in Mewshaw, *Playing Away*, p. 47.
20. Forsyth, *Remarks*, p. 135.
21. Byron, *Childe Harold*, IV, 146, in *The Complete Poetical Works*, II, p. 173.
22. James, *Letters*, p. 164.
23. Goethe, *Italian Journey*, pp. 125, 135.
24. Hawthorne, *Note-Books*, p. 187.
25. Batcheller, *Glimpses*, p. 258.
26. Smollett, *Travels*, p. 259.
27. *Nightingale in Rome*, p. 74.
28. Bowen, *A Time*, p. 174.
29. *Murray's Handbook*, (1871 ed.), p. 165.
30. Hawthorne, *Note-Books*, p. 95.
31. O'Faolain, *A Summer*, p. 129.
32. Trillin, *Travels*, pp. 168–9.
33. Harrison, *Italian Days*, p. 287.
34. Stendhal, *Roman Journal*, p. 213.
35. Hawthorne, *Note-Books*, p. 77.
36. Clark, *Rome*, p. 265.
37. Campbell, *Vitruvius*, I, Introduction.
38. Wright, *Observations*, I, p. 216.
39. Vance, *America's Rome*, II, p. 81; Crawford, *Ave Rome*, p. 326.
40. McCarthy, *Birds*, p. 264.
41. Longfellow, *Outre-Mer*, pp. 239–40.
42. *Murray's Handbook*, (1871 ed.), p. 96.
43. Smollett, *Travels*, p. 243.
44. Morse, *Letters*, p. 344.
45. Hawthorne, *Note-Books*, pp. 185–6.
46. Jannattoni, *Roma*, p. 87.
47. Morton, *A Traveller*, p. 290.
48. Lanciani, *New Tales*, pp. 47–51.
49. De Tuddo, *Rome*, p. 100.
50. Blotner, *Faulkner*, II, p. 1487.
51. Ibid.

8. Eighth Walk

1. Malamud, *Pictures*, p. 4.
2. Kémeri, *Rambles*, p. 259.
3. Bowen, *A Time*, p. 104.
4. Potter, *The Colour*, pp. 223–4.
5. Hawthorne, *Note-Books*, p. 86.
6. Lubbock, *Roman Pictures*, p. 183.
7. Le Vot, *Fitzgerald*, p. 181.
8. Fitzgerald, 'The High Cost', p. 15.
9. Ibid.; *Tender is the Night*, p. 226.
10. Harrison, *Italian Days*, p. 323.
11. Stendhal, *Roman Journal*, p. 119.
12. Hibbard, *Bernini*, p. 137.
13. Dupaty, *Travels*, p. 272.
14. Head, *Rome*, I, p. 238.
15. Vigée LeBrun, *Souvenirs*, p. 166.
16. De Brosses, *Viaggio*, p. 355.
17. Stendhal, *Roman Journal*, p. 120.
18. Clark, *Rome*, p. 274.
19. Howells, *Roman Holidays*, p. 174.
20. Lees-Milne, *Roman Mornings*, p. 120.
21. Varriano, *Italian Baroque*, p. 54.
22. Wharton, *Italian Backgrounds*, p. 186.
23. Simon, *Rome*, pp. 278–79.
24. De Brosses, *Viaggio*, p. 499; Richard, *Description*, V, p. 258.
25. Hawthorne, *Note-Books*, p. 93.
26. Elliot, *Diary*, pp. 299, 302–3.
27. Petrarch, *Rerum familiarum*, VI, 2, in Baxendall, *Giotto*, p. 51.
28. Shelley, *Letters*, in *The Complete Works*, X, pp. 42–3.
29. Pepper, *Guido Reni*, p. 43.
30. Richardson, *An Account*, p. 316.
31. Hawthorne, *Note-Books*, p. 91.
32. Jameson, *Diary*, p. 271.
33. Berenson quoted in Pepper, *Guido Reni*, p. 49.
34. *Blue Guide, Rome*, (1985 ed.) p. 175; (1989 ed.) p. 175.
35. Hutton, *Literary Landmarks*, p. 22.
36. James, *William Wetmore Story*, I, p. 286.
37. Ibid. pp. 28, 341.
38. Curran, *Shelley's Cenci*, p. xi.
39. Ibid. p. xii.
40. Hillard, *Six Months*, p. 233.
41. Witmer, *Wild Oats*, p. 133.
42. Nietzsche, *Ecce Homo*, p. 104.
43. Andersen, *A Visit*, p. 107.
44. Browning, *The Ring*, in *The Complete Works*, VII, p. 22.

45. *ROMEACCESS*, p. 19.
46. Andersen, *The Improvisatore*, p. 3.
47. Hawthorne, *The Marble Faun*, I, p. 226.
48. Fellini, 'Via Veneto', in *Fellini on Fellini*, pp. 67–8.
49. Hofmann, *Rome*, pp. 179–80.
50. James, *Italian Hours*, p. 211.
51. Stendhal, *Roman Journal*, pp. 124–5.
52. Lassels, *Voyage*, II, p. 171.
53. Rilke, *Letters*, p. 135.
54. Wilson, *Europe*, p. 72.
55. Vidal, *The Judgement*, pp. 54–5.
56. Jones, *Memoirs*, p. 91.
57. Addison, *A Letter*, II, pp. 87–8.
58. De Tuddo, *Rome*, p. 92.
59. Morton, *A Traveller*, p. 271.
60. James, *Italian Hours*, pp. 205–6.
61. Zola, *Rome*, I, pp. 216–17.

9. NINTH WALK

1. Kostof, *The Third Rome*, p. 15.
2. Gibbs, *European Journey*, p. 176.
3. Kidder Smith, *Italy Builds*, p. 106.
4. Spence, *Letters*, p. 121.
5. Stendhal, *Roman Journal*, p. 170.
6. Shakespeare, *Julius Caesar*, III, ii, 190–4, in *The Complete Works*, p. 833.
7. Byron, *Selected Poetry and Letters*, p. 416.
8. Potter, *The Colour*, p. 244–5.
9. Ray, *Observations*, p. 362.
10. Ibid. p. 405.
11. James, *Italian Hours*, pp. 109–10.
12. Masson, *Companion*, pp. 138–9.
13. Murray, *Italy*, p. 193.
14. Taine, *Italy*, pp. 218–19.
15. Zola, *Rome*, I, p. 47.
16. Richardson, *An Account*, p. 142.
17. *Nightingale in Rome*, p. 76.
18. Goethe, *Italian Journey*, p. 48.
19. Moore, *A View*, I, pp. 10–11.
20. Masson, *Companion*, p. 180.
21. Hawthorne, *Note-Books*, p. 209; Jameson, *Diary*, p. 189.
22. Greville, *Memoirs*, p. 266.
23. Bowen, *A Time*, p. 128.
24. Moryson, *An Itinerary*, p. 262.
25. James, *Roderick Hudson*, pp. 191–2.

26. Zola, *Rome*, II, p. 43.
27. Hare, *Walks*, p. 675.
28. Morton, *A Traveller*, p. 403.
29. De Tuddo, *Rome*, p. 6; Morton, *A Traveller*, p. 411.
30. Simon, *Rome*, p. 224.
31. Belli in De Tuddo, *Rome*, p. 47.
32. Elliot, *Diary*, pp. 31–2.
33. S. Hawthorne, *Notes*, pp. 283–4.
34. Harrison, *Italian Days*, pp. 225–6.
35. Eustace, *A Tour*, pp. 83–4.
36. James, *Letters*, p. 173.
37. Norton, *Notes*, pp. 44–7.
38. Taine, *Italy*, p. 269.
39. Simon, *Rome*, p. 234.
40. Stendhal, *Roman Journal*, p. 185.
41. Eaton, *Rome*, II, p. 137.
42. Ibid. pp. 137–8.
43. Peale, *Notes*, pp. 249–51.
44. Flaubert, *Notes*, p. 142.
45. Eaton, *Rome*, II, p. 138.
46. Eliot, *Life*, p. 345.
47. Winckelmann, *History*, I, p. 206.
48. Ruskin, *Diaries*, I. p. 128.
49. *Murray's Handbook* (1871 ed.), p. 189.
50. Gregorovius, *Rome*, VIII, I, p. 132; Clark, *Rome*, p. 255.
51. Lees-Milne, *Roman Mornings*, p. 70.
52. Morton, *The Fountains*, p. 170.
53. Longfellow, *Outre-Mer*, p. 242.
54. Martial, *Epigrams*, IV, 64, in Dudley, *Urbs Roma*, p. 219.
55. Melville, *Journal*, p. 207.
56. Chateaubriand, *Memoirs*, pp. 351–2.

10. Tenth Walk

1. Hillard, *Six Months*, p. 262.
2. Virgil, *Aeneid*, III, 62–5, in Dudley, *Urbs Roma*, p. 43.
3. Lassels, *Voyage*, II, p. 318.
4. Garrick, *Letters*, p. 396.
5. Smollett, *Travels*, p. 237.
6. Melville, *Journal*, p. 190.
7. Hawthorne, *Note-Books*, p. 65.
8. Rogers, *Letters*, p. 170.
9. Bonadella, *Fellini*, p. 267.
10. Smith, *The Tiber*, p. 40.
11. Taine, *Italy*, p. 16.

12. Ruskin, *Diaries*, pp. 132–3.
13. Trollope, *A Visit*, p. 184.
14. Montfaucon, *The Travels*, pp. 319–20.
15. Cellini, *Autobiography*, pp. 271–2.
16. Morton, *A Traveller*, p. 398.
17. Hugo, *Good Luck*, p. 23
18. Meeks, *Italian Architecture*, p. 353.
19. Clark, *Rome*, p. 209.
20. Harrison, *Italian Days*, p. 203.
21. Dickens, *Pictures*, p. 474.
22. Eliot, *Life*, p. 343.
23. Smollett, *Travels*, p. 255.
24. Zola, *Rome*, II, p. 130.
25. Ibid. pp. 252, 350.
26. *Nightingale in Rome*, p. 243.
27. Dostoevsky, *Letters*, II, p. 72.
28. Goethe, *Italian Journey*, p. 129.
29. Stendhal, *Roman Journal*, p. 54.
30. *Boswell on the Grand Tour*, p. 66.
31. Hillard, *Six Months*, pp. 144–5.
32. Ibid. p. 145.
33. Berlioz, *Autobiography*, p. 190.
34. James, *Italian Hours*, p. 152.
35. James, *Daisy Miller*, p. 180, quoted in Vance, *America's Rome*, II, p. 98.
36. Fauré, *Rome*, p. 87.
37. Browning, 'Christmas Eve', X, 560–8, in *The Complete Works*, V, p. 71.
38. Twain, *The Innocents*, p. 194.
39. James, *Portrait*, p. 272.
40. Byron, *Childe Harold*, IV, 158, in *The Complete Poetical Works* II, p. 177.
41. Smollett, *Travels*, p. 255.
42. *Murray's Handbook*, p. 110.
43. Lees-Milne, *Saint Peter's*, p. 313.
44. Lockhart, *Memoirs*, V, p. 402.
45. Milnes, 'Sir Walter Scott', in *Oxford Book of Travel Verse*, p. 112.
46. Raguenet, *Les Monuments*, p. 235.
47. Hillard, *Six Months*, p. 139.
48. Updike, 'Mea Culpa', in *Assorted Prose*, p. 218.
49. Ibid. p. 219.
50. Waterton, *Autobiography*, in *Essays in Natural History*, p. lxxi.
51. Wilde, *The Letters*, p. 825.
52. Ibid. p. 821.
53. Jonas, *Thomas Mann*, p. 8.
54. Chateaubriand, *Memoirs*, p. 350.
55. Jameson, *Diary*, p. 130.
56. Thomas, *Letters*, p. 627.

57. Winckelmann, *History*, in Vatican Museums, *Classical Art*, p. 14.
58. Goethe, *Italian Journey*, p. 393.
59. West, *The Life*, pp. 104–5.
60. Haskell and Penny, *Taste*, p. 243.
61. Byron, *Childe Harold*, IV, 160, in *The Complete Poetical Works*, II, p. 178.
62. *Boswell on the Grand Tour*, p. 67.
63. *Nightingale in Rome*, p. 61.
64. Dickens, *A Christmas Carol*, in *The Works*, p. 93.
65. Haskell and Penny, *Taste*, p. 312.
66. Hardy, 'The Vatican: Sala delle Muse', in *Complete Poems*, p. 103.
67. Wilde, *Letters*, p. 826.
68. Vasari, *Lives*, p. 52.
69. *Murray's Handbook*, p. 243.
70. James, *Letters*, p. 166.
71. Clark, *Rome*, pp. 268–9.
72. Simon, *Rome*, p. 22.
73. De Maupaussant, *Chroniques*, p. 328.
74. Taine, *Italy*, pp. 189–90.
75. Coleridge, *Notebooks*, n. 3286.
76. Eitner, *Géricault*, p. 100.
77. Tchaikovsky, *Letters*, p. 235.
78. Harrison, *Italian Days*, p. 270.
79. Melville, *Journal*, p. 200.
80. Chekhov, *Letters*, p. 191.
81. Stendhal, *A Roman Journal*, p. 23.
82. Emerson, *Journals*, p. 89.
83. Huxley, *Letters*, p. 201.
84. *Nightingale in Rome*, pp. 276–7.
85. Rilke, *Letters*, p. 133.
86. Hawthorne, *The Marble Faun*, II, p. 373.

BIBLIOGRAPHY

PRIMARY SOURCES

Henry Adams, *The Letters of Henry Adams*, Vol. 1, Cambridge and London, 1982.

Joseph Addison, *A Letter from Italy to the Right Honourable Charles, Lord Halifax*, 2 vols., London, 1709.

——*Remarks on Several Parts of Italy . . . in the Years 1701, 1702, 1703*, London, 1753.

Hans Christian Andersen, *The Improvisatore*, trans. Mary Howitt, Boston, n.d. (1st ed. 1833).

——*A Visit to Germany, Italy, and Malta, 1840–1841*, trans. Grace Thornton, London, 1985.

Mary W. Arms, *Italian Vignettes*, New York, 1909.

Richard Bagot, *My Italian Year*, Leipzig, 1912.

Tryphosa Bates Batcheller, *Glimpses of Italian Court Life, Happy Days in Italia Adorata*, New York, 1906.

Bernard Berenson, *The Passionate Sightseer, from the Diaries 1947 to 1956*, New York, 1960.

Hector Berlioz, *Autobiography . . . Comprising his Travels in Italy, Germany, Russia, and England*, trans. Rachel and Eleanor Holmes, 2 vols., London, 1884.

James Boswell, *Boswell on the Grand Tour: Italy, Corsica, and France 1765–66*, New York, 1955.

Elizabeth Bowen, *A Time in Rome*, New York, 1960.

Charles De Brosses, *Viaggio in Italia* [1739–40], trans. Bruno Schacherl of *Lettres familières*, Rome and Bari, 1973.

Robert Browning, *Christmas Eve and Easter Day* in *The Complete Works*, Vol. 5, Athens and Waco, 1981.

——*The Ring and the Book*, in *The Complete Works*, Vol. 7, Athens and Waco, 1985.

Michel Butor, *A Change of Heart*, trans. Jean Stewart, New York, 1969.

Lord Byron, *Childe Harold's Pilgrimage* in *The Complete Poetical Works*, Vol. 2, Oxford, 1980.

——*Don Juan* in *The Complete Poetical Works*, Vol. 5, Oxford, 1986.

——*Manfred*, in *The Complete Poetical Works*, Vol. 4, Oxford, 1985.

——*Selected Poetry and Letters*, New York, 1962.

Colen Campbell, *Vitruvius Brittanicus*, Vol. 1, London, 1715.

Antonio Canova, *I quaderni di viaggio (1779–1780)*, Venice, 1959.

Benvenuto Cellini, *The Autobiography of Benvenuto Cellini*, trans. John Addington Symonds, Garden City, 1961.

Chateaubriand, *The Memoirs*, trans. Robert Baldick, New York, 1961.

——*Recollections of Italy, England and America*, Philadelphia, 1916.

Anton Chekhov, *Letters*, trans. M. H. Heim, New York, 1973.

Susan Chitty, *That Singular Person Called Lear*, New York, 1989.

Eleanor Clark, *Rome and a Villa*, Garden City, 1952; 2nd ed., New York, 1982.

Samuel Taylor Coleridge, *Notebooks*, Vols. 2 and 3, New York, 1961–73.

James Fenimore Cooper, *Gleanings in Europe* [1829–30], Albany, 1981.

Joseph Cradock, *Literary and Miscellaneous Memoirs*, London, 1826.

Francis Marion Crawford, *Ave Roma Immortalis*, New York, 1906 (1st ed. 1898).

Dante Alighieri, *The Divine Comedy*, trans. Lawrence G. White, New York, 1948.

John Darretta, *Vittorio de Sica, A Guide to References and Sources*, Boston, 1983.

Charles Dickens, *A Christmas Carol* and *Pictures from Italy* in *The Works of Charles Dickens*, Vol. XIV, New York, 1900.

Scott Donaldson, *John Cheever, a Biography*, New York, 1988.

Fyodor Dostoevsky, *Complete Letters*, Vol. II, trans. David A. Lowe and Ronald Meyer, Ann Arbor, 1988.

Charles Dupaty, *Travels through Italy in a Series of Letters Written in the Year 1785*, London, 1788.

John Dyer, *The Ruins of Rome*, London, 1740.

Charlotte Eaton, *Rome in the Nineteenth Century*, 2 vols., London, 1852 (1st ed. 1820).

George Eliot, *Life and Letters*, Vol. 2, New York, 1901.

Frances Elliot, *Diary of an Idle Woman in Italy*, London, 1871.

——*Pictures of Old Rome*, Leipzig, 1882.

Richard Ellmann, *Oscar Wilde*, New York, 1988.

Ralph Waldo Emerson, *Journals*, Vol. 3, Boston and New York, 1903.

Erasmus of Rotterdam, *Correspondence* in *Collected Works of Erasmus*, trans. R. A. B. Myers and D. F. S. Thomson, Vol. 3, Toronto and Buffalo, 1976.

Rev. John Chetwode Eustace, *A Classical Tour Through Italy*, 2 vols., London, 1817 (1st ed. 1813).

John Evelyn, *The Diary of John Evelyn*, Vol. II, Oxford, 1955.

William Evill, *A Winter Journey to Rome and Back*, London, 1870.

Gabriel Fauré, *Rome*, London and Boston, 1926.

Federico Fellini, *Fellini on Fellini*, trans. Isabel Quigley, New York, 1976.

F. Scott Fitzgerald, *Correspondence*, New York, *c.*1980.

——'The High Cost of Maccaroni', *Interim* IV (1954), No. 1–2, pp. 6–15.

——*Tender is the Night*, New York, 1962 (1st ed. 1934).

Gustave Flaubert, *Notes de voyages*, in *Oeuvres Complètes*, Vol. II, Paris, 1910.

Joseph Forsyth, *Remarks on antiquities, arts, and letters during an excursion in Italy in the years 1802 and 1803*, London, 1816 (1st ed. 1813).

Paul Fussell, *Abroad, British Literary Traveling between the Wars*, Oxford and New York, 1980.

William Gardiner, *Sights in Italy*, London, 1847.

David Garrick, *The Letters of David Garrick* [1763–64], Vol. 1, London, 1963.

Edward Gibbon, *Autobiography*, London, 1970.

——*The Decline and Fall of the Roman Empire*, 3 vols., New York, 1946.

Philip Gibbs, *European Journey*, New York, 1934.

Nikolai Gogol, *Letters*, trans. Carl R. Proffer, Ann Arbor, 1968.

Johann Wolfgang von Goethe, *Italian Journey (1786–1788)*, trans. W. H. Auden and Elizabeth Mayer, New York, 1968.

Edmond and Jules de Goncourt, *Madame Gervaisais*, Paris, 1876.

Ferdinand Gregorovius, *History of the City of Rome in the Middle Ages*, 8 vols., London, 1909.

Charles C. F. Greville, *The Greville Memoirs*, Vol. 1, New York, 1875.

John Gunther, 'S.P.Q.R.', in *Twelve Cities*, New York, Evanston and London, 1967.

Thomas Hardy, *The Complete Poems of Thomas Hardy*, New York, 1976.

Augustus J. C. Hare, *Walks in Rome*, New York, *c.*1893 (1st ed. 1871).

Barbara Grizzuti Harrison, *Italian Days*, New York, 1989.

Nathaniel Hawthorne, *French and Italian Note-Books* [1858–9], Boston, 1894.

——*The Marble Faun*, New York, 1894 (1st ed. 1860).

Sophia A. P. Hawthorne, *Notes in England and Italy*, New York, 1869.

William Hazlitt, *Notes of a Journey through France and Italy* [1824–5], London, 1826.

Sir George Head, *Rome: A Tour of Many Days*, 3 vols., London, 1849.

Howard Hibbard, *Bernini*, Harmondsworth, 1965.

George Stillman Hillard, *Six Months in Italy*, Boston, 1866 (1st ed. 1853).

Paul Hofmann, *Rome, The Sweet Tempestuous Life*, New York, 1982.

Horace, *Odes*, trans. Christopher Smart, Victoria, 1979.

Horace, *Satires, Epistles, and Ars Poetica*, trans. H. Rushton Fairclough, Cambridge, Mass., 1978.

James Howell, *Instructions for Forreine Travell*, London, 1869 (1st ed. 1642).

William Dean Howells, *Italian Journeys*, Boston, 1867.

——*Roman Holidays*, New York and London, 1908.

Edward Hutton, *Rome*, London, 1909.

Richard Hugo, *Good Luck in Cracked Italian*, New York and Cleveland, 1969.

Aldous Huxley, *Along the Road*, New York, 1925.

——*Letters*, New York and Evanston, 1969.

Hendrik Ibsen, *Correspondence*, trans. Mary Morison, London, 1905.

Henry James, *Daisy Miller*, in *The Tales of Henry James*, Vol. 3, Oxford, 1984.
——*Italian Hours*, New York, 1979 (1st ed. 1909).
——*Letters*, Vol. 1, Cambridge, Mass., 1974.
——*Portrait of a Lady*, New York and London, 1963 (1st ed. 1881).
——*Roderick Hudson*, Harmondsworth and New York, 1969 (1st ed. 1875).
——*Transatlantic Sketches*, Boston, 1875.
——*William Wetmore Story and his Friends*, 2 vols., Boston, 1903.
Anna Jameson, *Dairy of an Ennuyée*, Boston, 1866 (1st ed. 1826).
Thomas Jones, *Memoirs* in *The Walpole Society*, Vol. 32, London, 1951.
James Joyce, *Letters*, Vol. 2, New York, 1966.
Juvenal, *Thirteen Satires*, trans. Alexander Leeper, London, 1902.
John Keats, *Selected Poems and Letters*, Boston, 1959.
Sándor Kémeri, *Rambles with Anatole France*, trans. Emil Lengyel, London, 1927.
Spiro Kostof, *The Third Rome 1870–1950*, Berkeley, 1973.
Rodolfo Lanciani, *New Tales of Old Rome*, London, 1901.
——*Wandering through Ancient Roman Churches*, New York, 1924.
Richard Lassels, *The Voyage of Italy*, Paris and London, 1670.
Vernon Lee [Violet Paget], *The Spirit of Rome: Leaves from a Diary*, London and New York, 1906.
James Lees-Milne, *Roman Mornings*, London, 1956.
——*Saint Peter's*, Boston, 1967.
Sinclair Lewis, *Babbitt*, New York, 1922.
Franz Liszt, *The Letters of Franz Liszt to Olga von Meyendorff 1871–1886*, trans. William R. Tyler, Washington DC, 1979.
John Lockhart, *Memoirs of Sir Walter Scott*, Vol. 5, London and New York, 1900.
Henry Wadsworth Longfellow, *Outre-Mer* in *The Works of Henry Wadsworth Longfellow*, Vol. VII, Boston and New York, 1886.
James Russell Lowell, 'Leaves from my Journal in Italy and Elsewhere', in *Fireside Travels*, Boston, 1865.
Percy Lubbock, *Roman Pictures* in *Percy Lubbock Reader*, Freeport, Maine, 1957 (1st ed. 1923).
Martin Luther, 'An Appeal to the Ruling Class of German Nationality as to the Amelioration of the State of Christendom', in *Martin Luther, Selections from his Writings*, New York, 1961.
Georgina Masson, *The Companion Guide to Rome*, New York, 1986.
Mary McCarthy, *Birds of America*, New York, 1965.
Rose Macaulay, *Pleasure of Ruins*, New York, 1966 (1st ed. 1953).
Bernard Malamud, *Pictures of Fidelman*, New York, 1969.
Hugh MacMillan, *Roman Mosaics or Studies in Rome and its Neighbourhood*, London, 1888.
Marcus Aurelius Antoninus, *The Communings with Himself*, trans. C. R. Haines, London and New York, 1924.
Henry Matthews, *The Diary of an Invalid*, London, 1820.

Guy de Maupassant, *Chroniques, Études, Correspondence*, Paris, 1938.

Carroll L. V. Meeks, *Italian Architecture 1750–1914*, New Haven and London, 1966.

Herman Melville, *Journal of a Visit to Europe and the Levant 1856–1857*, Princeton, 1955.

Felix Mendelssohn Bartholdy, *Letters from Italy and Switzerland*, trans. Lady Wallace, London, 1887.

Michael Mewshaw, *Playing Away, Roman Holidays and other Mediterranean Encounters*, New York, 1988.

W. J. C. Moens, *English Travellers and Italian Brigands, a Narrative of Capture and Captivity*, New York, 1866.

Michel de Montaigne, *The Journal of Montaigne's Travels in Italy . . . in 1580–81*, 3 vols., London, 1903.

Bernard de Montfaucon, *The Travels of the Learned Father Montfaucon from Paris thro' Italy*, London, 1712.

John Moore, *A View of Society and Manners in Italy*, 2 vols., London, 1781.

Ugo Moretti, *Artists in Rome, Tales of the Babuino*, trans. William Weaver, New York, 1958.

Samuel F. B. Morse, *Letters and Journals*, Vol. I, New York, 1914.

Francis Mortoft, *Francis Mortoft: His Book, Being his Travels through France and Italy 1658–1659*, London, 1925.

H. V. Morton, *The Fountains of Rome*, New York, 1966.

——*A Traveller in Rome*, New York, 1957.

Fynes Moryson, *An Itinerary*, Glasgow, 1907 (1st ed. 1617).

William Murray, *Italy, the Fatal Gift*, New York, 1982.

Murray's Handbook of Rome and Environs, 11th ed., London, 1872 (1st ed. 1843).

Thomas Nashe, *The Unfortunate Traveller*, Oxford, 1927 (1st ed. 1594).

Margherita Naval, *A Roma si racconta che . . .* , Rome, c.1978.

Friedrich Nietzsche, *Ecce Homo*, New York, 1911.

Florence Nightingale in Rome. Letters written . . . in the Winter of 1847–1848, Philadelphia, 1981.

Charles Eliot Norton, *Notes of Travel and Study in Italy*, Boston, 1859.

Sean O'Faolain, *A Summer in Italy*, London, 1949.

Francis Osborne, 'Advice to a Son' in Louis B. Wright, *Advice to a Son. Precepts of Lord Burghley, Sir Walter Raleigh, and Francis Osborne*, Ithaca, 1962 (1st ed. 1656).

Ottavio Panciroli and Francesco Posterla, *Roma sacra e moderna*, Sala Bolognese, 1977 (1st ed. 1725).

Francesco Petrarch, *Rerum familiarium Libri I–VIII*, trans. Aldo S. Bernardo, Albany, 1975.

Rembrandt Peale, *Notes on Italy*, Philadelphia, 1831.

Edgar Allan Poe, *Collected Works*, Vol. I, *Poems*, Cambridge Mass., 1969.

Olave Muriel Potter, *The Colour of Rome*, London and Philadelphia, [1909].

The Protestant Cemetery in Rome, Rome, 1982.

Abbé François Raguenet, *Les Monuments de Rome*, Paris, 1702.

John Ray, *Observations Topographical, Moral, and Philosophical: Made in a Journey through part of the Low Countries, Germany, and France*, London, 1673.

Ottorino Respighi, *The Pines of Rome. The Fountains of Rome*, Mercury-Wing recording, Antal Dorati and the Minneapolis Symphony, n.d.

Abbé Jerome Richard, *Description Historique et Critique de l'Italie*, 6 vols., Dijon, 1766.

Jonathan Richardson, Senior and Junior, *An Account of some of the Statues, Bas-Reliefs, Drawings, and Pictures in Italy*, London, 1722.

Rainer Maria Rilke, *Letters 1892–1910*, trans. J. B. Greene and M. D. H. Norton, New York, 1969.

Samuel Rogers, *Italy, a Poem*, London, 1830.

Will Rogers, *Letters of a Self-Made Diplomat to his President*, Vol. I, New York, 1926.

ROMEACCESS, New York, 1987.

John Ruskin, *The Diaries*, Vol. I, 1853–7, Oxford, 1956.

——*Ruskin in Italy, Letters to his Parents*, Oxford, 1972.

——*Modern Painters*, Vol. I, New York, 1858.

Marquis de Sade, *Voyage d'Italie* in *Oeuvres Complètes*, Vols. 15–16, Paris, 1967.

George Augustus Sala, *Rome and Venice with other Wanderings in Italy, in 1866–1867*, London, 1869.

William Shakespeare, *Henry VIII* and *Julius Caesar* in *The Complete Works*, New York, 1952.

Mary Shelley, *The Letters of Mary Wollstonecraft Shelley*, Vol. 1, Baltimore, 1980.

Percy Bysshe Shelley, *Adonais*, 'Notes on Sculptures in Rome and Florence', *Prometheus Unbound*, and *Letters* in *The Complete Works of Percy Bysshe Shelley*, Vol. II, VI and X, London and New York, 1916–30.

Martin Sherlock, *New Letters from an English Traveller*, London, 1781.

Kate Simon, *Rome, Places and Pleasures*, New York, 1972.

Louis Simond, *A Tour in Italy and Sicily*, London, 1828.

Sacheverell Sitwell, *Baroque and Rococo*, New York, 1967 (published simultaneously in Great Britain with the title *Southern Baroque Revisited*).

Strother A. Smith, *The Tiber and its Tributaries*, Geneva, 1871.

Tobias Smollett, *Travels through France and Italy*, New York, 1981 (1st ed. 1766).

Joseph Spence, *Letters from the Grand Tour*, Montreal and London, 1975.

——*Observations, Anecdotes, and Characters, of Books and Men, Collected from Conversation*, 2 vols., Oxford, 1966 (1st ed. 1820).

Madame de Staël, *Corinne or Italy*, trans. Isabel Hill, Philadelphia, 1973.

Stendhal, *A Roman Journal* [1827–9], trans. Haakon Chevalier of *Promenades dans Rome*, London, 1959.

Laurence Sterne, *A Sentimental Journey through France and Italy by Mr. Yorick*, Berkeley and Los Angeles, 1967 (1st ed. 1768).

Wallace Stevens, 'To an Old Philosopher in Rome', in *Poems by Wallace Stevens*, New York, 1959.

William Wetmore Story, *Roba di Roma*, 2 vols., New York 1887 (1st ed. 1862).

Hippolyte Taine, *Italy, Rome and Naples*, trans. J. Durand, New York, 1871.

Piotr Ilyich Tchaikovsky, *Letters to his Family, an Autobiography*, trans. G. von Meek, New York, 1981.

Pierre Teilhard de Chardin, *Letters from a Traveller*, New York, 1962.

William Makepeace Thackeray, *The Letters and Private Papers*, Vol. 3, Cambridge, Mass., 1946.

Calvin Trillin, *Travels with Alice*, New York, 1989.

Frances Trollope, *A Visit to Italy*, 2 vols., London, 1842.

Italo de Tuddo, *Rome, the Fourth Day*, trans. W. F. McCormick, Rome, 1968.

Ivan Turgenev, *Letters*, trans. David Lowe, Vol. 1, Ann Arbor, 1983.

Mark Twain, *The Innocents Abroad*, New York and Toronto, 1966 (1st ed. 1869).

The United States Catholic Magazine, VI (1847), August, pp. 401–12.

John Updike, 'Mea Culpa, a Travel Note', in *Assorted Prose*, New York, 1965.

Giorgio Vasari, *Lives of the Most Eminent Painters*, trans. Mrs Jonathan Foster, Vol. 2, New York, 1967.

Vatican Museums, *Classical Art*, Florence, 1985.

Elihu Vedder, *The Digressions of Vedder*, London, 1911.

Gore Vidal, *The Judgement of Paris*, New York, 1986 (1st ed. 1952).

Marie Elizabeth Louise Vigée LeBrun, *Souvenirs*, Vol. 1, Paris, 1869 (1st ed. 1837).

Mary King Waddington, *Italian Letters of a Diplomat's Wife*, New York, 1905.

Charles Waterton, *Essays on Natural History . . . with an Autobiography of the Author*, London, 1838.

Benjamin West in *The Life and Studies of Benjamin West Esq.*, comp. John Galt, London, 1816.

Edith Wharton, *A Backward Glance*, New York and London, 1934.

——*Italian Backgrounds*, New York, 1989 (1st ed. 1905).

Rev. Thomas H. White, *Fragments of Italy and the Rhineland*, London 1841.

Oscar Wilde, *The Letters of Oscar Wilde*, London 1962.

——*Poems*, New York, n.d.

Edmund Wilson, *Europe without Baedeker*, Garden City, 1947.

Johann Joachim Winckelmann, *History of Ancient Art*, trans. Alexander Gode, 2 vols., New York, 1968.

Theodore Witmer, *Wild Oats, Sown Abroad*, Philadelphia, 1853.

Virginia Woolf, *The Letters of Virginia Woolf*, Vol. III, New York and London, 1977.

William Wordsworth, 'The Pillar' and 'At Rome', in *The Poetical Works of William Wordsworth*, Boston, 1982.

Edward Wright, *Some Observations made in Travelling through France, Italy, Etc.*, London, 1730.
Marguerite Yourcenar, *Memoirs of Hadrian*, trans. Grace Frick, New York, 1963.
Émile Zola, *Rome*, trans. E. A. Vitzetelly, 2 vols., New York, 1896.

SECONDARY SOURCES

Diego Angeli, *Le croniche del 'Caffè Greco'*, Milan, 1930.
Maurice Andrieux, *Le Français à Rome*, Paris, 1968.
E. S. Bates, *Touring in 1600*, London, 1987 (1st ed. 1911).
Michael Baxendall, *Giotto and the Orators*, Oxford, 1988.
Jeremy Black, *The British and the Grand Tour*, London, 1985.
Joseph Blotner, *Faulkner, a Biography*, 2 vols., New York, 1974.
Blue Guide, Rome and Environs, London and New York, 3rd ed. 1985; 4th ed. 1989.
Peter Bondanella (ed.), *Federico Fellini, Essays in Criticism*, New York, 1978.
Tilmann Buddensieg, 'Criticism of Ancient Architecture in the Sixteenth and Seventeenth Centuries' in *Classical Influences on European Culture 1500–1700*, Cambridge, 1974.
——'Criticism and Praise of the Pantheon in the Middle Ages', in *Classical Influences on European Culture AD 500–1500*, Cambridge, 1971.
Vera Cacciatore, *A Room in Rome*, Rome, London, New York, 1970.
A. M. Canepa, 'From Degenerate Scoundrel to Noble Savage: the Italian Stereotype in Eighteenth-Century British Travel Literature', *English Miscellany*, 1971, No. 22, pp. 107–46.
Stuart Curran, *Shelley's Cenci, Scorpions Ringed with Fire*, Princeton, 1970.
Graham Dixon, 'Händel's Music for the Feast of Our Lady of Mount Carmel', in *Händel e gli Scarlatti a Roma*, Florence, 1987.
Donald R. Dudley, *Urbs Roma, a Source Book of Classical Texts on the City and its Monuments*, London, 1967.
Lorenz Eitner, *Géricault, his Life and Work*, London and Ithaca, 1983.
Margaret W. Ferguson, '"The Afflatus of Ruin": Meditations on Rome by Du Bellay, Spenser, and Stevens, in *Roman Images*, Baltimore and London, 1984.
Theodora Fitzgibbon, *A Taste of Rome*, Boston, 1975.
Robert W. Gaston, 'British Travellers and Scholars in the Roman Catacombs 1450–1900', *Journal of the Warburg and Courtauld Institutes* 46 (1983), pp. 144–65.
Laurance Goldstein, *Ruins and Empire*, Pittsburgh, 1977.
Thomas M. Greene, 'Resurrecting Rome: the Double Task of the Humanist Imagination', in *Rome in the Renaissance, the City and the Myth*, Binghamton, 1982, pp. 41–54.
Francis Haskell, *Patrons and Painters*, New York and London, 1971.
Francis Haskell and Nicholas Penny, *Taste and the Antique, the Lure of Classical Sculpture*, New Haven and London, 1981.

Francis W. Hawcroft, *Travels in Italy 1776–1783 Based on the* Memoirs *of Thomas Jones*, Manchester, 1988.

Laurence Hutton, *Literary Landmarks of Rome*, New York, 1897.

Livio Jannattoni, *Roma e i poeti*, Caltanisetta-Rome, 1960.

Isedore B. Jonas, *Thomas Mann and Italy*, trans. Betty Crouse, University, Alabama, 1969.

Raymond Keaveney, *Views of Rome from the Thomas Ashby Collection in the Vatican Library*, London, 1988.

Richard Krautheimer, *Rome, Profile of a City, 312–1308*, Princeton, 1980.

André Le Vot, *F. Scott Fitzgerald: A Biography*, Garden City, 1983.

Naphtali Lewis and Meyer Reinhold (eds.), *Roman Civilization Sourcebook II: the Empire*, New York, 1955.

Robert S. Miola, *Shakespeare's Rome*, Cambridge, 1983.

Oxford Book of Travel Verse, Oxford and New York, 1986.

Luigi Parpagliolo, *Italia (negli scrittori italiani e stranieri)*, I, *Lazio*, Rome, 1928.

Beverly Pepper and John Hobart, *See Rome and Eat*, Garden City, 1960.

D. Steven Pepper, *Guido Reni: A Complete Catalogue of his Works*, New York, 1984.

R. S. Pine-Coffin, *Bibliography of British and American Travel in Italy to 1860*, Florence, 1974.

J. J. Pollitt, *The Art of Rome c.753 BC–337 AD*, Englewood Cliffs, 1966.

Peter Quennell, *The Colosseum*, New York, 1971.

Neville Rogers, *Keats, Shelley and Rome, an Illustrated Miscellany*, London, 1957 (1st ed. 1949).

J. B. Ross, 'A Study of Twelfth-Century Interest in the Antiquities of Rome', in *Medieval and Historiographical Essays in Honour of J. Westfall Thompson*, Chicago, 1938.

Mark Schorer, *Sinclair Lewis, an American Life*, New York, Toronto and London, 1961.

Ludwig Schudt, *Italienreisen im 17. und 18. Jahrhundert*, Vienna, 1959.

George E. Kidder Smith, *Italy Builds, its Modern Architecture and Native Inheritance*, New York, 1955.

Richard Spear, *Domenichino*, Vol. I, New Haven and London, 1982.

Lucia Tresoldi, *Viaggatori tedeschi in Italia 1452–1870, saggio bibliografico*, 2 vols., Rome, 1975.

William L. Vance, *America's Rome*, 2 vols., New Haven and London , 1989.

——'The Colosseum: American Uses of an Imperial Image', in *Roman Images*, Baltimore and London, 1984.

John Varriano, *Italian Baroque and Rococo Architecture*, New York and Oxford, 1986.

Miller Williams (ed.), *A Roman Collection: Stories, Poems, and other Good Pieces by the Writing Residents of the American Academy in Rome*, Columbia and London, 1980.

ACKNOWLEDGEMENTS

Acknowledgement is due to the following for kindly giving permission to reproduce illustrative or copyright material:

Bibliotheca Hertziana, Rome, for Plates 1, 5, 9, 14, 15, 16, 17, 20; Estate of Elizabeth Bowen for *A Time in Rome* by Elizabeth Bowen; Brandt & Brandt Literary Agents for *Sinclair Lewis, an American Life* by Mark Schorer, copyright renewed © 1989 by Ruth Schorer; Cambridge University Press for *The Art of Rome: c.753 B.C.–A.D.337* by J. J. Pollitt; André Deutsch Ltd. for *Assorted Prose* by John Updike; Faber & Faber Ltd. for 'To an Old Philosopher in Rome' in *Poems by Wallace Stevens*; The Fine Arts Museums of San Francisco, Gift of Mr and Mrs John D. Rockefeller 3rd, for Plate 4; Freies Deutsches Hochstift for Plate 10; K. S. Giniger Company for *The Fountains of Rome* by H. V. Morton; Harcourt Brace Jovanovich Inc. for 'For the New Railway Station in Rome' in *Things of this World* by Richard Wilbur; HarperCollins for *The Companion Guide to Rome* by Georgina Masson, and for *Italian Journey* by Wolfgang von Goethe, trans. W. H. Auden and Elizabeth Mayer; Paul Hofmann, author of *Rome: The Sweet Tempestuous Life*; Keats-Shelley Memorial for Plate 8; Alfred A. Knopf Inc. for *Rome: Places and Pleasures* by Kate Simon. Copyright © 1972 by Kate Simon; Samuel H. Kress Foundation for Plate 3; Macmillan Publishing Company for *Artists in Rome, Tales of the Babuino* by Ugo Moretti; Martin Secker & Warburg Ltd. for *The Memoirs of Hadrian* by Marguerite Yourcenar; Methuen & Company for *A Traveller in Rome* by H. V. Morton; Michael Mewshaw, author of *Playing Away, Roman Holidays and other Mediterranean Encounters*; William

Morris Agency for *Rome and a Villa* by Eleanor Clark; W. W. Norton & Company Inc. for the lines from 'Castel Sant' Angelo' in *Making Certain It Goes On, the Collected Poems of Richard Hugo*, copyright © by the Estate of Richard Hugo; Peter Owen Ltd. for *A Visit to Germany, Italy, and Malta* by Hans Christian Andersen, trans. Grace Thornton; Sterling and Francine Clark Art Institute for Plate 18; Thames & Hudson for *The Passionate Sightseer* by Bernard Berenson; the Estate of Virginia Woolf for *The Letters of Virginia Woolf*, Hogarth Press.

Every effort has been made to trace copyright holders. In some cases this has proved impossible. The author and publishers of this book would be pleased to hear from any copyright holders not acknowledged.

INDEX